DEDICATION

In loving memory of my father, Irving Jaffe, my mentor, best friend, role model and inspiration. More fondly known as Papa Guido, my dad had a love and vision that touched the lives of countless friends, family and employees. Although he was the driving force behind our businesses, he never clamored for the credit he deserved. Papa Guido had the uncanny ability to make each and every person feel as though they were the indispensable one. But in reality, we were all just spokes within his greater wheel. As my eloquent mother, Eleanor, so aptly wrote on his tombstone: "He was the wind beneath our wings."

TURNING
CRISIS
INTO
SUCCESS

A SERIAL ENTREPRENEUR'S LESSONS ON
OVERCOMING CHALLENGE
WHILE KEEPING YOUR SH*T TOGETHER

RICHARD JAFFE AND CHARLY JAFFE

Waterside Productions

Printed in the United States of America First Printing, 2019

ISBN-13: 978-1-939116-67-3 print edition
ISBN-13: 978-1-939116-68-0 ebook edition

Cover design by DV Suresh

Waterside Productions
2055 Oxford Ave
Cardiff, CA 92007
www.waterside.com

A Boy Becomes a Man
January 12, 1980

A special kind of love attracts
A father and a son,
To share the wisdom of experience
Is a task that's never done.

From the moment we can crawl about
He teaches us to stand,
For the rest of life he's behind us
To provide a guiding hand.

For those of us so lucky
To work together and to share,
There grows a respect and admiration
No other love can quite compare.

Side by side we struggle
To build security and wealth,
Always remembering life's road to happiness
Must be filled with love and health.

Yet one day it must happen
That a father pass away,
And though his presence on earth is gone
His guiding hand will always stay.

For already he has taught us
Of the courage to be strong
And how to stand for what we believe
Though sometimes we'll be wrong.

So when you face adversity,
Search for strength to make you bolder,
Remember he's the guiding force

Whose hand rests on your shoulder.

For on the day your father died
A new stage of life began,
Because on that very same mournful day
A BOY BECAME A MAN.

TABLE OF CONTENTS

PREFACE

If you're looking for an old-school business book, focused on organizing your world around professional success over all else, this book is not for you. But if you demand more from life and are still trying to figure out how to get it, you've come to the right place. For me, the principles and practices that helped me start and sell two very successful businesses to Fortune 100 companies were the same ones that enabled me to be incredibly happy inside my own head. Personal fulfillment and professional success are not two separate journeys – at least not in my life – and not in my book.

My generation was taught to sacrifice marriage, family, and spirituality in the name of making a living. Many members of my age group made a great living, but did they really make a great life? I may not be the smartest man you'll ever meet, nor am I any sort of guru or advanced spiritual practitioner, yet somehow, I managed to find inner peace early in life, while also building two very successful public companies. What I learned throughout this process is that these two journeys share a common foundation. In the pages that follow, I will take you inside the workings of my heart and head throughout my roller coaster entrepreneurial rides.

This book is the result of countless hours of conversation and contemplation with my daughter and co-author Charly. I never imagined I would one day delve into my darkest thoughts and deepest insecurities at the direction of my offspring, but it has been one of the most rewarding experiences of my life. With wisdom and insight well beyond her years, Charly helped me understand the thought patterns that enabled me to maintain my emotional stability as I went from crisis to crisis, fell in love with my soul mate, avoided near certain bankruptcy and somehow came out deeply fulfilled in every aspect of life. Our biggest hope is that as you read through my experiences of building a mind for happiness and success in the face of high stress, the stories and lessons in these pages will help you do the same.

INTRODUCTION

Having hung up my entrepreneurial hat, leaving the nonstop hours and middle-of-the-night phone calls behind, I couldn't help wondering – how had I become so lucky? Reminiscing on my first 60 years of life, love and business, a few things became quite clear. It's not my innate abilities that got me here, nor was there one quick fix. I certainly had some serious advantages: an incredibly loving family, unfailingly positive attitude and endless persistence. Well, that and unbelievable luck; my friends tell me I am the luckiest person they have ever met. But as a man who's faced near business death more times than I care to count, and barely had time to breathe in those early years romancing and building a life with my incredible wife, I've realized that it's certain ingrained habits – helpful ways of thinking and doing – that led to my holistic, whole-life success.

While it has certainly been a wild ride, in retrospect, there are two key pillars that have been the driving force behind my greatest achievements – success in business and happiness in life. So if you take away only one thing from this book, make it these pillars.

In Business: Skate to Where the Puck Is Going to Be

You don't need to be the smartest, most well-connected or technologically advanced competitor to dominate your industry. The key is learning to be like hockey legend Wayne Gretzky. While Wayne was arguably the best hockey player of all time, he didn't have the all-star qualities one would expect from the king of the ice; he was not particularly big, didn't skate very fast, nor did he have the hardest slapshot. When asked how he became the best hockey player that has ever lived despite these disadvantages, his answer was both simple and profound: **"I just skate to where the puck is going to be."**

If you want to succeed in business, the most important skill you can gain is skating to where the puck is going to be; learn how to anticipate future customer needs, then give them products and services that satisfy those needs. This key is simple in theory; discover what customers really need before they do, and give it to them. But it requires listening to our customers very carefully and, most importantly, reading the meaning behind their answers to understand what they will really need. This invaluable life skill is not limited to business. We all have people we'd like to persuade. Learning how to give people what they really want is the secret sauce to getting what you want.

Henry Ford once said that if he had asked his customers what they wanted, they would have said, "Faster horses!" But he skated to where the puck was going to be. He developed the assembly line and gave them a car. I'm no Henry Ford, but as you'll see in the coming pages, pre-empting customer needs was the key that saved our businesses from the brink of bankruptcy and enabled us to soar to the top of industries I had zero background in – from creating the number one frozen novelty in America, to producing the top-selling medical glove in the world. So talk to your customers. Ask them what single thing they would like to do today that they are currently unable to, that would have the biggest impact on their business and life. Then, project customer needs into new products and services, solving their biggest challenges to drive your greatest successes.

As far as how successful we become, I have found that we always get rewarded in direct proportion to the needs we fill. If the need is small, so are the rewards. But if we find and satisfy a large and desperate need, the returns can grow far beyond our wildest imagination, and are measured in more than just money.

In Happiness: Self-Love is the Seed

While listening to my customers was the strategy that fueled my business success, learning to love myself was the secret sauce that made it all possible. Self-love gave me the strength of heart and mind to navigate through seemingly impossible moments and make it to the other side. But most importantly, loving myself gave me the inner peace to enjoy the ride. Far too many people have held onto this belief that happiness is a sacrifice made to achieve success. But for truly deep, whole-hearted success, happiness is not a sacrifice – it's a necessary ingredient. As Nobel laureate Albert Schweitzer explained: "Success is not the key to happiness; happiness is the key to success. If you love what you are doing, you will be successful."

So how do we get there?

It starts with self-love. We cannot deeply love what we don't know, so we must start by building an honest sense of self-awareness – including an acknowledgement of the nonstop stories running through our heads. So much of our society has bought into the idea that addressing challenging thoughts and emotions somehow makes us weak. But they couldn't be more wrong. When left unchecked, we give our stories all the power, allowing them to build us up or tear us apart as they please. Facing daunting feelings requires strength, but it also breeds greater strength and power in return.

From here we can build the ability to accept the things we cannot change, refocusing our efforts to work on those which we can, all while growing into our own invaluable best friend. In the coming pages, you will see how I learned to keep searching for solutions in the face of the constant turmoil surrounding the financial and operational issues of my businesses, rather than being angry at their presence. While I was incredibly fortunate to have such a supportive network of family and friends, finding worthiness within myself and being my own best friend is what gave me the stamina and mental strength to persist for so long without sacrificing my relationships or burning out.

I've seen some incredible returns on my investments as a businessman throughout the years, but all of the wealth, material gains and beyond-my-wildest-dreams experiences pale in comparison to the results of my deep self-love.

One important practice that's supported me throughout the way has been my poetry. An outlet I stumbled into as a broken-hearted twenty-something, doing anything I could to win back a love already lost, poetry became an integral part of my life the vehicle through which I could express my greatest highs and deepest lows. While desperation can be excruciating in the moment, it can also open us up to powerful paths we may not have found otherwise; the emotional intensity of my young heartbreak is nothing compared to the joy and meaning that poetry has brought into my life since then. So in addition to the stories, you'll also find a few of my poems interspersed throughout these pages, reflections of my mind throughout the years.

Quick Note from Charly

Thirteen years after my father sold his second company, I was a senior at Georgetown University anxiously over-analyzing potential job opportunities. It was a gloomy May afternoon, when my dad called with a question that would change our relationship forever. He had been speaking to MBA students about his key ingredients for happiness and success, and asked for my input as he began playing around with the idea of turning his talk into a book.

"What do you think about writing this together?" he asked in an inquisitive, no-pressure tone, "Would you be my co-author?" It was a no brainer for me; I loved writing and the idea of spending more time together. An enthusiastic "yes!" rolled off my tongue in an instant, and I had no idea what I was in for.

There was a special playfulness and intimacy about editing for my father; I often knew what he was trying to get across and could call him out far quicker and deeper than any outside ghostwriter could. He loved getting the feedback just as much as I liked giving it.

What I didn't realize in the moment I said yes, was that I had committed to an investigative journey inside my father's psyche – a life-changing journey for us both. It is our hope that in looking inside his greatest challenges and hardest moments, you're able to take some of my dad's most valuable lessons with you. In addition to his two key pillars, we have identified seven key ingredients that made them possible – ways of thinking and being that enabled him to skate to where the puck was going to be and experience a deep-seated sense of self-love and peace. While we don't interrupt the story to highlight them, these are the key ingredients you'll see in action throughout the coming pages.

1. **Controlling Our Thoughts**

    There is very little we control in life. We can't control much of what happens to us, or the thoughts that enter our minds – but we can choose how we respond to them. While it's by no means a simple skill to develop, learning how to control our reactions is one of the greatest determinants of meaningful happiness, and an invaluable tool in navigating the complex road to external success. There were certainly no shortage of challenging situations on my father's entrepreneurial ride, but as you'll see, controlling his reactions and taking responsibility for his perspective allowed my father to navigate through the seemingly impossible.

2. **Persistence**

    The more risks you take and the more you try to achieve, the more obstacles you'll find on your path. Success doesn't come from simply showing up; we have to find the lesson inside each rejection, get back up and come back smarter every time. **No is the first step to any sale,** regardless of what industry we're in. It's not simply talent, connections or luck – success is an unrelenting choice we make every day.

3. **Connecting from the Heart**

    Life is all about creating authentic, loving relationships with people we can trust. This isn't something relegated solely to our personal lives; great selling is all about connecting heart to heart. People do things for other people they care about, and as you'll soon see, my dad's businesses wouldn't have survived if it wasn't for the people he connected with going out on a limb for him.

4. **Do Today What Feels Good Tomorrow**

    Doing what feels good in the moment is easy, but success and meaning are built by acting upon what is best for us, our loved ones and customers tomorrow. Whether he was navigating extreme business crises or a personal experience of depression, doing today what feels good tomorrow is what helped my father move through the hard moments, keeping his winding trajectory geared towards his mountain tops.

5. **See the Outcome and Manage Backwards**

When building a house, we don't do it one room at a time; we start with a picture of the final outcome in hand. It works the same way with big goals; only once we visualize where we want to end up, will we be able to determine if our decisions today will get us closer or further away. It's also an incredibly helpful tactic in those overwhelming moments when the sheer size of obstacles ahead are blinding. In the face of his greatest business challenges, persistence alone would not have been enough; managing from the outcome backwards was the key tactic in creating his escapes.

6. **Find a Passion and Follow It**

Life is too short not to love what you do and the people you live and work with. For my dad, the passion wasn't in the product specifically, but in the greater goal of building a world-class company and fulfilling unmet customer needs. He needed a passion that burned so bright to fuel him through the 20 hour workdays and endless waves of crisis. Some find it at work, others in play; either way we only live once – we may as well invest our time in activities we love with people who make us feel alive.

7. **Leave a Legacy**

What do you want to be remembered for at the end of your life? Expanding our focus from success to significance, what we can create for others rather than what we can build for ourselves, can bring a depth of meaning and excitement like nothing else. Building a legacy should be something that shapes our journey – the culmination of our lives, not a rushed effort on our way out.

I never imagined I would spend so many hours exploring my father's psyche, or that it would involve so much joy and laughter. The process of putting a voice to his story has been one of the most meaningful experiences of my life, and getting to prod my unshakeable dad about his deepest insecurities and greatest heartbreaks has been equal parts enlightening and exciting. If you're lucky enough to have parents in your life, I hope you get the chance to spend some time exploring their past, and that you enjoy reading through the wisdom and shenanigans that my father shared with me.

As an added bonus, we've created free supporting videos where we dive deeper into the seven ingredients listed above.

Check them out and join the conversation at www. crisisintosuccess.com/resources.

The Garden of Our Mind
January 22, 2009

Our lives are true reflections of our thoughts and how we're raised,
Our confidence and self esteem measure how much we've been
praised.
Our programs are instilled in us the first eight years we are alive
The rest of life is spent discovering how best we can survive.

Some souls have had to deal with abandonment and abuse,
Having run away from their childhood they have a good excuse.
To question if they're worthy of a lifetime filled with love,
Or if there exists a higher spirit who guides our journey from above.

While others have been blessed with years
filled with warmth and love and caring,
Encouraged to explore their souls to
find comfort found through sharing.
But even souls so lucky to grow up within a loving past
Struggle with their constant inner voice whispering,
their worthiness shouldn't last.

It's not 'til we take responsibility for the life that we've created
Does the universe provide to us the goals and dreams we've stated.
Because the only thing we really control are our thoughts which
are never lost
When we fail to discipline the way we think
we pay a very heavy cost.

For our mind is the most fertile garden that will feed
any type of thought

It does not discern between good or bad,
it grows everything it's brought.
So if we only spend five minutes in our mind's garden every day
The weeds of negativity will flourish, our hopes and dreams will
fade away.

But constantly working in our mind's garden
with a clear focus that's brand new
Will provide an empowering energy that
will surround everything we do.
For you are a worthy, blessed soul deserving of
everything you create
Uncover an inner peace and happiness to share
with your true soulmate.

So do not waste another moment,
plant only thoughts that make you whole
Find the fire of white hot passion that burns
deep within your soul.

CHAPTER 1

DIVING IN THE DEEP END

In the early months of 1975, I was a happy-go-lucky senior at Cornell University having the time of my life. Living with my best friend in the woods, dating an incredible young woman and looking forward to one more year at school to complete my MBA I knew I was living out my glory days and loving every moment. But then, one warm early spring afternoon, my phone rang with the call that would change my life forever. It was my Uncle Bob. His Italian ices business in California had just gone bankrupt, and since my father had lent the business some money, he received the equipment as collateral.

"I'm really sorry to hear it," I sympathized, "But I'm a bit confused. Why are you calling me about this?" I asked. "The issue in California wasn't the business itself, but my partner," Uncle Bob explained. "So I was thinking, if we can get a small loan, we could use the equipment to launch the Italian ices business together in New York. With the two of us working on this, we can make more money than you've ever dreamed of!"

Humbled and shocked by his offer, I paused for a moment before explaining that I was in a five-year program; even though I was graduating in the spring, I still had one more year of school to get my MBA. But my Uncle Bob was a damn good salesman. Realizing money wouldn't pull me away, he switched gears. "Come on, Richard," he prodded, "Why sit and learn about running a company in a classroom when you can do it in real life? Business school will always be there, you can always go back." Despite my resistance, a part of me knew he was right. Business school could wait, but this opportunity wouldn't.

We went back and forth for a bit, and the longer we spoke, the more enticing the offer became. It was amazing how quickly this ridiculous idea started to seem like a realistic possibility. I asked for some time to think about it and spent the afternoon walking in the forest contemplating the offer. It was both incredibly exciting and terrifying. While I enjoyed frozen desserts as much as the next person, I knew absolutely nothing about the frozen novelty industry. I guess I could figure it out on the job, and at least it was a product I wouldn't mind taste testing!

Even though I knew I couldn't pass up this opportunity, I didn't feel ready. There was so much more to learn, I thought, what if I jumped in too soon and screwed it all up? My breath quickened along with the pace of my racing mind. It seemed like my worldview had changed over the course of a phone call. The more I thought about it, the more I realized that studying and having fun no longer had the same allure now that I had the possibility of starting and growing a new business. This was it, I told myself. I began shaking in anticipation, as the reality of the monumental leap I was about to take started to sink in. Diving into the real world with real challenges, earning my name in business – I was going for it!

I called up my father to talk things over. He thought this was a great opportunity and presented me with an offer; my father would give my brother, Jack, and me the equipment and loan us $50,000 to start the company with Uncle Bob, but only if I started the day after graduation.

The timing was not ideal. I had made plans with my best friends to go backpacking through Europe for one last hurrah before entering the real world, and I desperately wanted to go. But this would be worth it. So, after some long discussions with my parents, I decided to skip the trip, say goodbye to business school for now, and dive headfirst into the world of Italian ices.

• • •

So the day after graduation, I packed up my entire life into a baby blue 1967 Ford mustang, bid my college life adieu and drove two hours south to my new home in the sleepy town of Monticello, New York. My uncle had rented a small 1,200-square-foot garage with a small walk-in freezer, and as I wandered around the property that first fateful day of work, I was both excited and nervous. We already had six people working for us in the factory, and all of them were much older than me. It was a bit intimidating coming in as the younger boss, a month after everyone else had started.

As Uncle Bob and I sat down to kick things off, I was met with quite the surprise. He had forgotten to mention that he also had plans to start a frozen pretzel distribution company, which he would run with Jack. So after spending one week training me on how to manufacture the Italian ices from start to finish, he returned to Long Island with Jack, and I was on my own. "The hardest challenge you will have is learning how to manage the people. You are on your own for that one, but I'm sure you will figure it out quickly!" he assured me. Talk about on-the-job training!

Initially, I was totally consumed with the excitement of the new job and real life. But after a few weeks, the adrenaline wore off and the pangs of homesickness began. I didn't really know anyone and didn't have much of a life outside work. All my waking hours were spent making and selling the Italian ices. I missed my friends and college life, and my relationship with my college girlfriend, Debbie, was going downhill fast. This was lonelier than I expected. I kept reminding myself how lucky I was to have this opportunity and was determined to stay positive, but it all rang a bit hollow.

I buried myself in the work I was so lucky to have, but whenever I had a moment alone, I found myself engulfed in sadness and isolation. Suddenly, my baseline was different, with dark undertones I'd never experienced before. It was my first foray into really trying to regulate my thoughts and emotions, and I wasn't sure how to go about it.

My solution at the time was to throw myself into the business 24/7 – that way I had no time to think about how lonely I felt. All my energy went towards the success of the business as I tried to stay focused on the positive and direct my thoughts on making lists and executing my priorities. Avoidance didn't turn out to be as effective as I'd hoped. I found myself swinging between the enthusiastic highs of building a new business to despair when no one else was around. While the crew was there and the factory was bustling, I was fine. But late at night as I sat in the office preparing the paperwork for the following day, pangs of loneliness would envelop me, and I seriously questioned whether I made the right decision leaving Cornell a year early.

Regardless of my emotional state, it was summertime and as the thermometer crept up with the scorching summer heat, so did the demand for our Italian ices. We had to take advantage of the blistering heat; the days of summer were numbered, and we couldn't afford to waste a moment. I hit the ground running, working 20-hour days for months on end.

On a typical morning, I dragged myself out of bed before sunrise and was on my way to the factory by 5 a.m. After popping in to wish the entire maintenance staff good morning, I would go to the factory floor and prepare the machines and equipment needed to manufacture the flavored ices. After a full day on the factory floor, my afternoons were spent calling on hotels, camps and bungalow colonies, selling and delivering as many Italian ices as I could. Around 9 p.m., I returned to the factory where I would prepare and mix the batches for the following day, finally making it home around midnight or one in the morning.

Now I will admit that, on occasion, I would go home to shower and then go to local hotel bars to let loose. On these nights, I would stay out until 4:30 a.m., come home, shower, change and go right back to work without a wink of sleep. Even though I was only 22, this hurt, and words cannot describe the glorious feeling of falling back into bed for a few hours of sleep the next night.

This went on all summer and our Italian ices were an absolute hit! From hotel chefs to camp directors, our customers were blown away by the incredible taste. Bungalow colonies, where families gathered to escape the city for the summer, actually came and picked up their orders at our dock to ensure we didn't run out. Looking for a short, friendly, authentic Italian name, my father and Uncle Bob had decided to call ourselves Guido's Italian Ices (Jaffe's Jewish Ices just didn't have the same ring to it). Jewish and Italian families have plenty in common – a penchant for warm, loud family get-togethers and a love of food – and for the next several years, I can't tell you how many customers and suppliers set me up with their Italian daughters, nieces or granddaughters. I decided not to go out of my way to correct their assumptions about my background for fear of losing my dating pool!

One of my favorite blind dates occurred about a year or two into the job. One of our best customers insisted that I absolutely had to meet his gorgeous Italian granddaughter. While I was a bit nervous about the potential fallout from business-related matchmaking, he was insistent. So one fall evening, when business was slower, I made the two-hour trek down to Queens, NY, with the intent of picking up this (hopefully cute) Italian girl I'd never met, and heading to a friend's house for a party. As I pulled up to a picturesque red brick house, my hands clammed up and butterflies swarmed my stomach. "Be cool, Richard!" I shouted in my head, in a half pep-talk, half chastising tone, "It's no big deal!" So I took a deep breath, leaving any hesitation behind me, walked up to the front door with a confident stride, rang the doorbell and held my breath as I waited. As the door slowly opened, I looked up and just froze.

There in front of me was the most beautiful, dark-haired, brown-eyed girl I had ever seen. "Hi, my name is Giovanni but my friends call me Gi," she smiled welcomingly, "You must be Guido!" I tried to say my real name is Richard, but nothing came out. I just stared at her, frozen and engulfed by embarrassment. But Gi didn't seem to care a bit, "Please come in," she said as she motioned me inside, "I hope you don't mind but I thought we would stay for dinner with my family before we went to the party; everyone wants to meet the famous Guido!" She smiled with an irresistible twinkle in her eye. Finally, I caught my breath and smiled back as confidently as I could, "Of course we can stay for dinner, anything you like!"

We laughed, drank, told stories and had such a good time all night that we never ended up making it to my friend's party. Between the loud personalities, deep familial affection and peer pressure to eat until you burst, it felt just like our Shabbat dinners! While Gi and I never became a long-distance romance, that night remains my favorite, most family-fueled blind date ever.

Afew months into the job it felt like I was finally understanding the business and as I started thinking about the months ahead, it struck me – once it was cold, no one would want to buy our frozen desserts. It seemed like common sense, but I had dove straight into the business without thinking far ahead into things like seasonality, and my uncle never mentioned it. A wave of anxiety struck through me. We had never been through a winter before and hadn't done any forecasting. A dark premonition began surfacing in my mind.

And alas, as Labor Day arrived, demand for our Italian ices collapsed. Camps and bungalow colonies closed for the winter, and though the hotels were still busy, without the heat they didn't have the same demand for our desserts. Though we made good money over the summer, those profits simply could not sustain us through the winter while paying all our employees. As I began thinking about the upcoming production schedules, I realized I would have to fire most of our staff to preserve what little cash we had left. I decided to keep our head maintenance supervisor, Don, and his assistant as a minimal maintenance staff, but I would have to fire over a dozen employees.

I cannot tell you how heart-wrenching it was for me to fire someone for the first time. I still remember it vividly. I had asked Don to send over Marilyn, one of our packaging girls. I could not stop pacing the few steps across my cramped office, my hands wouldn't stop sweating and I was so filled with anxiety I thought I might throw up. Luckily for my waste bin, I was able to contain myself.

Marilyn was a soft-spoken, lovely-looking woman who always showed up on time and was very pleasant to be around. She was one of the four ladies responsible for taking the cups of Italian ices off the conveyor belt and packing them into boxes. Never one to complain, Marilyn was happy and willing to do whatever needed to be done, and I had grown very fond of her even in the short time we worked together.

When she opened the door to my office, a fresh wave of dread swept over me. I could not for the life of me figure out how to raise the issue. Though I had diligently practiced my speech throughout the weekend, when the time came, I just couldn't get the words out. So I ended up making awkward small talk for a few minutes until, with a knowing tone, Marilyn asked if I brought her into my office for any particular reason. I took a deep breath and finally managed to spit out that due to the lack of business we had to shut down production; with this, her job was being eliminated.

While I was a nervous wreck, Marilyn was very calm and understanding. She and the rest of the staff had seen it coming. "It's no surprise," she said, "It's happened to me before. I sorta expected this would happen at one point or another." All she wanted to know was when the work would stop, whether there would be any severance pay, and if she could apply for unemployment benefits. "Don't be so hard on yourself," she added gently, "This happens to most businesses in Monticello after Labor Day." Slowly rising out of her chair, Marilyn walked over and gave me a big hug goodbye. "If you ever need an extra hand, even for a day or two, just give me a call." Stunned, I stood there for awhile, grateful and amazed.

It took me many years to accept firing people as part of growing a business, but to this day, it's something I have never gotten used to. To me, it wasn't just work – employees were family. I would send special Italian ices to their kids on their birthdays, help them move on a rare Sunday I wasn't working or give them a ride home after work if their spouse got stuck at work. In turn, they would stay late, even until midnight, if we had an urgent order that needed to go out, and even come to work on a Sunday, without so much as a grumble. So firing never got "easy." Even when I've known that the person sitting across the table would find a better job, I've never been able to shake that empty feeling in the pit of my stomach of letting that employee down.

After our orders dropped off and the layoffs were complete, the factory was like a ghost town. I'd gone from working 20-hour days to not having enough work to keep me occupied for eight. Faced with all this newfound idle time, I couldn't stop replaying the layoff conversations in my head and thinking about the workplace community we had lost. We had spent every day side by side, moving as quickly as we possibly could to fill our orders. Though I didn't lose their friendship, we didn't have that day-to-day contact. I never imagined the emptiness the layoffs would leave behind.

While I had been busy building a business, summer had come and gone and I still hadn't made any friends in Monticello. The area was bustling as the population swelled throughout summer, but the town dwindled to less than 5,000 people after Labor Day. The town became as empty as my social life. While I'd initially hidden behind my work to avoid my loneliness, now I had basically no work, no community and no family around me. There was no one there who really loved me, and that quiet loneliness that had showed up a few weeks into the job snuck back in. This time it was tenfold.

I had never been all alone before. The second of four children, I grew up in a very close-knit family. While we fought constantly, the four of us loved each other as only siblings could. When I moved on to college, I gained a new set of siblings, my amazing fraternity brothers at Sigma Phi; we did everything together, and they were never far away. But now, I felt completely and utterly alone; there was no texting, no social media, no instant communication to diminish the sense of isolation. My mind became a very scary place to be, and for the first time in my life, I felt depression first-hand.

It was like an unwanted lens preventing me from seeing and feeling the world around me as it really was, as negative thoughts spiraled through my mind. In every interaction I felt like an unwanted burden to those around me, like it would be easier if I wasn't around. As this persistent fog set in, I started to get scared. Intellectually, I knew that my parents, siblings, family and friends all loved me very much, but with no one around me who cared, I couldn't feel it. Everything just felt heavy and dark.

This went on for several weeks. Growing up I had experienced the typical highs and lows of adolescence, but never anything like this. Many days my anxiety began the moment I woke up and lasted until I cried myself to sleep at night. I had never felt fear like this before. It was like sitting at the bottom of a deep, dark well; I tried to scale the walls, but each and every time a powerful force pulled me back down. I started to wonder if I would ever climb out.

One October morning, I remember gazing outside at the beautiful array of fiery red and orange leaves gently gliding with the wind, brightening the barren forest floor beneath them. Fall's natural beauty had always brought me such joy and wonder. But now, I could only think how the leaves were dying and so was I. How did I become like this? It was as though I became addicted to the negativity, and anytime I had a positive thought, my mind would turn it to darkness.

Finally, I'd had enough, and knew I just had to stop feeling sorry for myself and change my perspective. So I took a step back to reflect and figure out how to control my thoughts, take responsibility for my feelings and stay focused on a positive solution. No one else was going to figure it out for me and I had to find a way to pull myself out of my self-pity.

In moments of idleness, I focused my thoughts on what I did have and who did love me instead of all the things I didn't have. When I was able to keep my mind positive I felt fine, but it was all too easy to get sucked back into the negativity, and when I did all I could see was darkness.

After about a week of deep, concerted effort, I started to notice a small difference. As I became more aware of how much my family and friends really loved me, the sadness didn't disappear, but it's almost like the love and positive affirmations took the edge off. Slowly, I started to feel a little better each day. Several times I picked up the phone to call a loved one, but each time I put the phone down when I realized I didn't want to tell them how really miserable I was and I didn't want to lie to them either. Finally, after many failed attempts, I mustered the courage to start making calls to my parents and siblings.

The first call was to my mother. I was petrified while the phone was ringing; this depression was so far from who I'd ever been and my mother had no idea how I felt. My heart was racing and my palms were sweating. It didn't make any sense. Why would I be nervous to talk to the woman who loved me more than anyone else in the world? But then, the second my mother answered the phone, her beautiful, loving voice melted away my trepidation. As I started to explain my sense of despair, the words didn't make nearly as much sense out loud. Her warm words of unconditional love began to wash away my stubborn sadness. For a moment, I felt whole again.

I realized how much I missed being connected, and made it a point to talk more with my family and friends. Some days they answered, some days they didn't. But hearing their voices more often reminded me how much I was loved and how important I was to them. Even this little bit started to help me feel more hopeful. While things were still hard, the darkness felt a little less constant. I had more breaths of normalcy mixed in with the day-to-day struggle. At first, I felt entirely negative, but then my emotions started to feel more like a pendulum, swinging back and forth between sadness and happiness. Gradually, with each passing day, my happiness began overshadowing the sadness, and there was less and less space left for the darkness to live.

Energized by my small bit of initial success, I decided to sit down and reflect on what activities brought me joy. Basketball and tennis were two of my favorite sports growing up; I played both in high school and continued playing basketball at Cornell. So I decided to stop by the local hotels to play tennis with the pros on staff, and joined some pickup basketball games at a nearby gym. It wasn't always easy to get motivated. There were days and nights I wanted to go out but just couldn't find the energy to leave my apartment. It was hard to overpower every cell in my body begging me not to leave the house, but when I forced myself out the door to play, I usually felt at least a bit better and more human from it.

A few weeks into this new routine and a strict regimen of positive thinking and finding the silver lining, I started feeling infinitely better. While my environment hadn't changed – I still didn't have any good friends nearby, business was awful and I had no idea how we would make it through the winter financially – my approach to it had, and that made all the difference.

To be honest, I'm grateful for those few months of suspected depression. It taught me the importance of doing today what feels good tomorrow, especially when all I want to do is lie in bed and pull the covers over my head. Moreover, it highlighted the importance of acknowledging where I'm at emotionally, and taking action to shape my perception of how I see the world. Taking responsibility for our own perception is a lifelong practice, and there will never be a shortage of curveballs that can come our way. But the better we become at controlling our thoughts – the only arena we can truly rule – the better chance we have of feeling good about ourselves.

Depression taught me that in my sadness I was constantly looking at what I didn't have, while happiness stemmed from a focus and feeling of gratitude for all that I did have. In retrospect, I now see that my unhappiness was caused by a lack of joy, and my depression stemmed from a lack of hope. I have been filling the rest of my life with as much joy as possible, searching for passion and purpose, and remaining resolute in holding on to hope even when everything was crashing in around me.

We spent the next three years riding the same business roller coaster, albeit with a bit more emotional stability. Each summer we continued to build our customer base and raked in the cash, only to lose it all during the winter. I began a Labor Day tradition of opening up *The New York Times* to search for a second job to get me through another winter, but was never able to find one.

The second winter, our financial difficulties forced us to come up with some very creative solutions. At one point, things got so bad that we couldn't even afford to replace the worn-out freezer clothing our staff needed to stay warm. This created a big problem, as everyone I hired quit within days because they (understandably) refused to freeze their hands and feet for minimum wage. I racked my brain for a solution. Somehow, I knew there were people willing to do this work – I just couldn't find them yet.

Then, late one frosty Sunday morning as I skimmed through *The New York Times*, I came across an article about a well-known investor who was serving time in prison for embezzlement. The article mentioned in passing that the investor left the prison each morning, Monday through Friday, for a work-release program. A light went off in my head. I figured that inmates in a medium-security prison would do anything to get out into the real world there must be some who would be happy to work in cold conditions in order to do so! Energized and excited, I scoured through the local phone books and found a medium-security prison in Woodbourne, a quick half-hour drive away.

Monday morning, I called up the prison to talk about their work-release program. Much to my disappointment, not only did they not have one, but they had never even heard of it. Convincing a prison to start a work-release program was a much larger task than I had anticipated, but this was the perfect solution to my biggest problem, and I was insistent. After three weeks of several no's from half a dozen lower-level staff, I finally worked my way up to Patrick, the senior manager of administration. I knew he couldn't care less about my needs, and this project would require extra time and effort on his end, so I had to identify how I could make this a benefit for him.

Despite all the initial objections, I kept talking until I could figure out what would motivate him to say yes. Frustrated and eager to end our conversation, Patrick told me he and his team cared only about making the prison run more smoothly and making their own lives easier. Of course! I immediately reframed my pitch to speak directly to their needs; a successful work release program would improve morale and behavior, incentivizing other inmates to behave better in the hopes of securing one of these treasured jobs. I put on my best closing pitch and asked for not one, but three diligent workers.

Once I spoke to this administrator's self-interest, his entire attitude changed, and he finished the conversation asking when I would like to start the program. I was beyond excited. Once he signed onto starting a work-release program, that would mean having three workers dropped off on my doorstep at 7 a.m. every day – it didn't get more reliable than that! Quite pleased with myself, I was certain I had found the perfect solution to one of my biggest problems.

That first morning when 7 a.m. rolled around I was practically giddy. After getting out of the prison van, the officer introduced himself and the five of us walked into my cramped office. "OK," he announced, "This is Joe, Carlos and Tree. I'll drop them off each morning at 7 a.m. and be back to collect them at 5 p.m. Make sure to give them 30 minutes to walk into town for lunch," he droned on without much interest. "Any questions?"

"Nope!" I replied enthusiastically. After the officer left, I turned to the men sitting before me and somewhat awkwardly began, "Hi, I'm Richard and I'm very happy to have you working with us. Let's start with your names and what you're incarcerated for." Without hesitation, the largest of the group stood up first. "My name is Tree and I was set up and busted for dealing drugs. I never hurt or killed anyone, I really appreciate you organizing this and am really happy to be here. Just tell me what you need me to do." Weighing in at 6'5 and 265 pounds of pure muscle, Tree was actually more of a gentle giant than a fighting force. I never knew Tree's real name, but from that moment on, we clicked, and stayed in touch long after he got out of prison.

Both in for petty theft, Joe and Carlos continued their introductions, and everyone was ready to work. I was elated – at least for a few hours. Sadly, my newfound success didn't even make it through day one. The officer who dropped them off instructed me to give them 30 unsupervised minutes to walk into town for lunch. Lo and behold, Carlos ran for it at lunchtime and didn't return. I couldn't believe it. My perfect solution was off and running down some stupid highway! I called the prison officer, explained what happened and begged him to leave the other two workers there. But alas, no luck for me and even worse for Carlos. He was caught a few hours later in Middletown, only 30 miles away, while Joe and Tree were picked up immediately and the program canceled. So much for my perfect solution.

I spent the next two weeks pleading with the senior administrator, trying to convince him that one bad apple doesn't spoil the whole bunch. It may have been sheer annoyance with my persistent daily begging and pleading, but finally, the prison administrator relented. "One more chance," he warned, "and that's it." I couldn't wait to get the program started again, but until there was a van with three men at my doorstep, I had a nagging anxiety that someone high up at the prison would stop the program before they returned.

But my worries were unfounded, and the following day they brought back Joe, Tree and a new inmate named Juan. I decided to start by sitting everyone down for a little chat. Calm and confident, I tried to talk to them like an uncle, not a boss. "Listen," I explained, "You guys work here now and are a part of our family. That means I will do almost anything I can – within the law – to help and support you. But," I went on with conviction, "You need to be in this with me. So I expect that you will come talk to me before making any rash decisions, and absolutely no bolting. Look at the guys next to you; if you screw up or make a run for it, you won't just be ruining things for me but for them as well. So we need to hold each other accountable. Can we get on board with that?"

They all quietly agreed, and again thanked me profusely for getting them out of the prison and into the real world again. Working tirelessly without breaks or proper clothing, and only stepping out of the freezer for a few moments when they couldn't stand the cold, these three men were incredible employees, going far above and beyond what I'd asked of them. Not only did they become my best workers, they became great friends as well.

One day, a compressor on the outside of the building broke and needed to be replaced. Joe and Juan were standing outside on a break and I asked them if they could help me move the old compressor out of the way. It was only two feet tall, but must have weighed well over 300 pounds. They struggled and struggled and could not get the compressor off the ground. Just as we were about to give up, out of the freezer steps Tree, all dressed in his worn-out freezer gear. He asked what we were doing, and when I explained, he pushed Joe and Juan out of the way. "Let me take care of it!" he said. Squatting down, he put one arm under each side, lifted the compressor as he stood and asked ever so casually, "Where do you want it boss?" That was how the legend of Tree was made.

The program lasted several years until we moved out of Monticello. In the winter when we slowed down, the inmates would come to work only as needed. As Tree, Joe and Juan were paroled, other equally driven men took their place. Many of them would even come back in the summers to visit after they were released. I would take them to lunch and they would proudly share stories about their families, what they were doing with their lives at the time and how working for Guido's transformed their prison experience. While I'd started the program to fill a need, it led to some incredible friendships as well as a valuable lesson.

We all face seemingly unsolvable problems at one point or another in our lives; but in staying positive, controlling my thoughts and focusing on a clear outcome, I realized I could find a creative solution to almost any problem. I call it unrelenting persistence in pursuit of a solution! As the business grew, there was never a shortage of problems demanding creative solutions.

After three years, the business had become too complex for me to handle by myself. Trying to run production, keep the books, collect receivables, answer the phones, make the payroll, drive new sales and take care of existing customers had become overwhelming – even by my standards. What I really needed was an office manager and a sales and marketing executive, but I couldn't afford to pay either. So I called the only two people in the entire world who loved me enough to work for free: my mother and father. After taking a few days to talk it over, they couldn't see any reason not to give it a try. A few weeks later they packed up their car, made the two-hour drive from Long Island to Monticello and moved into my apartment until they could find a place of their own. In that moment, I felt like a pretty fine salesman!

That was another turning point in the business and my personal life. Having grown up with two amazing, loving parents, I've always been extremely appreciative of my family situation. But to have the chance to work together and to live together as equals was a rare and special privilege for which I will be forever grateful. While growing up, I lived in their home under their rules. Now as we worked and lived as equals, I was able to love them in an entirely new and even deeper way. My mom took over the office answering the phone, filling out payroll, paying the bills and doing the bookkeeping. Most importantly, my mother was the moral compass and driving force behind the scenes that kept the family and business together. My dad took over new sales and supplier relations, selling our Italian ices not just locally but to schools around the country. This allowed me to focus on running production, purchasing, supervising the employees, and developing new flavors and products.

My uncle Bob, who got me into this business, would show up unexpectedly every now and then in his pretzel truck. He started selling the Italian ices in two-and-a-half-gallon tubs to parks like Six Flags and state fairs. When the pretzel business was slow, Jack would show up for a few days to help as well. Eventually, they sold the pretzel business, which worked out great for me. Jack joined us in Monticello to work full time at Guido's. His energy, talent and whatever-it-takes attitude were absolutely crucial to surviving some of our hardest moments.

Though sales grew each summer, seasonality was killing us. Every year, orders plummeted with the falling temperature and each winter we kept running out of money. It was a mental, emotional and financial drain. After the first two summers we borrowed more money from my father. But once he had put in more than enough for him, we needed to find another source to support us. After much discussion, my parents and I agreed that Uncle George, who had a very successful electrical supply company, was our best hope. The next weekend we drove down to Great Neck, NY, and the three of us paid a visit to Uncle George and my mother's sister, Aunt Blanche.

Blanche and George were like second parents to me, and I'd grown up with their only son, Gary. Even still, I was beyond nervous about asking them for money. To calm myself down and give me courage, I recalled a lesson my father's best friend had shared when I was just starting out with Guido's: "When you are just starting out in business and have no money, don't be ashamed to beg for money. When you get on your feet and can make ends meet, you ask for what you need. When you are successful and making boatloads of profits, you demand what you want!" There was no question as to where we landed on this scale: it was time for me to beg.

After welcoming hugs, we sat around the table for a bite to eat. "So how are things going at Guido's?" George inquired. "I am glad you asked!" I responded with a smile and enthusiasm. I took the next 20 minutes to explain the formidable cash challenges and exciting opportunity we faced, and then asked quite directly, "Even though things are looking up, we need more money to get through the winter or we'll have to shut it down. Would you please consider making us a $40,000 loan that we expect to be able to pay back by the middle of next summer?"

His face turned from a smile to a frown. I could see his business mind working and assessing the danger. But before he could respond, my wonderful Aunt Blanche chimed in with, "Of course we will. We're family. In times of need family never lets each other down!" George threw her a look of disbelief, but realized Blanche would do almost anything for her sister. "I don't want to own any part of your business or take on any of your responsibilities," George began strongly, "Just give me a note and make me president of the company in title alone until I get my loan back, and we can work something out." Inside I jumped for joy. Having George on board also meant we were able to use his name, business experience, success and stature to give us more credibility when we applied to banks and suppliers for credit. Without his reputation and financial backing, Guido's never would have made it.

Despite all this, by the fall of 1979 we were broke again.

Now what?

CHAPTER 2

THE UNKNOWN UNKNOWNS

I knew we had the right product to be successful, and our customers loved us, but we needed to break this cycle of making money in the summer and losing it all in the winter. We just needed to find the right partner with the capital to get us through the winter, and more importantly, the contacts and a sales organization to expand our distribution. With this combination, we could increase our winter sales and become sustainable year-round. The question was, could we find this partner in time?

As things got more and more desperate, my parents and I started meeting for breakfast every Sunday morning with our accountant, Stanley Priskie, to review our cash position and discuss the company's future. But no matter how many times we talked, nothing seemed to be changing. We were heading towards bankruptcy, and it was another make or break point in the business. So very late one night after cleaning up, Dad, Mom and I sat down to talk about our next breakfast meeting with Stanley. We needed to convince Stanley to help us raise money. We knew he had many wealthy, successful clients, and agreed that we would not leave Sunday breakfast without convincing him to make a few introductions. The question was, what would motivate him to put his reputation on the line by recommending an almost bankrupt Italian ices company to one of his long-term clients? Dad reminded me that most business decisions are made based on one of two criteria: greed or fear. We decided to appeal to his greed.

We spent the next few nights planning and strategizing, and decided that I would make the presentation. That way, if Stanley didn't agree initially, Dad could use his close friendship with him to have another bite at the apple. That Sunday, as my parents and I piled into the car for a long and windy drive down to Stanley's house, I sat silently in the back, replaying my pitch over and over in my head.

After a few minutes of socializing and small talk about the family with Stanley, I took the reins and steered the conversation to business. "We need to find a true business partner," I explained, "One with contacts in the foodservice or supermarket business, who can invest hundreds of thousands of dollars into Guido's and help us grow our sales. If they do," I confidently assured him, "We promise they can make millions of dollars and we will pay you a percentage of the money they invest. Otherwise," I went on, "It's looking like we might have to shut down the company this winter. So this is a perfect opportunity for someone with capital who is already selling products in either of these markets."

Having finished my well-prepared pitch, I watched his facial expression closely. Nothing changed. Inside, my heart was pounding and my palms were sweating; if he turned us down, I knew that would likely spell the end of Guido's. Though my mind was racing, I forced myself to keep picturing him saying yes just as my father instructed me. Stanley stood up and slowly paced around the kitchen table, mulling over my heartfelt pitch. He turned to my father and asked, "Irv, what do you think?" Without hesitation, my father responded matter-of-factly, "This is a rare and valuable opportunity. For the right partner with money and contacts they could have a production facility run by Richard with the capability to make as much product as they could sell."

This was another one of those moments that felt like a lifetime. Finally, he turned around with a big grin on his face. "I agree!" he exclaimed. I nearly collapsed in my chair with joy and relief. Stanley said he would make the introductions but without getting paid a percentage; he had to convince his clients what a great deal this would be for them, and if he were getting paid to make the introductions it would taint his reasoning. In fact, he told us, he already had the perfect partner in mind. It took every shred of willpower not to jump up and bear hug him right then and there.

Once we got in the car and rounded the corner, I let out a big shout and my father congratulated me. "Way to go! You gave him just enough to make it interesting and then allowed him to make his own decision." My father's praise was almost as rewarding as Stanley's response. In a matter of minutes, I went from being distraught and almost out of work to ecstatic about our huge step forward.

That perfect partner Stanley had in mind was Murray Verlin, a tough, no-nonsense New Yorker whose food brokerage company represented Tropicana Orange Juice and Louis Sherry Ice Cream to supermarkets nationwide. As promised, Stanley scheduled the introduction, and a week later my dad and I drove down to Murray's New York office to meet him. Though very nervous that this could be our last chance to save our business again, we put on a smile and set out to convince Murray this was an opportunity he couldn't afford to miss. After a grueling hour and a half of very difficult questions – about the Italian ices business, the manufacturing process, the competition, how much money we needed and how we would spend it – Murray asked us to step outside the room while he spoke with Stanley.

While the two of them spent the next 15 minutes deciding the future of our company, I nervously kept pacing back and forth. As difficult as it was, I focused my entire mind's power into visualizing Murray opening the door with a smile, shaking our hands and announcing, "Congratulations, partners. We are going to make a lot of money together!" Finally, Dad and I were called back in for a decision, only to find Stanley in there alone. My heart dropped. That is, until Stanley gave us a big smile. Murray had just run out to another meeting but he loved the ices, and more importantly, he loved us! His company was already calling on many of the same supermarket buyers Guido's wanted to target, and having a new and exciting product would make him look innovative and different from most other food brokers.

He agreed on the spot to be responsible for all sales, marketing and financing of the business for 50 percent ownership in the company. All I had to do was figure out how to manufacture enough Italian ices for all the business they were going to bring in. In addition to funding the company, Murray offered to provide Jack and me with paid consulting jobs during the winter until they filled the factory with enough sales to keep us busy year-round. It was another near-death experience for the business averted, and I was over the moon about what a great partnership we thought we had found.

We began that first year in the blissful throes of the partnership honeymoon phase, with as much funding as we needed. Like many young romances, that first year was full of adventure, and Murray's support was crucial during one of the scariest, and now funniest, experiences I've had to date. Murray's salesforce didn't get the overwhelming response they had anticipated; we sold very little to the supermarkets in the summer of 1980. Unfortunately, my father had taken the lofty projections of how much Murray promised to sell and, in order to get the best price, simply placed a blanket purchase order for the full amount of packaging we'd need. Next thing I know, I received a surprisingly angry phone call from an ultra-Orthodox businessman in Brooklyn who printed inner cartons for us. Most of the packaging remained in his warehouse, and he was not amused.

One day, my father's not-so-friendly box maker called me to demand we pay him in full for all the boxes my father had ordered and move them out of his warehouse immediately. I calmly informed him that he should have made only the first shipment amount, not the entire blanket purchase order quantity, and that I had no money to pay him. This did not go over well. "Son, if you don't pay my bill in full this week, I will be paying you a visit," he said, his voice growing louder and more furious with each syllable, "I know where you work. *I promise I will break your legs, then shoot and kill you!*"

Shock would be an understatement, but that's what I blame for the most bizarre, reflexive reaction of my life: "Why waste your time breaking my legs," I asked mockingly, "if you're going to shoot and kill me anyhow!?" Click.

Did I really just taunt and hang up on a death threat? What was wrong with me? Slumping down in my office chair, nervous beads of sweat dripped down my forehead as I began hyperventilating, shaking and laughing all at once. In addition to fearing for my life, I was scared for our business. If we had to buy all those boxes right away we would be bankrupt and he would have killed our business instead of me.

Once I finally calmed down enough to breathe and form sentences, I called my father in hysterics. The boxes. The money. My looming death! "*How could you order all those boxes?!*" I demanded to know, taking out my fear and horror on my frustratingly calm father. Not one to lose his composure, he quietly told me to calm down, assuring me that everything would be all right. "Did you give him our address in Monticello?" I asked shakily, nervous that my potential assassin would show up on my doorstep the following week. Ignoring my inquiry, Dad just told me to breathe deeply and call Tony, Murray's Italian sales manager, to explain the situation.

My breath was a bit more even by the time I hung up with my father and I quickly dialed Tony to recount the horrible exchange.

"Calm down and talk slower," he patiently instructed me – I guess I wasn't as settled as I thought I was. "Your supplier just made the biggest mistake of his pathetic little life talking to you like that. Give me his name and phone number, go back to work and don't worry about a thing. I have handled dozens of calls like this before." The confidence in his voice was unusually comforting.

"In fact," Tony continued, "you should expect an apology by the end of the week." My emotions went from fear and shock to relief and amazement. I didn't ask how, I didn't ask why, I was just thrilled and relieved about my good fortune. I called my father back to explain how my call with Tony went and he acted as if he knew what Tony was going to say all along.

Lo and behold, within a week I received another call from the same infuriated supplier, but this time he was an absolute angel apologizing for the misunderstanding. "Everything has been taken care of," he kindly assured me, "You can go ahead and order the boxes whenever you'd like!" To this day, I have no idea what Tony said or threatened him with, but in that moment I was so relieved I couldn't care. This was my first big lesson in the importance of knowing the right people.

• • •

Though the supermarket business never really materialized under Murray's sales team the summer of 1980, my father and Uncle Bob had done a great job setting up a network of food brokers around the country to sell our Italian ices into school lunch programs. The school business had grown to almost a million dollars a year, and though it wasn't enough to support the business entirely, it paid some of the bills and gave us a bit of leverage when it came to negotiating with Murray for more money.

But just as we started to feel a sense of stability, we got blindsided again. That fall, the U.S. Department of Agriculture (USDA) made a ruling that junk food was to be entirely removed from all school lunch programs within nine months. That meant no soda, no potato chips and most importantly to us, NO ITALIAN ICES! One announcement, and bam – there goes the majority of our business.

As soon as I read the detailed report of the changes to the school lunch requirements in the *Food Industry News*, my emotions went wild. It felt like I was kicked in the stomach once again. Was this going to finally be the end of Guido's? I knew we couldn't do anything to change the USDA ruling so I immediately accepted it. But with no school lunch business and very little supermarket sales at the time, this seemed like the final straw that could close down the company.

Very quickly, however, I decided to reframe. Crises often can be the force that pushes us to pivot in a new and ultimately more successful direction. How could we turn this existential business threat into a lucrative opportunity? This was too important a decision to try to resolve myself, so I called for a meeting with my parents and Jack to explore all our options. We needed an action plan that night; speed was the key to survival, and this was going to take all the brainpower we could muster.

Late that same night the news came out, we sat around the

kitchen table debating what we could do next. Even though I recognized this was yet another episode in a series of regularly emerging crises, I felt like an emotional basket case. My fears about losing the business dominated my thoughts and I struggled to stay focused on finding a solution. I couldn't stop thinking about how much work was lost, and the massive scale of our challenges ahead was overwhelming. But when I stopped to observe my parents' reaction, they didn't seem frazzled or out of sorts. That was my reality check. Losing my cool wouldn't help anyone; if we wanted to save the company, I had to follow their example and learn to keep my emotions under control. Trying to take on all our problems at once would just overwhelm me, so I decided to let go of lost work and focus on the solution, one small step at a time.

With this adjustment in perspective, I found a newfound sense of focus reminiscent of my basketball days; time stood still and everything fell silent as I honed in on the immediate goal ahead. With a clear head and trusted team by my side, I knew we would find a way forward. After much discussion, we agreed this could be the seed of an even greater opportunity. "This takes a lot of food off the table for the kids to eat," my father commented, "But the kids in schools still have to eat something. If we can figure out what they are going to eat instead of junk food, we could turn this fiasco into a golden opportunity!" We all asked the same question: "How do we figure out what will be replacing the junk food?"

We agreed that the customers have all our answers, so I hopped on a plane to North Carolina to meet with some of our biggest school-food-service directors to find out what the kids were going to eat once all the junk food was removed. After about a dozen meetings, I heard the same answer across the board; if we could put two ounces of juice into Guido's Italian Ices, not only could the schools buy them, but they would be able to serve our product as a fruit or a vegetable, which is required in each meal. There were also tight cost constraints; school budgets required that they purchase each one for no more than a dime.

As a manufacturer, I knew that if we had to sell our Italian ices for a dime, we needed to be able to make them for a nickel. The good news was I had a clear vision of exactly what we needed to develop. The bad news was that the cup and lid alone already cost 4 cents.

I returned to the factory the next day and immediately began calling the chemists at our flavor suppliers. I knew very little about product development since our existing recipes came from my uncle's previous business, but figured with some ingredients and a little direction, Jack and I could start experimenting on a trial-and-error basis. We needed to find a new juice-filled recipe as quickly as possible. So I asked Jack to join me in Monticello and called up Uncle Bob to see if he could hire another driver for the pretzel delivery business to replace Jack until we figured things out. Next, I collected dozens of flavor samples from each of our suppliers, and spent hours speaking with their head chemists about how to blend flavors together when freezing them.

Exhausted but very excited, deep down I knew that this was the golden seed of opportunity my father had been talking about that anxious night sitting around the kitchen table. If we could quickly develop cost-effective, great-tasting Italian ices with two ounces of juice, we wouldn't just replace our existing business with school lunch programs, we could grow it exponentially. I had reignited this burning passion inside me. We were onto something very big, and instead of being down and distraught, I found myself excited and motivated to succeed.

Night after night, once all the machines were cleaned and batches for the next day completed, Jack and I would spend hours trying every combination of flavors we could think of to find one that would keep its flavor after freezing. The challenge was that unless the sweetness and acidity of the flavors and citric acid were *perfectly* balanced during the freezing process, we'd lose the strong flavored taste our customers had come to know and love. We tried batch after batch, but after freezing, each and every one came out tasteless.

As weeks turned into months, our enthusiasm began to wane as we tried every combination of juices that we could think of: guava, passion fruit, grape. Nothing kept a good enough flavor. To keep us motivated, I kept repeating how important our work would ultimately become, envisioning the future with a successful result and not getting bogged down in the disappointments of the present.

Then one night, exhausted and weary, Jack tried a new apple concentrate, and when we tried the frozen product it tasted amazing. This particular apple concentrate and the liquid sugar we were using had approximately the same brix (solids and sweetness), and the taste was bland enough that we could flavor over it to make the ices taste like cherry, grape, orange or, the hardest and most popular flavor, lemon. Eureka! After only a few months, we had stumbled upon a real juice product with similar cost that tasted great – it was exactly what we were looking for.

But that was only half the challenge. We still had to significantly reduce the cost of the cup and lid. I felt like a worn-down mountain climber halfway to the summit; exhausted by the path thus far but a long way from the top. While feverishly working to find a new formulation, I began scouring trade magazines for a package that would fit into our cost structure. One day, I stumbled across an advertisement for a product that came in a four-sided, twisted-paper package called a Tetra Pak. I recognized it as something syrup and nuts were packaged in. It required less material and was more affordable than the traditional cup and lid we had been using, but I had no idea if it could work for frozen products.

I called up Milliken & Company, who had the U.S. rights to the Tetra Pak, and was given the name and phone number of Hal Gibson, their northeast regional salesperson. After a few days of continuous phone calls (there were no cell phones, voicemail or emails back then), he finally called me back. A good old South Carolina boy, Hal talked slowly, moved slowly and at first didn't have the urgency that I desperately needed. He explained to me that their packaging cost only about a penny each, but they had never packaged a frozen product in it and he doubted that they could. I tried convincing him to visit us in Monticello right away, but Hal was on his way to Boston for a two-day convention and had to drive straight back to their South Carolina office for an important customer visit right afterwards.

Desperate and not to be denied, I tried everything I could think of to persuade him to visit us. Would he sympathize with a small, struggling company and do us a favor? No.

Then I tried appealing to his greed. Come visit and you'll see you could make a lot of money working with us, I prompted. I don't think he believed me on that one. Following the example my father set, I kept a pleasant, positive discussion going, learning about Hal in order to understand and overcome all his objections. However, Hal began losing interest and patience as I continued to push on. Our survival depended on him saying yes, and I began to panic. Clearly, I wasn't going to achieve this over the phone, so before he had a chance to shut me down completely, I told him my father would meet him in the lobby of his Boston hotel at 8 the next morning before his meetings for the day. Despite Hal's attempted protests, my father left Monticello at 4 a.m. the next morning and was waiting for Hal in the lobby of his Boston hotel by 8 a.m. sharp.

A polite Southern gentleman, Hal wasn't going to ignore my father after he drove four hours that morning to see him. It took

Dad only half an hour to convince Hal how big this opportunity was for his company, and how crucial it was for us. My father was one of the greatest salesmen I've ever known, with an uncanny ability to forge meaningful connections with mere strangers. I'm not sure exactly what my father said to convince Hal, but when he called to tell me the great news, I didn't have the energy to care how he did it. All that mattered was that Hal was coming to visit us in Monticello when his convention ended, and we desperately needed to convince him to install a Tetra Pak machine in our factory before he left. While many entrepreneurs can feel the need to solve problems ourselves, building a great team that can shine where we need them is often key to survival.

Finding an affordable package was not my only critical challenge at the time. Having dealt with all our business problems and near shutdowns for over five years, Don, our head maintenance and refrigeration manager, was considering leaving us for a better, more lucrative position at a nearby company. Without him we were done. While I had learned how to run a business (or run it just well enough to avoid bankruptcy), I had no idea how to oversee or maintain the Freon refrigeration units needed to support our freezers and blast tunnel. Much to my relief, Don said that when he saw my father leave at 4 a.m., drive four hours for a half-hour meeting and return the same day, he knew there was no way we would ever fail. That was the moment he decided to stay – one more crisis averted.

Two days later, Hal arrived as promised and was shocked to see how small our operation was, especially after my father insisted that we'd be such a valuable customer. When we finished touring the facilities, he asked me where the rest of the factory was. This came out of left field for me; I had been so busy running the business, I never stopped to think that our size might be a concern!

My stomach dropped and hands clammed up, and I feared Hal might up and leave without even sitting down to talk to us. Quick on my feet, I assured him we were large enough already. We could run three shifts, 24 hours a day, seven days a week, and ship right from the back of the blast tunnel onto waiting trucks when the demand surged. I don't think he truly believed me, but he was interested (or polite) enough to hear more and come to a decision himself.

After moving into our cramped offices, Dad, Hal and I spent the next six hours talking about everything and anything. During those talks, we got to learn about Hal as a person – his childhood, his education, how much he enjoyed working for Milliken & Company. As luck would have it, Hal also began his career working inside a close-knit family startup. Our plan to appeal to his heart and not his brain or pocketbook worked perfectly as we bonded over the trials and tribulations of keeping a small family business afloat. After all was said and done, Hal agreed to place a Tetra Pak machine in our factory. Guido's was still alive!

As Hal packed up to leave, I walked out with him, adding an uncomfortable addendum to our conversation. "I hope you realize I can't afford to pay for the machine upfront," I blurted out, with an apologetic look in my eyes. I had been dreading this bit, especially after our operation hadn't lived up to his expectations. But, I knew in my gut that now was the right time to bring it up. He paused, smiling gently and answered with the grace of a father speaking to a child. "I can see from our conversation today that you are just starting out. I believe in you and your father, and that you will do everything possible to be successful. I will work out a special deal for you to pay a little extra for each package you buy until you pay off the machine." I could not contain my excitement and instinctively ran over to give him a huge hug. "Thank you so much, Hal, you won't regret it!" Little did I know that I had just met a man who would not only become a very important supplier in the future but an incredibly special friend. That night as I sat basking in my newfound relief, I took a moment to reflect on how we had been so lucky yet again. Why is it that Hal agreed to install the Tetra Pak machine and cut us a special deal to pay for it over time? The first step to any deal is identifying a want or need the other person has, and filling it. We didn't have anything Hal needed. But people in business do special things for people they care about. Our challenge here had been to get Hal to care about my father and me, to foster a desire to help us.

When Hal saw that my father drove four hours to arrive at 8

a.m. for a 30-minute meeting that had such a low probability of success, he realized how much this meant to us. Our effort and commitment struck a human chord inside Hal. My father quickly built just enough of a connection and business opportunity for him to agree to visit our factory on his way home.

Once Hal had arrived, the real work began. Given the small size of our business, we needed to make both a strong business case and a genuine connection with him. Probing questions about Hal's life and business gave him the space to talk about whatever he felt like until we could unearth some common ground to bond over. Having been part of a close-knit, struggling family startup meant Hal could empathize with us. He had been us. And once we connected heart to heart, he would go out on a limb to try to help us. It's funny, but by the end of our conversation, I felt the same way about him. The secret to success in this case was uncovering common values and shared experiences, making his decision both business and personal.

In applying this approach, there are many times where we can't find anything in common with the other person. In those instances, I like to ask one of my favorite questions: "What would you like to do today that you can't that would have the biggest impact on your life?" When the other person asks if I mean business or personal, I always say both, but lead with your personal life. It is amazing some of the stories I have heard. One buyer told me he would like to cure cancer because his mother was dying of cancer. Another told me her child had a heart defect and if she could find a cure it would be the most impactful thing in her life.

Over and over people have turned from indifferent and aloof to vulnerable and caring. Of course, I would then follow up with some sort of connection from my life that would show my empathy and compassion. It's not a foolproof approach, and there are some people who simply won't care, but the vast majority of the time when I've asked that question I've been able to break the ice and find a channel for meaningful connection.

When Hal left our factory that day I was full of enthusiasm and excitement. Once the Tetra Pak machine was delivered, however, the warmth and good feelings of our initial meeting quickly dissipated into the cold hard facts of reality. Though this packaging was clearly our answer for the price, it wasn't working for our frozen products. We tried everything they knew but could never get it to seal properly, and our ices were leaking everywhere. Yet again, just when I thought I had a perfect solution, something new would turn up. Going back and forth from elation to disbelief was deeply draining, but no matter how mentally and emotionally exhausted I was, I refused to give up my positive attitude. Eventually I realized that these constant fire drills are just the way life and business really work. So, I changed my expectations and was no longer surprised (though still frustrated) when problems arose.

After weeks of trying to fix the leaking package problem, the engineers finally concluded that the Tetra Pak machine we had would not seal a package around the ices. Not to be denied, my father and I called Hal's boss to find a solution. As Ray, a senior executive at Milliken, began to relay the same sorry conclusion his engineers had come to, my father stepped in. "If we can find a way to put a man on the moon," he asserted, sternly yet politely, "Your guys can find a way to make the package seal our Italian ices." Though he did not appreciate my father's analogy, Hal's boss did agree to instruct their engineers to find a solution.

After extensive discussions between our maintenance manager and theirs, they came to the conclusion that the only possibility was to exchange our small machine for a much bigger, stronger and more powerful industrial sealing machine. They said it would take a week to prepare a larger machine for shipment and then another week for delivery. However, this was urgent and we couldn't wait another day, let alone two weeks. So my father, Jack and I huddled together to figure out what to do.

My father came up with the solution, as he often did. We would load the small machine on the back of a rented 16-foot truck and Jack would drive straight to the Milliken facilities in Spartanburg, South Carolina. The fact that the bigger machine was not ready, that Jack had other plans that night and that the current machine did not fit into the back of a 16-foot truck did not stop my father. Those were my problems, he said. My father did not let the obstacles stand in the way of the best solution. A key to being successful in business is knowing when and how to take risks, he often liked to remind me. As a small and struggling business, we had no choice but to take chances; often our only options were to take a risk or fail.

I called Hal and told him that Jack would be at the loading dock of their factory in South Carolina the next morning with our smaller machine ready to pick up the larger machine. When he protested that the machine would not be tested and ready, I told him to load all the new machine parts on our truck, and they could assemble and test it in our factory. Jack was on his way and would wait there until the larger machine was loaded on the back of his truck. With time quickly running down until our Italian ices were kicked out of the schools, we did not have an extra moment to spare. Without waiting for his approval, I thanked him and got off the phone.

The next challenge was to get Don and his maintenance team to rent a 16-foot truck (that was the largest truck Jack could drive with his license), disassemble the current machine and load it onto the truck in parts. Later that afternoon, the machine was loaded in the back of the truck, the route was mapped out for Jack and he was on his way for a 14-hour drive south. He drove straight through the night speeding past the truck scales he was supposed to stop at because he was late and the truck was overweight. The next morning as the Milliken factory opened the loading dock doors, they found Jack sleeping in the cab of his truck, which happened to be occupying one of their three loading dock bays. We had instructed Jack not to leave without the new machine, so when they told Jack he didn't have an appointment and had to move out of the way, he refused until they unloaded the small machine from the back of his truck.

The dock supervisor was mad as hell. But, after several threatening phone calls and some smooth talking from Hal, they unloaded the smaller machine, placed the parts of the new larger machine onto Jack's truck without even testing it, and sent Jack on his way. I can still see in my mind that irate dock supervisor wagging his finger, telling Jack never to come near his dock again. Lucky for us, we had Hal. He knew we had no choice but to just show up, and like all great salespeople, he represented our best interests, not those of his company. Some time before midnight that night Jack pulled into our loading dock as I was finishing cleaning up. The next morning Don and his team unloaded the new machine and assembled it to the best of their ability. I called Hal to let him know we were ready for a serviceman to fine tune the machine. I'd lost track of all the "crisis averted!" high fives by this point.

After about a week of testing, changing out parts, significantly upgrading our electrical service for the new machine and several other unforeseen challenges, we were ready to start testing it with real Italian ices. To everyone's surprise and excitement, though not perfect, the new machine actually sealed the packages!

My emotions were flying again as I saw us getting closer to finally delivering the product we knew our school customers would love. This was truly an example of "necessity is the mother of invention." I had been riding this roller coaster for half a decade, building up the business throughout the spring and summer and nearly going bankrupt each winter. We were determined to break this cycle, to develop a product that could generate enough cash to keep us in business year after year.

Having combined our new, juice-packed, great-tasting product and a novel new package that fit into our cost structure, we went back to the schools to see what they thought. Bingo! The kids loved it, and with two ounces of juice and a 10-cent price tag, the school buyers loved it too. We did have one small hiccup; the buyers had a hard time tearing open the package and started to put up a stink. The kids, on the other hand, just used their teeth to rip it open and had no problem. Ultimately, we figured out how to put a notch in the top of the package to help adults open it as well. With a great-tasting, juice-containing, cost-effective product, we had hit the nail on the head and didn't realize the magnitude of what we had created.

Packaging for our low-cost, fruit-juice-infused products that would explode across America in 1981.

With a great new product ready to go to market, we needed all the help we could get, so we dug deeper into the family Rolodex. My sister Susan left her successful real estate career to work tirelessly alongside my father and Uncle Bob introducing our new product to the schools around the country. My cousin Idonna also joined on board, representing Guido's at school food shows and stepping up to fill whatever responsibilities arose.

With real fruit juice in our product, we decided to change our name from Guido's Italian Ices to Guido's Icee Juicees, highlighting our fantastic new selling point. We had printed up thousands of new packages, and I was walking with my head held high when, within weeks of introducing our product, we were served with a lawsuit demanding we cease and desist using our new name. As it turned out, there was another frozen product at the time called Icee, a frozen slushie sold in many movie theaters. While Icee hadn't made it big yet, they had already copyrighted their name and were pursuing their legal rights over it with full force. This was the first time I had ever been sued, and I was just about pissing in my pants with fear.

Immediately, scenes of courtroom and jail time filled my mind. I had no idea what it meant to be sued, and I naturally thought of the scariest possibility. The good news was I didn't have time to dwell too long on these courtroom drama nightmares; there were too many other problems to deal with. After calling up an attorney for advice, it was just another few items on my never-ending to-do list, and I felt fine. In the end, after several tense discussions and realizing we were (unintentionally) in the wrong, we came to an agreement. Guido's would change our name to Ice Juicee (not Icee Juicee) and Icee would drop the lawsuit and allow us to use up existing packaging.

Just when we thought we were out of the woods and on top of the world, I received my second life-changing phone call. A month after we shipped our first Ice Juicee orders to the schools, our financial partner, Murray, called explaining that he was not happy with his investment. Since Guido's Ices did not sell as well as he had expected in supermarkets the previous summer, he would now have to invest significantly more money to keep the company going for another year – something he had not anticipated.

Looking for the quickest way to get his investment back, Murray was informing me of his decision to stop paying any bills, shut the company down for 30 days and then reopen it in time for the summer season. He figured that with no other alternative, we would take a very small amount for our half of the shares and he would own the entire company himself. He said I was welcome to come back and work for him running the factory, but my parents weren't needed since he would be in charge. Shocked was the least of my reactions.

My fingers gripped tightly around the receiver as I attempted to contain the rage shooting through my veins. Who did this asshole think he was? My blood felt like it was literally boiling, and I broke into a sweat. Was this the end, was all we had worked for over the past five years going down the drain with one phone call? Just when it seemed like we had turned around the business with our new Ice Juicee, Murray couldn't just whisk it away in a moment. What about firing all our employees? I still hadn't gotten over my initial distaste of firing Marilyn and her entire team that first winter, now I might have to fire everyone. It felt like my whole world was collapsing. NO. Absolutely not. This was not happening.

After what seemed like several minutes of expletives, I slammed down the phone. Very rarely do I lose it, but I was livid. After taking quite awhile to get myself together, I walked into the adjacent room and explained the situation to my father so we could figure out what to do next. Instances of outrage can be the most challenging times to forget about the problem and focus on the solution – but these are the exact moments when we need it most. As we sat down, my father didn't get upset at all but rather asked me to start listing all the good things we had going on our side.

The good news was that we had already begun receiving checks from schools that had been buying our new Ice Juicees. The big challenge was that when Murray invested, he set up a check-writing system where we would need two signatures to send out any checks to pay bills. My mother would make out the checks, I would sign them then send them down to his New York office, where his finance VP would countersign and send them out. We hadn't objected to this arrangement since it was the only way he agreed to invest in our company in the first place and we never thought he would try to take advantage of us like this. At this point I knew they would no longer sign any checks I sent to them.

We had come too far to lose it all now. From the prison work-release program to the Tetra Pak machine, my experience thus far had illustrated that just because a problem seems insurmountable doesn't mean there's no workaround – it was just a matter of finding it. For two days I racked my brain without any luck. My emotions swung between utter exasperation and an inexplicable, quiet confidence that the perfect solution would soon surface.

Finally, I realized that I was mistakenly looking at the problem, not the solution. So I took a step back and evaluated what we did have: customer checks, but no way to pay our suppliers. Then a light came on. We had a local payroll bank account that needed only my signature. Maybe we could deposit and issue checks from there to pay our invoices!

I ran to the local bank, but much to my chagrin, the teller explained that we could only issue payroll checks from that account and couldn't use it to pay our suppliers. However, he continued, if we had a petty cash account, we could deposit the customer checks and make payments from there. Murray set us up with only a payroll account at that bank, but I thanked the bank officer and went out smiling. Murray had also organized a petty cash account at another bank for things like deliveries, postage and office supplies. The greatest part? With a $500 limit, this account only required my signature! We began depositing all the customer checks into the petty cash account and paying $2,000 invoices with four $500 checks. This enabled us to pay all our past-due invoices and continue paying our bills as they came in. Business was booming, and we were working around the clock as springtime steadily approached. I had never been so excited about our business outlook, and with this turnaround the stress stemming from Murray's harrowing phone call slipped away.

A month later, we received another call from Murray inquiring how we could possibly have kept the business open without him. Rather than telling him to screw himself (though that sounded immensely rewarding), I told him that I had lost all respect for him, didn't need him and would prefer to have nothing to do with him from here on out. Whatever he wanted to know, he could ask his accountant, Stanley Priskie. Then, I hung up. Boy did that feel good!

It wasn't even an hour before I received a note that Stanley was irate and on the line with an urgent call. As he explained to my father and me how deeply I had pissed off Murray, I realized that my pride may have gotten the best of me. Murray was threatening to sue us and shut us down completely. He was the nasty type of businessman who loved a good legal fight, and knew he had much more money than we did if it ever got to court. I didn't feel like a big shot anymore. We might have had more orders than any other point in Guido's history, but we certainly didn't have the time or the money for a lawsuit.

We agreed to discuss it at our Sunday breakfast meeting. The rest of the week flew by as I was buried in work. On the drive to Stanley's, my parents and I discussed the possibilities. Though he disagreed with the way I acted, my father understood where I was coming from and was confident this could be the seed of an even greater opportunity. If we could only get rid of Murray and keep the company to ourselves, it would work out great for us in the end. Stanley was livid and not as kind to me. Berating me for my immature behavior, Stanley could not fathom how I could put the company in such danger just as we were turning the corner.

Having worked with Murray for many years, Stanley saw him put numerous young companies out of business. Now I had poked the bear, and he was planning to do the same to us. I felt awful. While I took a moment to mope, my father wasted no time. Reminding Stanley that we couldn't do anything about the conversation I already had with Murray, my father informed him that it was his job to fix the problem and find us a solution. If fear and greed were the only two things that motivated a man like Murray, that left us one option. Murray clearly had no fear of us at this time, so we had to go for greed. We instructed Stanley to call Murray and see if we could offer him half his original investment to buy out all his shares, since the company was worth nothing at the time. While he thought we were out of our minds, Stanley told us he would see what he could do.

On the ride home I was feeling down and my father could tell. When he pressed me about it, I explained that I had plenty of challenges without creating more crises for myself – it seemed like crisis creation was his job! My dad laughed and said we were in an exciting time and he had been through much worse. Confident that we would work out a solution with Murray, he explained that my first priority should be filling the rush of orders and running the business. I wasn't as confident, but decided to defer to Dad and not worry about it at the time.

The following Sunday at our breakfast meeting, Stanley said he had made a small amount of progress with Murray. As a favor to Stanley, he agreed not to sue us but still wanted to teach us a lesson I would never forget. So he informed Stanley that we could give him double his money in cash up front for his share of the company, or he would see us in court. We didn't have that kind of money and this offer was completely ridiculous. My father told Stanley to go back and use his long-standing relationship with Murray to work something out that was fair. We knew Murray would never do anything for us, but maybe as a favor to Stanley, he would agree to something reasonable after cooling off. My father also told Stanley that with whatever deal he was able to work out, he'd also have to find a way for us to finance the terms. Though not happy about it, Stanley accepted it and knew it was true.

For the next few months Murray came back with nasty threats and ultimatums. But my father held his ground and explained he had dealt with all sorts of unethical businessmen in the past and no matter how much money they had, guys like this didn't like to lose money no matter how little. It made them look bad to their friends and executives if they couldn't get their money back from a little business like ours. Again, my father was right. After a few months of difficult back-and-forth negotiations, Stanley finally cut a deal we could live with. We would repay Murray's original investment over the next three years if he gave us all his stock back. I was ecstatic. Business was booming, I had learned so many valuable lessons and we had bought our own company back from a tyrant. What a relief!

Our issue was no longer survival. It was growth. So what exactly were we supposed to do next?

CHAPTER 3

EXPANSION

After six years of struggling just to keep our business alive, we were walking on air through summer of 1981. From being fired, broke and hopeless a few months earlier, all of a sudden we were hitting on all cylinders. Schools were buying as many Ice Juicees as we could churn out, and as we approached the summertime, orders began coming in from the camps, hotels, and bungalow colonies alike. We were running production 24 hours a day to keep up with the demand. Guido's Ice Juicees were the new rage and it felt *great*.

Needing to expand production to keep up with demand, we bought six acres of raw land 30 miles closer to New York City and started building a new factory. My Uncle Bob sold the pretzel business so he and my father could sell Guido's across the country. Meanwhile, Jack moved back to Monticello to help me run the Guido's production while I built the new factory. Once it was ready we would move closer to the new factory, so when my lease expired I gave up my apartment. This meant Jack and I had to sleep on the same couch in my parent's place for the summer while working 19-hour days. He worked from noon to 7 a.m., catching a few hours of sleep during the morning shift. Meanwhile, I ran the morning shift, built the new factory throughout the rest of the day and after helping Jack clean up, slept from 1 a.m. to 6 a.m.

While certainly not the most luxurious of living situations, I didn't realize quite how ridiculous it all was until one morning when Jack managed to finish work a little early. Overworked and sleep deprived, he was so exhausted when he came home that he didn't have the energy to lift up the covers. He collapsed face first onto the couch, not realizing I was still sleeping. I don't know which of us was more shocked and confused! Still, we had turned the corner, we were making money and it felt so good.

Later that year, I received a phone call from a parent of a student in North Carolina. Her child loved Guido's Ice Juicees and was buying them at school, but where could she find them in supermarkets? I took her name and phone number and told her I would call her back. Instantly, I realized she couldn't be the only parent whose child enjoyed the Ice Juicees at school and wanted them at home. So I looked up all the large supermarket chains in North Carolina and found the biggest one, a company called Food Lion. I called up its headquarters and asked for the purchasing department for frozen novelties. My call was transferred to an older gentleman who was very courteous, but in the end said he was not interested in our product.

Extremely disappointed, I felt like I had not done a good enough job explaining the merits of our Ice Juicees. I was certain he needed our product, one that was in demand but hard to find. I just failed to convey the true value and how we filled his needs. It was then that I remembered: No is the first step to any sale. If he had said yes, I would just be filling an order. With that first no, the sale process had just begun, forcing me to better understand my client's needs and therefore build a stronger, lasting relationship. The next day I called back and asked for a frozen novelty buyer. When the operator asked me which one, I asked her to list their names and then chose a different buyer than the original. This time I engaged the buyer in discussion, listening very closely and trying to understand just how he chose his new products and what his objections were to our Ice Juicees. His goal, I learned, was to choose products that would sell quickly. Since we weren't in any other supermarkets, we had no name recognition, no large marketing budget and no proof that our products would sell, so he, too, turned me down. But all was not lost, as he had given me great advice on what was important to the buyers at their company and how they decided to bring in new products. This time when I got off the phone I was not dejected, but rather excited by the conversation.

After one day, I couldn't wait any longer. I was so anxious to call them back. I had to calm myself down in case I was rejected again. But deep down inside, I knew I could get to yes. When I called, I asked for a third, different buyer. This time I explained the benefits of our new product: how sales had exploded in local schools and how parents would come into Food Lion stores to buy Guido's Ice Juicees and leave with other staples like milk, bread and eggs. This was an opportunity for them to grow their customer base as well, I told him.

Now that I was speaking to his needs, this buyer agreed that Guido's Ice Juicees was exactly the type of new product they were looking for. In the back of my mind, I was thanking the previous buyer for doing such a good job explaining the company's decision-making process. The first buyer taught me that I needed to listen. The second showed me that I needed to ask the right questions. In the end, the third buyer said yes because we overcame all his objections and gave him what he needed.

He placed a small initial order for several of his test stores and said if it sold well he would expand it to all of their stores. We had to work very hard and fast to design and order new retail boxes to take advantage of the summertime business. With no money to promote or market it, I didn't know how we were going to ensure that our ices would move off the shelves. My father and I went to several supermarkets to study the frozen novelty case where our product would be placed. We evaluated the competition's boxes, trying to figure out a way ours could stand out; frozen novelties were an impulse buy and we needed our box to jump off the shelf.

Since we didn't have the money to draw customers to the frozen novelty case, we needed to make sure we got their attention once they were there. Most of the other frozen novelty boxes were white or very light in color. Therefore, we designed ours in all black with red, orange and purple lettering for the different flavors. No one had done that yet, but we didn't mind being unorthodox. Our box jumped out as if to say, "Here I am, try me!" It didn't cost much more to create a package that looked special; we just had to be willing to try something new. Then, as luck would have it, Dole introduced its Frozen Fruit Bar on a stick in 1982. With it, Dole rolled out a multimillion-dollar advertising promotion to bring new customers to the frozen novelty case. So even without a marketing budget, Guido's Ice Juicees jumped off the shelf and took off like wildfire – our retail business was an instant success!

That fall, my father and Uncle Bob went out and set up a network of retail food brokers to sell Ice Juicees to supermarkets across the country. By the summer of 1983, Guido's Ice Juicees variety pack (Cherry, Grape and Orange) had become the No. 1 selling frozen novelty product in the United States. We were shipping five, 40-foot truckloads of Ice Juicees per week to our California distributors to meet the massive demand and we needed even more than our new factory could produce.

As we sat down to breakfast with Stanley one Sunday morning, we began discussing when, where and how to expand. Originally I favored the simple solution: buy more land next to our new factory and double our size while keeping things easy to staff and oversee. However, as my father pointed out, the freight costs and cross-country shipments were becoming an unmanageable challenge. Our business was growing quickest on the West Coast, and in order to properly take care of our customers, we needed a manufacturing presence there. I was a little intimidated at first; building a new factory while running the existing one only 30 minutes away was already challenging enough. But doing so across the country would completely change the nature of our company; we'd have to say goodbye to our days as a small, family-run business and hire professional management to run both factories. The whole thing made me very nervous.

We agreed to think about it for a week and make a decision the following Sunday; no time to dilly dally with decision making. As my parents and I drove back home that day, Dad helped me look at the bigger picture and made the case to embrace this massive change. "Timing is everything in business and life, and this is our chance to really grow," he explained. "If you truly do believe in our vision of becoming a leader in the frozen juice bar business, it's time we make a decision, or let the rest of our competitors pass us by. We've got the right product and the time is right. The question is do we have the balls to roll the dice and go for the gold ring?"

While I appreciated the pep talk, I still spent the rest of the week going back and forth over what to do. Staying and building another factory right where we were in New York was certainly alluring; it would be a smoother, easier expansion allowing me to be closer to my family and existing suppliers. However, we were already spending almost a million dollars a year on freight to ship truckloads of Guido's to the West Coast and that number would only go up. Plus, doubling our capacity probably wouldn't be enough, so even if we expanded locally we'd probably have to come back to this conversation sooner than later.

When I kept my emotions out of the decision-making process and focused on the facts, it became increasingly clear that expanding to California was the best move. Finding an existing factory to install our blast freezers and production lines in would be quicker, we would have multiple factories we could ship from and it would establish us as a big-time player in the frozen novelty industry. I just kept worrying that running multiple locations so far apart would keep me constantly on an airplane flying back and forth between the two.

On the ride back to Stanley's house for breakfast the next Sunday, my father asked me to talk about my concerns. I immediately dove into the challenges that were keeping me up at night: finding the right factory, hiring a new management team in California and designing and building an entirely new production facility 3,000 miles away. Keeping up with demand for the existing orders was already more than challenging, and by the way, where were we going to get the money to do all this? When I finally finished rambling on about just a few of our many major issues, I was hoping to get some sympathy. Instead, my father laughed out loud and gave me a big light-hearted smile, "Is that all? I thought you had bigger concerns. Let's discuss it with Stanley and see where we come out." I loved my father and I loved working with him, but he had the infuriating yet visionary ability to see past all the obstacles and focus on the strategic results, while leaving the execution of it to me.

His strength lay in seeing the big picture rather than the details. It was as if he would spot a gorgeous mountain peak and shout, "Let's go!" and I would have to figure out how to get up and down all the dangerous valleys and canyons. When I complained that he kept creating unnecessary crises, he informed me that he was just trying to help me. "You see," he said, "Crisis is actually change over a very short period of time. I am just trying to help you to change quickly!" How exasperating. I wish I had as much faith in myself as he did.

The discussion with Stanley was more like my father's one-man show, as he went right to explaining our need to find a California factory. After a short exchange of ideas, we all agreed to keep our excellent management team running the existing business in New York, with my mother and Jack overseeing operations and reporting back to me. My father would hire a real estate broker in Southern California to find multiple factory locations for us to evaluate, and he had already spoken to my Uncle George and Aunt Blanche. They recently sold George's business and agreed to move to California, where George would oversee the factory on an interim basis until we found a permanent general manager. Meanwhile, I needed to hire a whole new management team, design the factory and set up the manufacturing process and supply chain.

After laying this all out, my father turned to Stanley and finished up by saying, "And you figure out how we are going to pay for all this." He seemed to have thought out the entire process. Everything was moving so fast my head and heart were spinning out of control. On the drive home, I asked myself, apparently out loud, if we really just made the decision to expand in California. "Yes, son," my father said, calm and quite matter-of-factly. "We're going to California." It was a massive leap, and though I was excited, I was petrified by how much I didn't know and had this sinking anxiety that I might be in over my head.

The next few months just flew by as supermarket sales continued to skyrocket. Even the nation's biggest chains wanted Guido's, and the orders were larger than even our most optimistic predictions. I called up Hal to see if he could help, and he sent in a team of production consultants to advise us how to increase our shifts to produce in the factory 24/7. Turns out, people don't particularly love getting scheduled for graveyard and weekend shifts, and I never imagined how difficult it would be staffing them. Though I didn't have a free moment to rest, it was truly intoxicating making so much money after all those years of struggling. We were running production 24 hours a day, seven days a week, and still couldn't keep up.

We got very lucky, and late that summer my father let me know he'd come across the perfect factory for sale in Southern California. We hopped on a plane together to Orange County, spending the entire flight talking big plans and business ideas before driving over to inspect the factory. We returned to New York on a red-eye that night. It was just what we were looking for. In November 1983, we bought the Hawaiian Punch factory and officially established Guido's operations in California.

With our newfound success, we needed more money both for working capital and to buy the California factory. To do this, we could find a new investor, borrow a huge sum of money or take the company public. Having had such a miserable experience with our last investor, I wanted to avoid this like the plague. We realized that at the rate we were growing, a loan could cover our shorter-term cash flow needs but wouldn't be enough in the long run. So Dad and Stanley decided it was time to start discussing taking the company public and arranging a loan to cover our current costs in the meantime. Most banks didn't want to take on the risk of loaning money to a small, startup company with only one year of profits, but luckily for us, Stanley had a close connection with Bank Leumi, an Israeli bank with branches in Manhattan, and they agreed to take on our risk.

Going public was a big decision for a small, fast-growing company and it was something I knew nothing about. Overwhelmed with my existing responsibilities, I tried to object to yet another massive undertaking to no avail; Stanley and my father were sure it was the only way we could finance our new factory and rapid growth. I wasn't entirely sure if they knew what they were doing, but they had no doubts. We'd have consultants to coach me through the process, they explained, and all I'd have to do was get up in front of potential investors, tell our story and convince them what a great opportunity this was.

While every cell in my body resisted the idea of putting more on my plate, I knew we needed the money to grow the company and I was the only one who could pull it off. It would take a few months for Stanley and the company to prepare documentation and bring the consultants up to speed before my road show, so there would be plenty of time to keep focusing on my insane workload before I had to start preparing for our public offering. While I had no idea if I could pull this off, there was no sense in worrying about it now. Like it or not, we were off to the races!

CHAPTER 4

CUPID'S ARROW

On Christmas Day in 1983, I found myself staring out a frosted airplane window, waiting for the maintenance crew at JFK airport to defrost the wings for takeoff. Between moving across the country and gearing up to go public, an exciting new stage of my life was about to begin but, honestly, I was too tired to give it much thought. After a lengthy delay, we were finally able to fly high above the blizzard, descending into a sunny California afternoon only hours later. Enjoying the unusual day off, I spent the rest of the afternoon playing tennis in 80-degree weather and the sheer contrast from the frosty, East Coast tundra was disarming. "Where has this place been my whole life?" I wondered. The daydreaming was short lived, as I had to hop straight back into business, but I immediately fell in love with my new California home.

The first month of 1984 was incredibly hectic, even by my standards. Hiring the right people is both crucially important and time-consuming, and in those first few weeks I needed to hire 40 new workers, buy new equipment and most importantly, hire a foodservice broker to get Ice Juicees into school-lunch programs across the West. All this needed to be done while maintaining a manufacturing facility back in New York and preparing to take the company public in 90 days' time. It took multitasking to a whole new level.

It was a full-on family effort: my Aunt Blanche and Uncle George made the move from New York to oversee operations at the California factory when I wasn't there, while my father and I focused on establishing a network of foodservice brokers. We settled on Food Sales West (FSW), a regional powerhouse in the school foodservice industry. Charlene, our account representative, informed me that if I wanted to sell to the biggest school-lunch buyers, I needed to go to the annual School Foodservice Industry Seminar down in San Diego at the end of January to meet them. While I began with my instinctive "I don't have time!" response, I knew she was right; sales is all about personal connection and this was my golden chance to connect with the biggest buyers in the school-lunch business.

As I pulled up to the beautiful Hotel Del Coronado in San Diego, it looked more like a summertime movie set than a wintertime foodservice conference. But once I walked through the elaborate entryway, it was straight to business. A few minutes late and a bit of an outsider, I hustled into the ballroom and grabbed one of the last empty seats at a dinner table. Turns out, I had joined the Los Angeles, Oakland and New York City food service directors, who couldn't have been more welcoming. Charlene was right, this was exactly where I needed to be.

After spending the first day and a half in meetings and classes, we had the second afternoon free. Charlene asked me to join her for a game of mixed doubles tennis. I originally protested the intrusion upon my precious little work time, but she reminded me that I'd come here to meet buyers, and there was no better way to connect than over a casual game of sport. She was right (again), and I tried to ignore the alarming amount of unanswered work queries to focus on being present and available for networking opportunities.

As we warmed up, I couldn't help but notice a very attractive, petite young lady playing tennis two courts over from us. My heart skipped a beat as I realized she was partnered with the only other person at the conference I knew, a pizza salesman named Bruce. I spent every moment between points watching this beautiful young lady run around and chase the tennis ball. Suddenly this perfect stranger had stolen all of my precious attention without so much as batting an eyelash – butterflies erupted every time I looked her direction. I felt an indescribable excitement I had never experienced before. Despite my best efforts to stay focused, I was smitten from afar.

After our match, all the tennis players went inside to the bar to have a drink. I strategically worked my way over to Bruce and was ecstatic when his cute partner sat down next to him. After drinks, Bruce smiled at me and challenged, "Hey Richard, why don't you and I go play some real tennis?" I guess he didn't get much of a workout either. "Sure," I replied, my heart pounding as I tried to sound as casual as possible. "But only if our partners come along to watch. Who is the lady you were playing with, anyway?"

I thought for sure he would see right through my attempts to play it cool. "Ah sorry, I thought you knew each other," he responded nonchalantly, as he turned to get his partner's attention. "Ann, this is my friend, Richard Jaffe, President of Guido's Italian Ices. Richard, meet Ann Levinson. She's the foodservice director for the Escondido Schools." My heart skipped a beat as she looked straight into my eyes and then, out of the blue, started laughing. For half a moment I panicked, wondering if I had forgotten to zip up my fly or something else completely mortifying.

"Guido's!" she exclaimed with a smile. "We haven't met, but I've been buying your Ice Juicees for several months now. My family is from Monticello, so when I saw that's where they're made I gave them a try, and I must say they're delicious. The kids love them as well!" I tried with all my power not to blush, but to no avail. My cheeks were on fire as I pulled myself together to feign casual confidence. "Thank you for the compliment, and I look forward to getting to know you better!" Before I could think of anything brilliant to say, Charlene jumped in: "If you two are going to play tennis, get going or we will run into dinner time!"

Charlene and Ann sat on a short cement wall next to the tennis courts, chatting away while Bruce and I played a very competitive set of tennis. I must admit, even though she wasn't paying attention, I found myself pushing myself to my physical limits to try to impress Ann. When Bruce and I finished our match and shook hands at the net, I asked him if he knew anywhere in Orange County where I could find an apartment and meet some nice, preferably Jewish, young ladies, secretly hoping he would redirect me to Ann. It worked like a charm! Bruce immediately asked what I thought about Ann, insisting that she was a great lady.

It's not that I needed someone else to suggest it, but I was more nervous around Ann than most women, and Bruce's recommendation gave me that extra little boost to go for it. My heart pounded as I pondered the best way to ask her out. Unbeknownst to me, Ann and Charlene had spent the entire tennis match making a list of all the things they were looking for in a man. Charlene, a little older and recently divorced, pointed to me on the court, "What about Richard?" she had asked Ann. "Not my type, he's too tall," Ann said, writing me off without much thought. She was 5'0, over a foot shorter than me. Luckily I had no idea of her hasty dismissal, and spent the next few days doing everything I could to meet her again.

There was just one problem. This conference was full to the brim of men, and Ann, the radiant woman she was, was constantly surrounded by numerous suitors everywhere she went. I was getting a little nervous that I'd never find a chance to speak with her alone! Finally, after lunch around the pool the last day, my first opportunity presented itself. As everyone began making their way inside to the next session, Ann fumbled around under her lounge chair to find her purse. This was it – my one chance.

I took a deep breath and walked right up to her, reintroduced myself as Bruce's friend and, after some very brief small talk, asked her if she would have dinner with me that night. "Aren't you going to the Gala dinner tonight?" she asked with a quizzical look on her face. "If you like" she added, "You can sit at my table." Though it wasn't exactly the response I was hoping for, it wasn't a no. So, half elated and half disappointed, I agreed, thanked her and headed into the next session. We were both a little late arriving and though we had walked in through different doors, we met up in the middle of the room looking for seats. "There's two seats in the front row," I whispered, "Come join me!"

The motivational speaker for the next session was a short, African-American man with a booming voice, named Cecil Reeves. He spent most of his talk trying to inspire everyone to think more highly of themselves. When he stopped and asked the audience, "How many of you think that you are God's miracle?" I raised my hand without hesitation, and noticed Ann's hand go right up as well. They were the only two hands I saw in the air. Years later she pointed out that we were in the front row and couldn't see the majority of the room, but I didn't notice that at the time. I just remember a shot of excitement running through my body. "Hmm," I remember saying to myself with a smile inside my head, "This could be trouble!"

The next session on world hunger featured Muhammad Ali among its panelists, one of the keynote speakers of the weekend and the one I was most excited to hear. But, struggling with Parkinson's Disease, Ali didn't say a word throughout the entire presentation. He just sat there, silent and shaking. It felt like this hadn't been thought through, and seeing one of my greatest idols like this made my heart sink. What was far worse, though, was the fact that after presenting on world hunger to the largest food companies and school foodservice directors in the country, there were no plans for taking donations. We all had the ability to help, a call to action to do so, but no way to do it.

Heartbroken for the hungry and unnerved by the lack of preparation of the presenters, I asked Ann to take a walk on the beach with me after the presentation to calm down and unwind. It wasn't at all the vibe I would have gone for to begin an impromptu first date, but it actually set a deep and beautiful tone. For the next 20 minutes as we walked along the beach, she shared the key foundations in her life: her childhood, close-knit family, and how her Jewish heritage had fueled her desire to make the world a better place as a registered dietician feeding hungry kids. She was one of the youngest school foodservice directors in the state, responsible for feeding over 5,000 children per day.

With each story and each stolen glance, my admiration for her grew. Not only was she beautiful and smart, but she was also compassionate and caring. I had never met anyone who made me feel like this before. Entranced by her every word, I barely noticed the beautiful beachfront atmosphere. With the sunset and crashing waves on one side, rows of palm trees swaying on the other, Ann asked about my story. I told her I had been writing poetry for years, and had outlined my philosophy in a piece called *Eternal Happiness*.

I paused for a moment as my hands began to shake. "Would you like to hear it?" I asked. As she nodded yes, I reached out for her hands and suddenly became overwhelmed with fear that I would forget the words. But as I stood there, flushed with excitement and desire, I took a deep breath, looked straight into her beautiful brown eyes and hoped for the best.

Eternal Happiness
Feb 14, 1979

Our lifetimes pass so swiftly in the search for what is real,
It often takes another's heart to know what we can feel.

And though love's bond with friendship is the strongest ever known,
It is inner peace and happiness we must discover on our own.

For love that brings us happiness blinds with strength knowing we
are sure,
But what if we awake one day and that love remains no more?
Our souls will fill with loneliness and emptiness abound,
We will have lost our happiness until another love is found.

But a happiness with one's own true self, not an easy bond to
make…
Allows our hearts to pour out love without the need to take.

And then if we be blessed with love found only "wished upon a star,"
Do we first begin our journey in search of who we really are.

So if we find everlasting love, the one fate has meant to be,
Together, we will inspire Him to set our spirits free.

But if it's just another love to teach us how to care,
We each will have our own happiness and inner peace still left to
share.

As I recited the last word, my eyes and heart still locked with hers, it was clear something magical had connected between us. I yearned to kiss her but didn't know if it was too much, too soon. I was scared she might pull back, or I might chase her away. But it just felt right. There was no thought process, only the sound of my heart pounding through my chest and a magnetic pull drawing my lips closer to hers.

Our first kiss was like nothing I had ever experienced. Her lips met mine with force and passion, and time stood still. Overwhelmed by an all-consuming spark, our eyes remained locked well after our faces pulled away. There was never a question as to how Ann felt; her hands grasped mine and, in that moment, we both knew our souls had found their perfect match.

The rest of the night was like a dream come true. We both went back to our separate rooms to change clothes and then met for dinner. She later confessed that, when she had gone back to her room, she called her best girlfriend and told her she had met the man she was going to marry. But Ann's attention was not mine alone to hold. One distracting contender at dinner was Muhammad Ali; he was sitting right behind Ann and kept tapping her on her shoulder throughout the evening, wowing her with different magic tricks.

I took a moment to appreciate the fact that, despite my attempts to avoid another distraction from work, in a few short days I'd met the woman of my dreams and competed with one of my greatest idols for her attention. Sometimes love really does strike when we are least expecting it. Four months later Ann and I were engaged, and by December we were married. As it turned out, attending the School Foodservice Industry Seminar was the most important decision of my life.

Walking down the aisle with Ann less than a year after meeting, brought more joy than I knew was possible. She continues to make me a better person every day, in every way.

CHAPTER 5

GOING PUBLIC

While my heart was swirling around somewhere out in the universe, my mind and body needed to return to work. Though the conference had been productive in more ways than one, I returned to the factory only to be met by mountains of incredibly urgent work demanding my immediate attention. While the New York factories were smoothly churning away, getting things up and running in California was a monumental, time-consuming task. A few weeks later, as we were pulling all the pieces together to get production off the ground in the hectic final stretch, my father called from New York. It was time to return to New York and start the public-offering process.

It would have to wait at least a week, I protested, noting my calendar full of critical production meetings. My father brushed off my concerns without a thought. "It's now or never," he insisted, "Delegate. Uncle George can handle things in California for the next few weeks, but there's no one but you who can make these presentations. Figure it out!" I knew he was right. It was useless to disagree, so I fought the desire to protest and decided to dive straight into planning mode. There went my dreams of resting up a few days and spending time with Ann.

I used the next day to reassign my top priorities, gathered all the folders and plans I needed to make important equipment decisions, and packed my bags for how long I didn't know. I called Ann that night and tearfully explained the change of plans. Though sad and very disappointed, she said she understood. She'd known I would need to spend a few weeks on the East Coast, but neither of us expected it so soon. I promised to call her every night and come back as soon as I could.

The next night I hopped on a plane to New York for what turned out to be a two month whirlwind adventure. Dad and Stanley had hired a very professional public relations firm called The Wall Street Group, and handed me a jam-packed schedule with plenty of training to somehow squeeze in. I tried explaining that I needed time to run our business and at least a week on and a week off. But no dice.

After my arrival, Dad, Stanley and I spent the next two days in a large, fluorescent-lit conference room as our consultants walked us through every detail of my presentation and the challenges that lay ahead. In order to persuade any major Wall Street firm to take us public, we had to convince them that Guido's would continue to increase profits year after year. While many tech companies today are able to go public based solely on revenue projections with huge future earnings, this was 1984 and most investment firms wanted to see at least three years of profits to ensure we weren't just a flash in the pan.

Despite being warned that one year of very high profits would be a tough sell, we were unabashedly optimistic that at least one firm would want us. Several meetings later, that optimism began to fade. No matter how well I sold our story, each firm told us the same thing: come back in two years when you have three profitable years under your belt, then let's talk. We were growing too fast for that, I explained, we needed money now to supply the incredible demand for our products! However, everyone came back with the same response: grow more slowly and keep to a pace your profits can support.

Dejected but not defeated, Dad, Stanley and I huddled with our consultants to figure out another tack. Taking us public would require time and money, the consultants explained. If we did not hit our forecasted projections and the stock price tumbled, the investment firm would lose face with their investors and have to explain why their due diligence failed. With so many other companies boasting longer profit histories to choose from, the risk of investing in Guido's was not worth the reward.

We racked our brains for hours trying to overcome the problem, but no matter what angle we took, there didn't seem to be an answer. Late that night, frustrated and groggy, my father and I hit a breaking point. But instead of losing it, we both decided to take a deep breath and realized it was time to reframe. We were looking at this all wrong. "Let's stop looking at the problem," I thought out loud as I paced around the room. "Let's start with the solution instead," my father finished with a smile.

We had been going to all the big firms without any success. We didn't fit their bill. With plenty of options to choose from, they all wanted reliable wins and it wasn't in their interest to take risks. I started questioning whether we could ever find an investment firm to take us public. While I was overwhelmed with nerves and emotion, my father was calm as a rock. What we really needed, he explained, was to find a smaller investment firm with fewer companies to choose from but enough big clients that could buy all our shares. We could minimize much of their costs by doing the legwork ourselves; all they needed to do was make an introduction. This way we could convince them that the potential gains with

Guido's were worth the risk. To pull this off, we'd need a Wall Street insider, someone with credibility who knew all the players and could use their personal relationships to support our case.

As luck would have it, we had the perfect person within the family tree. Uncle Ted, my mother's older brother, had been a Wall Street stock trader for years. We called him up and explained the situation. It was a long shot, he warned us. Still, he agreed to at least call in a few favors to get us meetings with some of the smaller firms he knew. The response wasn't great. Unsurprisingly, our short profit history was a concern for everyone. However, he persisted and found a small investment firm, The Mueller Group, who agreed to introduce us to all their customers if their executives liked our story. "Yahoo!" I shouted, giddy as a schoolgirl. I couldn't believe our luck.

"Hold on a minute," Ted continued calmly. "There's still a lot of work ahead. First you and Mueller Group will need to agree on how much the company is worth, and how much you are willing to sell. Then you'll need to lay out how much the firm would be paid, and these guys are in it for the cash. Lastly, the only thing they're giving you is an introduction to their investors; you will need to do all the legwork and cover all the costs."

The warnings didn't diminish my excitement in the slightest. While I was new to the IPO process, none of this seemed like too much to ask. My father and Stanley, however, knew the odds were stacked greatly against us and were not nearly as excited as I was. Either way, it felt like another catastrophe avoided. I was simply thrilled to be moving forward.

We spent the next day and night negotiating a value for the company with their president. Going in, we knew we needed at least $3.5 million to buy the factory and support our growth, and were looking to sell as little of the company as possible. He knew we didn't have many choices and was extracting every last cent he could from us. I was getting madder than hell listening to him claim we weren't worth much, belittling the company we worked so hard to build. But my father and Stanley just sat there and took it. "Relax," Stanley coached me as we stepped out for a break. "This is just how negotiations begin. They want to do a deal or we wouldn't be meeting with their president. Let your father and I do the negotiating, and I promise you we'll come out with a fair deal."

When we returned to the room after our break, they had written a proposal on the whiteboard. Based on our current sales and profits, Mueller valued the company at $15 million, and wanted us to sell at least 30 percent of the company. My father thanked them for their offer, but insisted it was way too low. Based on next year's revenues and profits Guido's was worth $40 million, he explained, and we didn't want to sell more than 20 percent of the company. We were at a standstill and the tension to see who blinked first was excruciating.

At the perfect moment, Uncle Ted stood up and said, "I know both parties very well. I know there is a deal to be made so let's stop pretending and find a middle ground that is fair to both sides. Guido's needs enough money to build their factory and grow their business, and Mueller needs to make enough money to make it worthwhile. Let me talk to both sides separately, and come back with what I know is a fair deal."

We all consented to trust Uncle Ted and in the end we agreed to value the company at $20 million: five million shares at $4 per share. While this was far less than we thought fair, they relented on allowing us to sell only 20 percent of the company. This would land us about $3.5 million after expenses and commission, which was enough to buy the factory and run the company.

All we needed to do now was convince their investors to buy all the Guido's shares; I was just praying that they were not as tough as the Mueller executives. Our consultants and Mueller executives walked me through which investors I would be presenting to, what they were looking for and what I needed to say. The presentations weren't difficult, in fact, I loved getting up and telling the Guido's story. I was actually excited about this aspect of the process.

The next month just flew by with multiple presentations a day, sometimes in multiple cities. Every night I would call Ann and describe the reception and excitement we received that day. It was hard being so far away, but she did her best to pump me up each night and it felt like we managed to share this experience in a way. Everything seemed like a bit of a blur but after awhile I got the feeling people really liked our story. I could feel myself getting better and better as I began pre-empting investors' questions by integrating the answers into my presentations. It was one big sales game, and this time I was selling our story! I fed off the excitement and adrenaline, and I think the investors could feel it. Truth be told, I was actually a little disappointed when the presentations came to an end. But we sold every share we needed and that's what mattered: Guido's had the money necessary to keep growing.

By the time we finished the road show for our public offering, George and the California team had done a great job of installing the new machinery and getting the factory ready for production testing. There were surprisingly few crises, and when I returned, we had entered the final phase of testing all the new equipment to ensure we were producing identical products in New York and California. Despite having done everything we could for a smooth startup, with a new team, equipment and production line, I was nervous about all the unknowns that could pop up and derail things.

But after only a few minor hiccups and some expected challenges, such as broken chains and missing parts for conveyors, we commissioned the factory ahead of schedule and began making

Ice Juicees just in time for the summer rush. Things seemed to go from fast to faster, but somehow we had made the transition. Both factories were up and running full tilt and we had become a profitable public company.

Making the transition from a small, struggling startup, to a fast-growing public company with many shareholders and high expectations was daunting. I felt out of my element, as usual, and had no idea what was needed to run a public company. However, having been a bit out of my element since day one, I had gotten used to the discomfort and was confident I could learn on the fly. With my father, mother and Stanley by my side, and a slew of experienced businessmen as board members and advisors, I wasn't on my own. There was time and space for trial and error.

We had built our board prior to the public offering around two major needs: experts who would help advise us on our current fast-growth challenges, and the people who would help us find solutions to our future challenges. Our seasoned board members helped me see around corners and preempt a great deal of challenges before they grew too big.

All the while, business kept getting crazier and crazier. Running production around the clock, we still couldn't keep up with demand. We bought a small juice and ices manufacturing company in Florida, and I spent my time flying between the three factories and visiting important customers around the country. Somehow, I never stopped thinking about Ann no matter how sleep deprived I became. As I bounced from place to place, the one constant was my late-night phone calls with her. I yearned to be near her, but we knew this craziness was only temporary, and had the rest of our lives to look forward to.

Ever since I fell in love with poetry, I dreamt of proposing through a poem. I knew Ann was the one for me the night we met.

But when I was ready to propose to her, I had been so busy working, I hadn't written a poem in two years. So for my next cross-country trip in June 1984, I set a goal to write a poem on the plane ride there and back to ask her to marry me. As my first flight took off, I eagerly pulled out my pen and paper, and the words flowed right through me as if I was just their vessel. The whole trip I couldn't wait for the chance to finish it on my return flight home. By the time I returned to California, I had finished the perfect proposal poem, bought a beautiful diamond ring and couldn't wait to ask Ann to spend the rest of our lives together.

The next few days were torture; I could barely contain myself talking to Ann each night that week. Finally, the weekend came and I took her to one of our favorite restaurants. The ring was burning a hole through my pocket but I somehow managed to hold out until our dinner plates were cleared before asking if I could recite a poem I had just written. Her eyes sparkled yes, and I could feel her anticipation as I began:

Eternal Love
June 10, 1984

While life consumes our mortal souls first spank 'till final death, Our spirits search for happiness far beyond our final breath. For already days are numbered that we walk upon this earth, But forever has no boundaries just a beginning we call birth.

So while exploring life's true meaning our hearts fell helplessly in love, Like two feathers floating freely with His guiding force above. But once our separate paths engaged the outcome left no doubt, We've only just begun to learn what 'eternal love's' about.

For deep beneath the solitudes our inner peace reveal, Lay depths of
endless happiness two hearts in love can feel.
And never have I met someone whose soul is so pure and sweet,
Through laughter, trust and tenderness you fulfill my needs
complete.

For my heart aches when I'm without you but a moment or a day.
I need to live my life with you in love and health, I pray.
For you are who I've dreamt about to share my family and life, With
all my love, I ask you, Dear, will you forever be my wife?

After what seemed like a couple minutes of ecstatic tears, she leapt into my arms. "Yes!" she shouted, "Yes, yes, yes!" A month later, she made the move from San Diego to Orange County and agreed to join Guido's marketing team. We were both traveling nonstop for the next few months and would actually meet running through airports as we both crisscrossed the country visiting customers. It was an exciting yet exhausting time in our lives.

Ann and I would talk every day, dreaming about the future when we would be able to wake up in each other's arms every morning. We both realized that we had a lot more work and sacrifice before that would become a reality, but placed our focus on savoring the few moments we had together. The business needs would come first, and we both knew that one day we could slow down and reap the benefits of our hard work. With a lifetime ahead of us, we were betting that a short-term sacrifice would be worth it. The fact that we were sharing it together made it that much more special.

CHAPTER 6

THE SALE

One night, after returning from a grueling cross-country trip, I had a message to call our board member Eddie Epstein. When I finally got in touch with him, he explained that he had some good news: one of his clients was interested in acquiring Guido's. "Which one?" I asked with cautious optimism. "Coca Cola," he replied, with a smile in his voice. I couldn't believe my ears!

Eddie explained that, as the owners of Minute Maid (the leading juice company in the world), Coca Cola wanted to make its stake in the exploding frozen novelty category. Rather than spending two years building factories and a product line, they wanted to buy a leading brand with a great product and manufacturing capacity ready to go; this way they could expand the salesforce and production power, crushing the competition before they had enough time to get close. Time was of the essence, they wanted to move quickly and were willing to pay for it. We seemed to be the perfect fit, and once they realized that the Eddie Epstein who was on our board was their consultant, Coca Cola called him up to approach us about a sale.

While it was incredibly exciting to think that someone would pay us for the years of hard work, it felt too early to sell. After taking a few days to mull it over with my mother and father, I let Eddie know that we were growing exponentially and weren't ready to sell yet, but to send our appreciation and let Coca Cola know we would get back to them if we changed our minds. I never actually gave any thought to what it would feel like not owning Guido's. A part of me felt relief at the idea, but the other part felt a massive, sharp resistance, like I was selling my firstborn.

I had spent my entire career learning on the fly, doing everything I could to keep up. I knew that at some point, if all went well, we would outgrow my abilities and someone else would be better fit to run the company. But Guido's had been my life for a decade, and I was only just realizing how much my identity was tied to my company. Having built my self-confidence around much more than just my job, I was able to prioritize the company's success over my personal needs. We were so fortunate to be in a situation where the company was outgrowing my skills, and I chose to take that as a testament to my abilities rather than a dismissal of them. The time was getting closer for me to find my own replacement.

One of the most important factors to a successful startup is knowing when to sell. Many of us who experience rapid growth after so many years of struggle somehow believe the growth will go on forever. But the majority of young companies on *Inc's 100 Fastest Growth Companies* are hard to find five years later. Most often, it's lucky timing rather than individual brilliance that leads to such rapid growth, and whether it's large companies entering the market, competitor copycats or customer needs that change faster than a company's ability to adapt, success is easily lost.

It is incredibly important to be willing to sell a company while it is still growing quickly and can project future profits for potential buyers. Far too often, executives and board members drink their own Kool-Aid, overestimating their strength and ability to overcome the challenges ahead. Keeping an eye on the future competition and a realistic perspective on where one is in the industry curve is crucial for good timing. Skate to where the puck is going to be, or get off the ice before you get hurt. We did not have that foresight at the time and almost waited too long ourselves.

By early 1985, several large food companies such as General Foods and General Mills entered the frozen novelty category, completely changing the playing field. Supermarket buyers started demanding "slotting allowances," which meant that, instead of getting three full rows of space in the supermarket frozen cabinet at no extra cost, we had to start paying big dollars for just one row. My first step was denial, clinging to the hope that we could convince buyers to give us more space. But my father wasn't fooled for a moment. The pendulum was swinging back to the stores, he insisted, and manufacturers would need to start paying a hefty price to stay on the shelf. The end was coming.

Once I realized there was no negotiating myself out of these exorbitant fees, I began to panic. The big company competitors had plenty of other products to absorb the additional costs and could take the blow, but these would tank our profits. While I paced and felt entirely overwhelmed, my father was calm and calculating. "The elephants are starting to dance," he said simply, "If we don't move quickly enough, we'll get crushed." It was time to make our exit – and fast.

With Eddie's introduction and a newfound fire under our asses, we entered direct negotiations with the president of Coca Cola Foods six months after their initial inquiry, in what turned out to be the most agonizing summer I could have imagined. Business was getting harder just as my father predicted, and as I built our forecasts for the winter it was clear we wouldn't survive it. On one hand, we had to put on a face that it was still too early to sell the company, but on the other hand we knew we were running out of cash and had to take any deal we could get. We were the only ones who knew that, with the new slotting allowance, we wouldn't have enough cash to make it through the next winter.

If we were still a private company, we could have found creative solutions to keep the business afloat. We could have borrowed the money we needed quickly, most likely through a personal guarantee. But as a public company we did not have the same flexibility; it took longer to raise additional cash and there were tons of eyes on every move we made. Every time I turned to my somehow calm and collected father, he just encouraged me to visualize us closing a deal, assuring me he had been through much worse times and come out the other side.

While I wanted and willed myself to believe him, I couldn't shake this all-encompassing fear that we would run out of time and money before closing a deal. The sense of dread and negativity was like nothing I had ever experienced. My early depression was horrible, but it only affected me. This was so much heavier and much more public. With so many people counting on us, and the general expectation that our rosy reality would go on forever, I felt crushed by the impending sense of doom.

To the outside world I looked fine, but alone with my father I finally let my guard down and admitted I was drowning in anxiety. "I ran the numbers again and again and there is no way we can hit our fourth-quarter sales or profit projections. What are we going to do?! Do we need to tell the board?" My mind was racing so quickly I could barely get the words out.

"Keep your head up and keep driving the business as best you can," he assured me, with confidence. "We've already got negotiations with Coca Cola underway. It's in their best interest to close a deal as quickly as possible, so let's help them. I'll talk to Eddie and see if we can speed things up; maybe he can tell them we have another suitor calling." Luckily, Coke didn't want to wait another season to get into the frozen novelty business.

For the next few weeks my emotions were all over the place. It was only through daily communication with my father that I was able to get up every day and keep pushing through. When we had a good meeting or phone call I felt rejuvenated and hopeful, but the moment we hit a snag I would plummet, nearly dissolving into tears after getting off a bad-news call. A day later things could be back on again and I'd perk right back up, imbued with newfound enthusiasm. While I darted across the emotional spectrum, my father was as cool and even as could be. I found the negotiations tortuous, but Dad actually looked like he was having fun. It's not that he wasn't struggling, he had his low moments right alongside me, but the moment negotiations started he was strong as a bull.

After a few weeks of some incredibly stressful meetings with the Coca Cola Foods CEO, we were able to craft a financial deal that we were thrilled with. The only caveat they insisted on, was waitingtoseeoursecond-quarterfinancial results beforefinalizing the deal. The quarter ended on June 30 and our financials didn't need to be filed until the end of July. We had never had a problem filing on time and were exceeding our forecast for that quarter, so we happily agreed.

Then one day in the middle of July, Stanley called to talk to my father and me. "We have a major problem," he said, sounding unusually grave. "This could be a deal breaker." My heart stopped as his words knocked the wind out of me. "What could possibly be bad enough to stop the whole deal?" my father calmly asked. "Well, it seems our friends at our accounting firm have changed the way they want us to recognize revenue," he began, clearly exasperated, "They're insisting we only book revenue once the trucks arrive at our customers' locations, or they won't sign off on the filing." We had always claimed our revenue the moment our customers' trucks picked up the product at our dock, so this sudden change seemed absolutely ridiculous.

"Those slimy little bastards don't realize it will kill our deal. There's no way we'll meet our forecasts for this quarter with this, and Coke will walk away from the deal. I have seen it before," Stanley continued, "Irv, you need to convince them to sign off on the numbers the way they are. I don't care how you do it, but find a way to get it done – and fast!" I had never heard Stanley order my father or use such a stern tone before.

"I will handle it, we have no other choice," my father said matter-of-factly. Apparently, in trying to protect themselves against any possible future lawsuits, our large accounting firm had different standards for companies being sold. They wanted to make sure if the deal didn't work out for any reason, Coke couldn't come back and accuse the accounting firm of wrongly stating our financial numbers. This meant that, come July, they were unwilling to sign off unless we agreed to the new calculation. I couldn't believe my ears. For four quarters in a row since going public, we reported revenue the exact same way and the accounting firm signed off immediately. I couldn't believe they were pulling this shit, changing the way we recognize revenue at the last moment of our deal. Here I was on the verge of going broke yet again with the perfect solution right in front of me, and our accountants would be what could kill us? Any semblance of emotional control was out the window. I was furious.

Of course, when Coca Cola learned that we had not filed our quarterly results on time, they called to back out of the deal. Their Chief Financial Officer, Doug Ivester, said he smelled something fishy. We were small potatoes to our big accounting firm, and much to our fury, it had taken over a week to get our issue bumped up to someone high enough to overrule our representatives and sign off.

I felt sure the deal would fall through, and there was no chance we'd be able to make it through the winter. Exhausted and frightened, I was pushed to my limits. But my father reminded me we had to keep fighting. "We just need to convince the accountants to sign off on our numbers, so we can file and get Coke to revive the deal," he said. "It still makes sense for Coke to buy us so don't give up hope yet!" It was a draining battle, and the accountants only relented when we threatened to sue them if our deal fell through due to their change in revenue recognition.

By then, Coca Cola was not returning our calls. So close to a home run and yet closer to going bankrupt than anyone else knew, those were two of the most difficult weeks for my parents and me to live through. I was doing my best to keep my shit together, but it was almost impossible. I kept meditating and visualizing success like I knew I should, but didn't really believe it would help. Putting on a strong face at work, I was being pulled from all sides with customers and employees coming to me with other urgent problems. But I couldn't bring myself to care, not when my mind kept returning to Coke and what would happen if we couldn't get them back to the table. It took another week and several phone calls from Eddie Epstein, but we were finally able to explain the situation and reassure them that we had in fact exceeded our forecasts.

With some reservation, Coca Cola agreed to move forward with the deal, but now informed us that they couldn't buy a public company unless we were represented by an investment-banking firm to give them a fairness opinion. Exasperated, I tried to calmly push back, noting that we had agreed to all the points they requested, but they stood firm. Get an investment bank fairness opinion or there would be no deal, we were told.

I called another one of our board members, Bernie Myerson of Loews Theatres, for help. He used his connections to get our foot in the door with Goldman Sachs, who would never have represented a company so small otherwise. The company was given instructions to get us the best deal they could, but I firmly explained that we were very happy with our deal and only needed a fairness opinion from them. Despite all this, our lead banker at Goldman Sachs went for a better deal and contacted Coca Cola with a few more requests. Coke refused and told him not to call again – they were no longer interested in buying our company.

When Stanley called and told my father what happened, we were dumbstruck. Sick from the nonstop tension, I finally lost it. Immediately, I picked up the phone, called the investment banker and ripped him a new one. "What the hell do you think you were doing?! We specifically said we didn't even want to hire you, but Coca Cola demanded a fairness opinion. I gave you specific instructions! Why in the world would you do anything else?!" I demanded, fuming with uncharacteristic fury.

"You pay us a nice fee to represent you. It's my job to get the best deal I can," he explained in a calm and apologetic tone, "I have dealt with Coca Cola before and never had a response like this." I hung up without even bothering to finish the conversation and turned to my father. "So what do we do now?!" I don't think he'd ever seen me so wound up.

After telling me to take some deep breaths, he brought me back to earth. "Son, we are in the middle of negotiations; each one has a life of its own and it's always an emotional roller coaster. Somehow they usually get done," he assured me. "Let's call Eddie Epstein and have him get us back to the negotiating table. This deal is a long way from being over, but also a long way from getting done. Expect more highs and lows and learn to ride the waves." I calmed down a bit and started to look at things with more reason. "Why are these lessons so hard to learn? Why can't things just go as planned?" I lamented.

My father laughed with a love that only a parent could project. "Get used to it!" he chuckled. "Next time you go through negotiations you'll be much better prepared." We called Eddie to explain what happened. He understood and told us not to worry; the Coke executives were just offended by the investment banker and trying to teach him a lesson. The CEO still wanted to do the deal, and though it might take a few days to reach him, he was sure he could get the ball rolling again. "Get the fairness opinion going and I'll convince the CEO to accept our original terms," Eddie promised. Three days later Eddie called us back; Coke finally agreed to the deal on our original terms. Ecstatic and relieved, I thanked him profusely and sank back into my chair. Never again, I thought, never again will I let myself get so emotional throughout negotiations.

The final deal required that I stay on as president of the Guido's subsidiary, with my father continuing as chairman for four years to ensure we hit our financial forecasts. Public shareholders couldn't get less than the public price (around $10 per share at the time), so Coke insisted that the deal could go through only if the Jaffe family took $4 per share upfront, with an earn out over the next four years. With Coca Cola as a partner, we were confident that we would not only hit our projections but exceed them over the next four years, and make more than the public shareholders when all was said and done. However, we were wisely counseled to make sure we'd be happy even if we never made another penny from the deal.

We were thrilled even if it ended with $4 per share, and in reality, we had to take any deal they offered or go broke that winter. Coke Foods pushed hard to have our family return some of the purchase price if we failed to hit our minimum targeted profits. However, we refused to allow a "claw back" of anything they paid up front. They finally agreed, and for the next few months we were on pins and needles. We had to make sure we hit the financial numbers we promised while also informing our employees and distributors of the sale, who then decreased their orders so they wouldn't have as much inventory in case Coca Cola changed the name of the product.

The day finally came when the entire Coca Cola board met to approve our acquisition. Our board had already approved the sale, so this was the last big piece standing between us and closing the deal and I thought the anxiety would swallow me whole. The day ticked by without a call, and while I kept trying to stay positive, focusing on the outcome and putting on a happy face to our executive team, my mother and father saw right through it. All I could think about was that the longer we had to wait, the less chance we had to get their board approval. Had Mr. Ivester poisoned the board with his reservations about missing our filing? My mind began racing through countless imaginary factors that could surprise us. This was life or death for us, but for Coca Cola it was just a small distraction.

Hours after the phone should have rung, I pulled myself out of my chair, my heart heavy and mind racing as I began gathering my things to leave. With dashed hopes and bankruptcy notices flashing before my eyes, it took every ounce of effort to keep myself from dissolving into tears. Just as I was heading for the door, my phone rang. I dropped my briefcase and held my breath for a moment before picking up. Mr. Amoroso, the CEO of Coca Cola Foods, greeted me and apologized for the delay. "Not a problem!" I assured him with a fake smile in my voice, as if I hadn't been on the verge of a breakdown the entire time. He had been tied up on other board matters, he explained, but as promised, the entire board had unanimously approved the transaction and was looking forward to integrating us into the wider Coca Cola Foods organization. I graciously thanked him for his effort and support, assuring him how excited I was to be able to work together.

After putting down the receiver, I collapsed to my knees, releasing a decade of stress and anxiety with the strongest, most violent shriek my body has ever produced. I felt years lighter as my father came running through the door, and I leapt into his concerned arms. "It's approved, it's approved!" I cried out, smiling hard enough to nearly crack my face in half. "We're alive! Dad, we made it!"

We knew there were still a lot more things that could go wrong, but we also knew we could figure out a way to get the deal closed. After the high of the approval faded, the next month provided a new dose of gut-wrenching stress as we waited the necessary thirty days before closing. Once we publicly announced the approval, what little business we had all but disappeared. Customers were afraid that Coca Cola would change the name and packaging, leaving them stuck with whatever old product they had in inventory. At this point, if there were any regulatory objections and the deal didn't go through, we would probably have to shut down the company.

Though we were all ecstatic about the deal, I woke up every day knowing our job was not done until the money was in the bank. The first two weeks I somehow managed to keep my anxiety under control as we overcame the small challenges and requests for information. Then, two weeks before closing, I got a request from Mr. Ivester for an updated financial forecast for the fourth quarter and began to panic. Grabbing my father by the arm, I pulled him into my office and quickly explained the situation. "If he saw how little business we had and how much money we lost this quarter would he cancel the deal?" I asked, my breath quick and shallow, face red and flushed.

"Relax," my father said. He calmly reminded me that Steve Poley, the Coca Cola Foods marketing executive in charge of the acquisition, put together the financial forecast with me for the fourth quarter, as well as the following four years. "Send him the request and let him respond to Mr. Ivester and answer any questions they still have." Brilliant! Why didn't I think of that? With another doomsday avoided, I took a deep breath and did my best to focus on the tasks at hand. But in reality, I was a mess. The anxious electricity pumping through my veins was growing stronger by the day. While daily meditations and the occasional run helped take the edge off, I wouldn't be able to escape the stress until the money was in the bank.

By the time we flew to New York City for the closing, I couldn't eat or sleep and it really pissed me off how calm and relaxed my father appeared. Yet somehow, when Ann and I awoke the day of the closing, I was stunned at a newfound sense of calm and ease. I couldn't believe that we were actually selling the company that had been my blood, sweat and tears for the last 10 years. My experience at Guido's began the day after my graduation – I had loved it, hated it, and most importantly, been completely transformed by it. Though we didn't have any children at the time, it felt like I was selling my firstborn. Don't get me wrong, I didn't have any seller's remorse; I knew we either sold the company or went broke. But as I reflected on all the crises and near-death experiences we somehow pulled through, there was a pang of sadness like I was losing a best friend. So it was with mixed emotions that I walked into the Coca Cola law firm offices that chilly December morning in 1985. But as I stood alongside Ann and my parents, my heart swelled, and what I felt most of all was pride.

All the Coca Cola Foods executives raved about what a great job we had done starting, growing, going public and especially working through the acquisition process. They couldn't stop talking about how excited they were to take our company and grow it into the leader of the frozen novelty category. Their excitement, like that of adopting parents, was surpassed only by our excitement and relief to hand over our baby. After exchanging pleasantries for at least an hour, the lawyers finally walked in, told us all the paperwork had been filed and handed each of us a seven-figure check for our share of the proceeds.

After exchanging handshakes and congratulations, followed by hugs with Ann and my parents, we exited the building to a beautifully crisp and sunny December day. Drenched in relief and gratitude, Ann and I went for our first horse-drawn carriage ride around Central Park. No longer constrained by the weights and responsibilities of owning a struggling business, I was free at last!

Coke's Steve Polay (left) with Richard Jaffe (center) and Irving Jaffe in a Houston supermarket
Merging entrepreneurial spunk with marketing muscle.

Smiling with the relief of my last great Guido's crisis averted, in this Forbes story on our acquisition.

CHAPTER 7

INSIDE THE BIG POND

Once we returned home to California and the euphoria of closing the sale to Coca Cola wore off, I had to address the very thorny and difficult deliberation of deciding where to live, and more specifically, how to get Ann on board with my relocation plans. Technically, I didn't have to move; Coca Cola only required that I be present in the Houston corporate office every Monday morning at 8 a.m. for the operating committee meeting. This meant that I would either fly from San Diego to Houston every Sunday night, or move there.

With the new reality of being a very small fish in Coca Cola's giant pond, I had already made the decision in my mind that we'd be better off moving to Houston. Now that we would be using their sales and marketing teams, I knew I needed to be close in order to influence the Coke executives to spend more time on our products so we didn't get lost in their portfolio of priorities. I just didn't know how to convince Ann to leave California. When I asked her to move after we got engaged, she was less than enthusiastic about relocating just an hour and a half north to Newport Beach. Now I had to figure out how to ask her to move all the way to Houston, Texas.

Having been married only one year, I still got nervous trying to convince her to do something she really didn't want to do. No matter how hard I tried, I couldn't figure out how to convince her that this move would be in her best interest. Our first evening back at home, we were relaxing on our patio and reminiscing about the early struggles at Guido's when I decided to take the dive. "Honey, even though the deal with Coca Cola has closed, we still have one more major issue to address," I began, focusing on maintaining eye contact and a calm smile. "I thought the deal was done?" she said, her head perking up as concern rang through her voice. "We're no longer a public company and agreed we'll just continue working the same way as before?"

I guess my facial expression and tone of voice gave away the seriousness at hand. I decided to be direct and not beat around the bush. "That's true, but now that we're part of Coca Cola, I think we should move to Houston," I all but blurted out. Her eyes grew wide, like a deer in very unwelcomed headlights. "What are you talking about?! Why would we do that?" Panic filled her gaze, and the knot in my chest expanded as tears began to well in the delicate corners of her big, brown eyes. "I thought you said we could stay in California after the sale," she said, sounding desperate and caught off guard.

I knew she wouldn't like this, but took a deep breath and explained. "Originally I thought we could, but I've been working long and hard to figure out how we're going to operate the company, and I don't think I can do it from California. I have to be in Houston every Monday morning for the operating committee meeting, and need to be in front of the sales and marketing executives throughout the week if we're going to get our Ice Juicees sold. That means I'd fly out Sunday night and come back Thursday or Friday night. I love you, and I want more than just weekends together." The tears had begun rolling down her cheeks. "I don't know how long we will be there, but whenever the time comes to leave Houston, we can move anywhere in the world that you choose," I promised.

This pitch wasn't working. Her voice broke as she almost begged, "Please, is there any way possible we could stay in California?" My heart crumbled in her sadness. I loved her so much and would do almost anything to keep her happy, but I knew it wasn't realistically possible to do my job well when all the people I would be managing would be working in Houston. There had to be a reason why she would agree to move, I just had to quickly figure out what would motivate her to sign on to this temporary relocation.

I refocused onto her perspective and tried a different route; in California, we were never able to really get away from the business. Between my business-obsessed father next door and the crisis-ridden factory nearby, I continued to get phone calls at two or three in the morning several times a week. It never bothered me, as that was my job, but Ann never got used to the middle-of-the-night phone calls and never understood why people couldn't wait until 7 a.m. to call me.

"If you think about it," I proceeded with cautious positivity, "If we moved to Houston, my family, the factory and all the other middle-of-the-night interruptions would cease. We would have a lot more alone time there. We could enjoy our life so much more." I knelt in front of her, catching her gaze and clasping my hands around hers as I went in for a final plea. "Please, my love. It's the best of our options, and I promise next move we'll go anywhere in the world you want." Although she loathed the thought of moving to Texas, she quickly realized that this was, in fact, the best of all options. Being the loving and incredibly supportive life partner she is, she begrudgingly agreed. Ann knew that being inside a large, bureaucratic company would be an enormous change for me and wanted to be there to help me through it. We rang in the new year and flew directly to Houston to start looking for an apartment.

The next two years were filled with new challenges and lessons, but the excruciating, personal financial pressures were gone. The challenges of a big corporation are much different than those of a startup. Startup life is a crazy, unpredictable sprint. We wear so many hats that we can work 24/7 and never catch up – the most important task is often deciding what not to do. However, we are also able to make instant changes; we can talk directly to almost anyone in the organization, and people have more authority to make decisions.

Big companies are another beast. With many more people and more defined roles and responsibilities, communication becomes a much bigger and harder task. It felt much like the game of telephone, where messages are passed along by a number of people and morph into something entirely new by the time they reach the last person in line. The first year we introduced a smaller package of our Ice Juicee product through the Coca Cola Foods salesforce and, after recognizing a packaging mistake, I tried to recall the presentation so we could quickly fix it. However, I was told once the presentation was released to the salesforce there was nothing I could do to pull it back and change it. The message was off and running, and out of our hands.

The second new obstacle we faced was going from the only fish in a tiny, water-starved pond to becoming one minuscule fish amongst a giant school in the sea. While we were fighting to stay afloat at Guido's, Ice Juicees were the only product we sold. However, at Coca Cola, each product competed for time and attention from salespeople promoting orange juice, frozen mixers and several other products on their sales calls. We had to convince the sales executives to incentivize their people to sell our recently renamed product, Minute Maid Fruit Juicees, or we would quickly get lost in the myriad of products they were selling. Struggling to get my own sales team on board was something I never imagined, and I was never able to completely overcome it my entire time at Coca Cola.

Going from being my own boss working alongside my father and mother to working inside a $2-billion corporate infrastructure took getting used to. Most entrepreneurs find this transition of working for someone else the most difficult aspect of selling their companies. Large corporations have rules and guidelines for everyone to follow, ensuring consistency and efficiency across the board. At Guido's, we tried to do the right thing for the customer and employee whenever a unique situation came up. When a buyer made a mistake and forgot to order enough Ice Juicees before a major holiday weekend, we occasionally flew product to them at a loss just to keep them in stock. When a long-time executive needed a short-term loan to close on his house because his bank papers weren't ready in time, we advanced him the money.

At Guido's, situations like these were brought directly to me and I had the authority to make it happen, earning us long-term commitment and loyalty. But at Coca Cola, certain rules were necessary to create efficiency at scale; if treated on a case-by-case basis, the sheer volume of exceptions would overwhelm the system. While I could appreciate the logic of it all, losing the authority to make these type of judgement calls was a tough pill to swallow. I figured out how to do the best I could within the constraints I was under, and escaping the stress and financial strain was well worth it. Every other executive in the organization had the same rules, so I just accepted them and went about my business.

While I was young and flexible enough to shift with the circumstances, my father didn't put up with arbitrary rules and being told what to do. This became an issue when he and my mother would fly out from California for quarterly meetings. Coca Cola had a strict no-hats policy inside the corporate headquarters, but my father had created an image as Papa Guido, wearing a big, white cowboy hat religiously for years. It had become his persona. After a few quarterly meetings, I was called into Mr. Amoroso's office and told, in no uncertain terms, that from now on my father would need to remove his hat before entering the corporate offices.

I knew instantly I was stuck between a rock and a hard place. Coca Cola Foods would not change their rules, and the chances of convincing my father to remove his hat were slim to none. Still, I knew I had to try. One night when Ann and I were enjoying a relaxing dinner with my parents, I saw my opening. "How is everything going and how are things different than when we ran the company without Coke?" my father inquired, always one for reflective, bigger-picture conversations. I held my breath and decided to give it a shot. "Well, most things are still the same, but they do have a few rules that we would never think of." I tried to sound nonchalant as I set the bait, dreading the moment I knew he'd take it. "Like what?" he asked, brow raised with a sense of curiosity. "Well for instance, no one is allowed to wear a hat inside the corporate headquarters." I looked up nervously as I went on, "That means even you need to remove your big, white hat when you come to meetings here from now on."

"Absolutely not!" he barked, almost before I had finished my response. "Coca Cola sets the dress code rules for their employees, not me. I am Papa Guido and I don't take my hat off for anyone!" he asserted, proud and stern. "Well, maybe just for your mother," he corrected himself, winking at her for approval. I knew this wasn't a battle I'd win, and decided not to press him on it. My father had been his own man his entire life; he was not going to change for anyone, not even Coca Cola. Unsurprisingly, my father refused to take off his hat and decided not to visit the Houston headquarters ever again.

My father was a man of principle. I, however, have always been a pragmatist at heart. And it was no different at Coca Cola. My very first week, Mr. Amoroso, Coke Foods CEO, opened the operating committee by letting us know we were in for a rare treat; Coca Cola's iconic Chairman Roberto Goizueta would be speaking and joining us for lunch. We were given strict instructions not to approach Mr. Goizueta and to be respectfully brief if asked a question. Mr. Amoroso checked in with me personally after the meeting to ensure that, as the new kid, I'd understood his instructions and would let the more seasoned VP's chat with him first. I thanked him for the opportunity to be there, assuring him I got the message.

Twenty of us sat spellbound as Mr. Goizueta spoke brilliantly about the future of Coca Cola; he was as informative as he was charming. When he finished speaking and the applause died down, we were told to find seats at the three or four tables set up for lunch. As most people fell into groups of friendly hellos and familiar faces, I scanned the room like a new kid in the high school cafeteria. I watched as Mr. Amoroso escorted Mr. Goizueta to a table and sat down next to him.

Noticing an empty seat on the other side of Mr. Goizueta, I figured if everyone else was busy catching up, I could easily justify joining his table. Everyone else had plenty of time to take the spot, and it was a once-in-a-lifetime opportunity I just couldn't pass up. "Excuse me, sir, but is the seat next to you taken for lunch?" I tried to conceal my sweaty palms and shallow breath as Mr. Amoroso shot me a pointed frown. "No, not at all," Mr. Goizueta chirped back, gesturing to the chair alongside his. "Please sit down and join us!" My excitement was beyond words as I sat down to dine with the business legend, unmoved by Mr. Amoroso's displeasure.

We spent the next 15 minutes discussing his Cuban childhood and my experience starting Guido's. "I hope you can bring some of your entrepreneurial spirit inside our big organization," he said, wishing me luck in joining the Coca Cola family. "Don't get discouraged if you can't change things as quickly as you're used to. Just do the right things and don't give up on the issues you believe in." I was on cloud nine; I couldn't have dreamt up a warmer welcome!

This turned out to be one of my Coca Cola highlights, and Mr. Amoroso never mentioned it afterwards. The next day, every vice president came to my office, enviously inquiring as to how I got to sit next to Mr. Goizueta my first week on the job. I told them I simply saw the empty chair and asked to join the table. They were astounded by my audacity and good fortune. I was probably able to get away with more than most officers in the company because I didn't fear getting fired, nor did I care what others thought. In this instance I decided it was better to ask for forgiveness than permission, and it paid off in spades.

Though the personal financial pressures of running our own company were gone, we still struggled to grow a profitable business. While we continued to hit our promised revenue targets, we missed our profit forecasts by a long shot. Because of Coke Foods' expenses and increased slotting fees that supermarkets were charging, I knew it would be practically impossible to make our forecasted profits. It was why we were so desperate to sell the company. But the executives responsible for purchasing Guido's built the revenue and profit forecast for the first year, and I wasn't going to tell them to adjust them down to pay us less.

Guido's revenues had grown from $1 million in 1981 to almost $20 million when we sold in 1985, reaching nearly $50 million the second year after our sale. But between the cost of slotting allowances and supermarkets' expectation that Coca Cola would invest more marketing dollars, our costs skyrocketed. I knew we'd miss our forecast, but I didn't anticipate how far off we'd be.

While I tried to rationalize the gap, attributing much of it to the unfamiliar way Coke did business, failing to meet my forecasts felt absolutely horrible. I tried challenging the status quo, asking the VP of sales about reducing the costs and paying less slotting allowances, but was quickly brushed off. This was the way Coke Foods did business, he assured me, and the salesforce wouldn't pay any attention to our product if we made it difficult for them to sell. Despite our best efforts, we never did figure out how to significantly reduce our costs of sales. While it was common sense that salespeople would always sell whatever makes them the most money, I never imagined what big dollars would be necessary to incentivize our own salespeople to get our product out there.

Missing profit forecasts made for very challenging and uncomfortable board meetings. Our new board included Doug Ivester, the CFO of Coca Cola, as well as the CFO of Coca Cola Foods. They were numbers guys, and after paying a very high price for quick entry into the frozen novelty category, they expected to start making money immediately. Gaps in expectations were not tolerated.

"Richard, I know you are new to the way we do business at Coke Foods, and you are not solely responsible yet for delivering the profits you forecasted when we acquired your company," Mr. Ivester compassionately began, before sternly dropping the hammer. "But we do not miss our financial forecasts more than once. Fix it or tell us what advice you need to deliver the results you forecasted." My hair stood on end; I had never been spoken to in such a tone, especially in front of other executives.

I nearly threw the Coke Foods salesforce under the bus, itching to note that they had given away far more slotting allowances and marketing dollars than the team had forecasted. But thankfully, I caught myself. "Do I want to be right or do I want to be successful?" I asked myself. It didn't take a stroke of genius to realize that throwing blame wouldn't get me anywhere. If I wanted to survive and do well here, my best option was to respect my superiors, thank them for their advice and focus on executing whatever was needed to achieve our goals.

"I am still new to Coke Foods," I agreed, refocusing on Mr. Ivester's expertise and interests. "How do you suggest we reduce the marketing expenses demanded by the sales and marketing team while still delivering the projected revenue?" I decided to ask for advice rather than trying to be right. An eerie silence fell over the room. I don't think he had ever been spoken back to like that, especially in front of other board members. Waiting for his response, I was proud of what I had said but unsure how he would react. I already was disappointed about not delivering on our acquisition projections, but I was setting the tone for how I would engage with the board, and felt it was worth the gamble. "That is a very good question," Mr. Ivester said, sounding encouraging, "Let's go talk to Tim [VP of sales] after the meeting and see what choices we have!"

Phew! I think he actually respected me for engaging with his criticism; he was on my side and willing to help. The rest of the board meeting went smoothly and, true to his word, Mr. Ivester accompanied me to Tim's office right after our meeting. The shock on Tim's face when we walked in was apparent. "Good afternoon, Mr. Ivester, is there anything I can do to help you?" Tim nervously greeted us. Mr. Ivester proceeded to facilitate a fruitful discussion around how Tim could help sell Guido's Ice Juicees and reduce our marketing costs.

From that day forward Tim knew that, if needed, I could always call Mr. Ivester. I never held it over his head, and Tim was always as warm and cooperative as he could be. But we still had a long-term problem delivering revenue without spending enormous marketing dollars. As part of a bundled sale, we couldn't disconnect from the other brands to sell on our own; we were glued to the slotting allowances Coke Foods committed to. While sales volume grew significantly, we missed every profit projection that first year, and began each board meeting by combing over the sales and marketing costs to rectify the problem.

After just two meetings, the board seemed to realize that the forecasts were flawed, and they probably paid too much for the business. Despite this, we were doing everything we could to turn it around, and while I didn't feel good about missing our forecasts, I wasn't embarrassed. I was actually very proud of our team's efforts and knew we were setting ourselves up for success the following year. By the spring of my second year, it felt like we had turned the corner.

After some protracted and difficult discussions, I convinced our board to let me make up a new budget for the second year with a similar revenue forecast and a break-even profit. Though these were different than the forecasted profits from the acquisition, I justified it by promising we would make up the lost profits in years three and four. Coca Cola operated more like a bank with each of its brands than a consumer products company. So as I put in a budget and asked for money to grow the business, Coca Cola Foods evaluated how much return they would receive for their investment and how secure it was. I am not sure they believed that I'd make up the profits that quickly, but either way they agreed to make a more realistic budget.

Meanwhile, business was on the up and up. We had grown from being sold in 10% of supermarkets across the country before the acquisition, to over 70% nationwide by year two, and the school business was expanding as well. As our volume continued exceeding the forecasts, it looked like we had a chance to become profitable that summer. With newfound access to a research and development team (R&D), I was excited to explore expanding our product offerings. At Guido's, we never had the time or money to do anything but manufacture and sell the basic products we'd come up with, but now that I had the power of a corporate salesforce and manufacturing support behind me, I was able to spend more time working with their product development team. But yet again, I found myself struggling with the big company learning curve.

As with every other team, we had to fight for the time and attention of our R&D team. And it seemed like no matter what I suggested, I got nothing but constant pushback on all our ideas. I quickly realized that even with a company as great as Coca Cola there was still the "not invented here syndrome"; people would invest more time and energy into their own ideas than the ones I asked them to create. Then it hit me. All I had to do, I realized, was figure out how to make the new products their ideas.

So I made a plan. I took each of the R&D associates assigned to Ice Juicees out to lunch, getting to learn more about them as people, their families and their perspective on how to introduce new products at Coke Foods. "You know, Ray, we are doing pretty well, sales are good," I explained to one of the associates, giving an update on my life, "But there's such a focus on getting in shape for the summer, I feel like if we could find a way to come up with a health-conscious product, we could unlock a whole new portion of the market."

Ray's eyes lit up, and he nearly cut me off before I finished my sentence. "You won't believe it," he blurted out, "But we actually just got approval to use a brand new low-calorie sweetener called

Nutrasweet. I hear there are some challenges when you heat it, but it would be perfect to put in a frozen product. Can I try putting it into the Ice Juicees and taking out some of the sugar calories?" I could see the excitement dancing on his face. "That would be great!" I said, thrilled with his response. "As long as you don't lose our great taste, you can try anything you like!" I challenged, gleefully egging him on.

I did the same type of thing with Pat and somehow coming up with Coca Cola flavored Italian ices. He was so excited he had thought of adding Pop Rocks to the ices to emulate the carbonation of Coca Cola that I had to calm him down, reminding him this was a confidential product development project. After letting them know I had the authority and budget to initiate a new product introduction, I gave strict instructions not to disclose the project to anyone without my approval, and ensured our associates that once we rolled out the new product, they would receive full credit for developing it.

The secrecy and novelty of the projects added an excitement I don't think they ever experienced before. After that, there was no struggle for attention; they wanted to prove they were right, and suddenly things started moving much more quickly. I was so excited about creating the first zero-calorie frozen dessert and Pop Rocks Coca Cola Ices, I couldn't wait to tell my board members.

Meanwhile, an entirely new adventure reared its head; Ann was pregnant! In March of 1987 she gave birth to a baby boy we named Brett, a surreal experience that brought me to new levels of joy and love. I was so grateful to really be present for the beginning of Brett's life, and as it turns out, the constant demands and sleep deprivation of startup life had been incredible preparation for parenthood.

I was in complete awe and overwhelmed with emotion as we welcomed our son into the world. While Ann and Brett rested comfortably in the hospital that first night, the nurses sent me home to get some sleep, but I was too excited to close my eyes. Instead, I sat down to write a poem to my newborn son, and polished it throughout the week. Overcome with emotion, the words came pouring out through my pen. It's one of my favorites, and expresses my deep hopes for all children.

My Newborn Son
March 13, 1987

Today is your Bris, my newborn son
The miracle of life has only begun.
Though the Mohel may cut outer flesh and take skin
Happiness in life resides deep within.

For already you're blessed with my very first goal
A healthy body, sound mind, and a pure, peaceful soul.
As destiny beckons you to come forth and share
Challenge yourself to be as great as you dare.

For I'll always be there with a supporting hand
When you stumble and fall down, I'll help you to stand.
My father taught me to be successful in life
By confronting adversity and conquering strife.

But the ultimate person you grow up to be
Depends on your choices and not upon me.
For I've had my chance to experience life
I've been blessed with much love and a kind, caring wife.

But when it's your turn to stand on your own

Remember I love you, you're never alone.
As you travel life's journey and search high above
Turn your eyes inward and express all your love.

For you are a leader, compassionate and strong
Trust your own instincts and you will never go wrong.
Because when you don't worry what others believe
No limits exist to what you may achieve.

So if you select to build castles of wealth
Remember your loved ones, your morals, your health.
But if inner peace is your ultimate goal
Its secret is waiting within your own soul.

Whatever you choose I'll be there to share
To love and to cherish just to show that I care.
For I'll always provide you a wise guiding hand
Like Moses, who led our people to the promised land.

For life is the journey to who you will be
Only you are the author to your own destiny.
Today, I thank God, his greatest miracle well done
For health and shalom for my dear newborn son.

Just when I thought I had everything firing on all cylinders, I received yet another phone call that would change my life. Mr. Roberto Goizueta, Coca Cola's inspirational Chairman of the Board who visited for lunch my first week on the job, was sending his plane to pick me up at the end of the week for a meeting in Atlanta with him and Donald Keough, the President of Coca Cola. While it was an honor and privilege to meet with two great icons of the soft drink industry, I had a sinking suspicion it would not be good news.

Though we reported through the Coca Cola Foods division (think Minute Maid Orange Juice and Hi-C Fruit Drinks), Coca Cola Atlanta made the actual acquisition. I never reported to or communicated with Coca Cola Atlanta, and had a hunch that people this important wouldn't be flying me in to congratulate me on a job well done. Plus, I hadn't done anything well yet.

Right after my secretary told me about Mr. Goizueta's invitation, I immediately called up my father to ask why he thought they wanted to see me. He had no idea either, but decided we should make a list of all the possibilities. After racking our brains there were only a few options:

1. Our financial performance was so poor they wanted to sell the company back to us or shut it down.

2. They found something terribly wrong in the original purchase transaction and wanted an explanation.

3. They heard about our Coca Cola Italian Ices idea and were going to shut it down.

4. They were going to berate me for missing the acquisition projections by so much and wanted to know what I was going to do to fix it quickly.

While I tried to keep my thoughts and emotions positive, I was consumed with dread, and couldn't shake the uncomfortable feeling in the pit of my stomach all week. Though I'd held my own during uncomfortable meetings with my own board, dealing with two industry legends was a completely different ball game.

By this point in time, I was seasoned in the art of facing high-stress conflicts, so I fought the impulse to think emotionally. I took a step back to remind myself of my priorities and rationally think through the worst-case scenario. Regardless of Coca Cola's disappointment, there was no way they could take back the cash they had already paid us. And while I liked my job and living in Houston, I was not dependent on it for my happiness. With poetry as an outlet, family for unconditional support and a wife I was madly in love with, I knew that no matter what happened I still had the most valuable things in life.

Most importantly, I had learned that what I did was different than who I was. My self-worth was tied to how much I loved and respected myself, not my business accomplishments. Being able to separate those two gave me a greater sense of contentment and quality of life, but it also helped in high-stress situations, giving me the ability to maintain focus and composure. I loved myself for who I was, I reminded myself, and whatever happened to me next would be to teach me a valuable lesson, one way or another. Figuring the fourth option was their most likely motive for calling me in, I was prepared to walk through why our lack of profits was Coca Cola Foods' fault, but realized that I was better off not making excuses and just agreeing to fix the problem. "Do I want to be right or do I want to be successful?" I kept asking myself. "Successful," I answered, again and again. Keeping my focus on the desired outcome and working my way back, I first needed to define success for this meeting.

For starters, I wanted Mr. Goizueta and Mr. Keough to respect and believe in me as a competent executive. Second, I wanted them to believe that I was the best executive to fix the problem. Finally, I wanted to convince them to see the same profitable future that I did at the end of our earn-out in three more years. I knew I had the confidence and enthusiasm to pull it off, I just wasn't sure that they would give me the chance to articulate my future vision.

All they had to do was agree to invest the necessary dollars to allow us to introduce the two new products we were working on, and I was sure we would make all the money promised in the acquisition forecasts. We could sell our new products at a premium, factoring Coca Cola's high sales and marketing costs into the price. By using the Coke or Minute Maid name, along with our existing distribution, new products were sure to fly off the shelves and deliver the profits we had promised. When I arrived in Atlanta and walked into the building, I felt prepared both emotionally and professionally, confident that I had thought through all the possible conversations. But once we sat down, it became clear that my confidence had been misplaced.

After some brief pleasantries, the two executives quickly got to their reason for summoning me. Mr. Goizueta explained that Coca Cola Foods was having challenges in their core orange juice business; Tropicana and Citrus Hill (Procter & Gamble) were taking large market shares away from the Minute Maid brand. They told me confidentially that they would be replacing Mr. Amoroso and the leadership team at Coca Cola Foods, and that the new CEO would focus strictly on growing their orange juice business. Applauding me for my efforts, the two icons assured me this was in no way a reflection of their opinions about me, but I would not be getting the resources necessary to grow the Fruit Juicee business. They needed me to be patient and just maintain our current operations for a few years.

Without hesitating, I thanked them for their kind words but told them if I can't grow a business I can't breathe. I am not the right leader for just maintaining a business, I explained, but rather a fast-growth one. Though I made the decision in an instant, it was not a hard one to make. I knew myself quite well, along with what I could and could not commit to. Being unhappy for two years wasn't worth the earn-out that came with it, even if Coca Cola was prepared to pay me big dollars to stay. I had to follow my passion.

These words unleashed a flurry of emotions as everything began to sink in. I knew that nothing I said would change their minds. All the preparation I had done for this meeting was meaningless; I wasn't being berated or fired, but emotionally I didn't quite know how to react or respond. I never knew if I was going to work for Coca Cola for four years (the length of my current contract and our earn-out) or 20, but I certainly did not expect to be cut off from all the capital necessary to grow our business. Had I just resigned? Was I just fired? I gave my best shot at a stoic look of calm, but my heart pounded and sweat dripped down my temples as I tried to process the situation.

Mr. Goizueta looked at Mr. Keough and nodded. Mr. Keough then thanked me for my honesty, and noted that they were not surprised by my response. However, they had made up their minds and asked if I would stay on as president of Guido's until the end of the year to effectuate a smooth transition. Of course I agreed, and I asked if there was anything else they wanted me to do. Then it hit me that I *was* just fired. Since this was my first real job working for someone else, I had never been fired before.

I didn't know if I should be happy or sad. All I could feel was an emptiness like I had just lost a best friend. The many years of near-business-death experiences and struggling to grow Guido's all flashed through my mind in an instant. I knew I wasn't going to be working at Coca Cola forever, but this was not how I envisioned it ending. But regardless of how I felt, Ann would certainly be thrilled to leave Houston. We shook hands and they thanked me for my service to Coca Cola, and the professional manner in which

I handled myself in what must have been a very surprising and somewhat upsetting encounter.

While I was driven back to the plane, it struck me that my world was about to turn upside down. As the wheels of the plane left the runway, I no longer needed to put on a brave face, and the reality started to sink in. The adrenaline subsided and I felt my heart tear open with an overwhelming wave of deep sadness and emptiness, and I allowed myself a moment of grief. Then, I refocused and spent the next two hours reflecting on all the memorable moments, thinking to myself how lucky I had been to have a chance to live out a dream. By the time I landed in Houston, I was somewhat relieved to know that at the end of the year I could take some time off before starting the next chapter of my career. It was almost surprising how quickly I was able to process and accept the new change in my reality.

As I drove from the Houston airport home, I called my father and explained what had happened in Atlanta. His response shocked me. "Not surprising," he shared, completely unmoved by the meeting. "I am very proud of you. You lasted longer at Coke Foods than I expected and I think you did a great job." His words of praise provided a soothing comfort, like the exclamation point I needed to complete the Guido's experience. He wasn't upset that we would not make the money we expected in our earn-out, nor was he annoyed about how I was treated. He was simply happy to watch me successfully close one chapter of my life and prepare to open the next exciting stage.

CHAPTER 8

STARTING OVER

While I was still taking in the magnitude of what had just happened, I knew Ann would be thrilled to hear we were no longer tied down to Houston. After a big hug and kiss, I recounted the entire meeting, watching her face closely as I explained that I would stay on until the end of the year to help with a smooth transition. A sense of unbridled joy swept over her as she realized what this meant. She grabbed my hand, jumping up and down with excitement. "Does this mean we can go back home to San Diego?!" she practically squealed. Her joy was contagious. "Yes," I beamed back at her, "But not until the end of the year!" I could barely get the words out before she smothered me with kisses. So far, losing my job was going famously.

In December of 1987, Ann and I packed up our belongings and young Brett into the car, and drove from Houston to San Diego. When my Coke Foods colleagues asked what I planned to do as a 34-year-old entrepreneur, I let them know I was ready for a break. After spending my 20s in a constant state of near bankruptcy, followed by the stress of running a public company and navigating the frustrations within a large corporation in my 30s, I thought I would be relieved to take a year off and just enjoy life. I had grand plans of simple life pleasures – watching my young son grow, writing more poetry and learning to play golf. It was a life most people only dreamed of. But deep inside something was still missing.

The first few weeks I basked in the lazy mornings, taking leisurely walks on the beach and enjoying a full night's sleep, free from frantic business calls. For the first time in over a decade, there were no massive business challenges hanging over my head, and the world felt lighter as I began to unwind. Tired and burnt out, I thought it would take awhile before I felt like myself again. But I was shocked at how quickly the years of stress and struggle seemed to melt away. I was more surprised still at the unexpected void that filled their place.

While the endless demands of entrepreneurship had taken a toll on me, I didn't quite know how to exist without them. Two months into my "funemployment" family time, I was getting antsy. Building things and being part of a team were part of my identity; no matter how much I loved my wife and son (which I did immensely), I realized that without that sense of challenge, I wouldn't feel complete. I called my parents to confide my conundrum, explaining that I needed to find something to build. Knowing all too well how hard I had been pushing myself the past 12 years, they urged me to have some patience and enjoy the moment. "Spend time with your beautiful wife and son, travel and enjoy the fruits of your labor," my mother advised. "There will always be business opportunities waiting whenever you are ready."

While I understood their concerns, patience wasn't always my greatest gift, and I decided it was time to broach the subject with Ann. "I just want you to be happy," she assured me, after I explained my feelings over dinner. "Whether that means going back to work or staying home with me and Brett, only you will know. But I love you and I believe in you, so whatever you choose I will support you 100%!" I had been head over heels for Ann the moment I met her, and always knew I was lucky. But her compassion and endless support never ceased to amaze me. Even just putting it out there and discussing my dilemma with her started to help.

Then, as luck would have it, my father received a phone call the next week from an acquaintance of his in Florida; he had invested in a startup company that needed more money and someone with operating experience. Having heard that I'd finished my two years at Coca Cola, he wondered if I might be interested. This was just what I was looking for! I immediately asked my father when we could fly to Florida to investigate things further. So far, all I knew was that this was a latex glove startup called SafeSkin, but I was so eager to get back in the game I would have jumped at just about anything. The following Wednesday, my father and I flew to Miami to meet with Neil, the company founder and president.

My dad and I met Neil at his office just outside Miami on a Thursday morning, not knowing what to expect. I had done some quick research on the latex glove industry and after a few phone calls, I learned that the existing latex glove shortage was quickly devolving into an all-out crisis due to the AIDS epidemic. Huge numbers of previously healthy young people were dying from the disease at an alarming rate, and latex gloves were the front line of defense in keeping uneasy healthcare workers protected. This was definitely a product that mattered.

Originally from New England, Neil was about 15 years my senior, a tall, thick-built man with a matter-of-fact manner. As anyone looking to woo a new partner might do, he began by sharing a bit about himself, going over his childhood, education and business background. An options trader with a degree in engineering, Neil was new to the medical field but had spent the past 25 years manufacturing assorted products in Asia. There was a global latex glove shortage due to the new government regulations to address the AIDS epidemic, he explained, which required all healthcare workers coming in contact with bodily fluids to start wearing gloves, masks and gowns, and change them for each patient they treated. Existing supply could not meet this massive new demand, and recognizing the lucrative business opportunity, Neil began building a latex glove manufacturing machine in Malaysia, home to the world's largest supply of raw latex.

"While the conditions are perfect to enter this market, we need to raise more money in order to finish the first machine. We're looking for someone with funds, as well as business and sales experience to help run the company," he concluded. "That's why you're here today." Though thoughtful and cordial in the discussions, he had an all too familiar sense of urgency about him, and I could tell that he was under a lot of pressure to raise money for the business – and fast.

Neil told us that he could do all the engineering and manufacturing but needed someone who could handle all the sales, marketing and distribution of the gloves. It sounded like a perfect fit for me. As the day flew by, I was getting more and more excited. Neil seemed like a straight shooter we could work well with, and he had identified a product with tremendous need in the marketplace. Though I knew nothing about the medical industry, I was an avid customer advocate and very confident I could sell boatloads of any product.

The big disadvantage we would have, I realized, was that all the contacts we had developed in the food business over the past 12 years were now running many of the top food companies and they would be of zero help to us in the medical device industry. We would need to start all over and build up a new network in the medical field. In my head I was already planning how to hire experienced medical device salespeople who could introduce us to their contacts and teach us everything they knew.

By the end of the day, everything seemed to be falling into place. After Neil's pitch, we spent the afternoon recounting our success with Guido's, and how those selling skills were transferable to SafeSkin. He loved the fact that we had started a company from scratch and taken it all the way from a tiny seed to a public company sold to a Fortune 100 company. We didn't delve into the details of our constant state of near bankruptcy or how lucky we had gotten in the end, but once we were interested in SafeSkin, we were quick to sell Neil on why we were the right partners for him.

When we finally got down to discussing the finances of the deal, Neil said he was looking for $1 million cash for operating capital and $1 million of collateral to borrow against, in exchange for 45% ownership of the company. This meant we would be equal partners, with 10% owned by initial investors who financed the company up until that point. We had not anticipated moving this quickly, and didn't have much to go on besides the fact that this looked like a great opportunity with a very large market. "Sounds like you have an amazing operation here, Neil," I assured him enthusiastically. "Give us a few days to mull things over, and we'll get back to you."

When I am hiring an executive or investing in companies, it is much like dating someone. My first meeting is to find out whether or not I am attracted to them and if I want a second meeting. Thereafter, each meeting needs to feel better and better. In most early-stage investments it is almost always about the people and never just about the technology; things never work out as originally planned, so I would always rather have great people with good technology than good people with great technology. That night as my father and I ate dinner back at the hotel and discussed the events of the day, we agreed that with his experience and expertise,

Neil seemed the type of partner we could work with. Though it was very early on, both of our gut instincts told us we should take the next step.

My father and I agreed that before we invested millions of dollars, I needed to fly to Asia to see the glove machine in action.

Over the next few weeks, we needed to identify the targeted customer, understand which needs weren't currently being met, study up on the competition and figure out how to differentiate our gloves from the ones currently in circulation. "Most shortages come to an end quicker than expected," my father reminded me, "So we need to develop the best product that the customer really needs, and establish a distribution network that can deliver our products even when the big guys try to squeeze us out."

After hashing things out with my father, I spent an hour on the phone with Ann that night sharing my impressions, explaining the size of this opportunity and the role I would play. "Tell me more about Neil, and your dynamic with him," Ann inquired, always taking an active role in my big decisions. "Was he a good listener or did he spend most of the time selling you on how great things would be? Did you and your father feel energized or drained when you left the meetings? All work aside, is this a man you'd want to be friends with?"

She bombarded me with so many great questions I had to cut her off. "It's hard to tell what someone is really like when they are trying to excite you to invest in their company," I reminded her, trying not to get overwhelmed myself. "But both dad and I had a positive impression of him. The only thing I can think of is there was some underlying impatience in his voice. But I could have very well been like that too, during my early days at Guido's," I said. "It's hard to tell if we can trust someone just by meeting them for a day," I admitted, worn out by my intensely focused day. Supportive and familiar with the unpredictability of startups, Ann was happy for me and recommended we wait and see how much of what Neil said was actually true. She was always the more pragmatic one. I had an extra bounce in my step the next morning, and my flight home was absolutely dreamy! There was something mystical and exciting about manufacturing in Asia and not being the executive responsible for factory operations. Though I had overseen manufacturing and even built factories from the ground up, sales and marketing were my true strengths and loves.

My love affair with selling started as a teenager. However, I wasn't one of those natural-born salesmen, inherently comfortable chatting up strangers. I was actually quite shy and insecure as I approached my Bar Mitzvah at the tender age of 13, officially entering adulthood in the Jewish tradition. My father sat me down, congratulated me on becoming a man and invited me to come work with him on Saturdays at his appliance store.

I can't express the joy and excitement that flowed through me, as I would have done anything to spend more time with my father. He worked dawn to dusk six days a week, and my siblings and I would fight just to sit next to him whenever he was able to make it home early enough for dinner. Now I would have him to myself for a whole day?! "Yes, yes, yes!" I burst out, nearly jumping out of my seat. "What will I do all day while you are doing your work?" I asked. "Will I follow you around?"

His facial expression hardened, and he spoke with a level of seriousness I hadn't seen before. "No," he sternly corrected me, "I will teach you how to sell just once, and then you speak with whoever walks in the store, helping them buy a TV, air conditioner or any other appliance they are looking for. It will be great experience for you!" My heart sank into my stomach. "How am I going to talk to people I don't even know?" I asked myself. Walking up and selling things to pure strangers? My heart pounded and hands clammed up just thinking about it. I was even considering changing my mind, but I just couldn't turn down a chance to spend more time with my father.

That first Saturday of work I cherished our 30-minute car ride together while secretly dreading the moment we'd arrive at the store. As we walked through the front doors, my father called over two of the top salesmen and explained that I would be joining their ranks every Saturday, and unless people specifically asked for them, I should get my turn with new customers just like everyone else. I couldn't tell if they reacted with a smirk or a chuckle, but they weren't amused. Any customers I closed would take away from commission they could have earned, but they knew there was no use arguing with my father. "All right," Tony conceded, "but if they are Italian then I get first shot!"

"Yeah," George agreed, "If they are Greek, they're mine!" Cheeks aflame, I kept my gaze glued to my shoelaces as they hashed things out. "OK, OK," my father assured them, "That's fine. It's only on Saturdays and there are plenty of customers for all of you." Tony and George nodded and begrudgingly agreed. I never dreamed that I would start a controversy and I hadn't even started working yet!

Much to my relief, the first few customers who entered the store were returning customers for Tony and George. When the next middle-aged couple entered the store, my father and I approached them and he thanked them for coming in to see us. He introduced me as his son and let them know this was my first day on the job. Would they mind if I listened in, he asked. "Of course not," they gushed, "We think it's great!" Over the course of the next 10 minutes my father asked them a host of questions, going over where they were from and how many kids they had before asking how we could help them. Not once did he talk about selling them anything. I later came to learn that he was starting by making a personal connection so they would trust him.

Once he finally got around to ask what appliances they were interested in, the couple let us know they were just beginning to look for a new TV and unsure of whether they were ready to buy one. "We're just here to learn about our choices," they said. Happy to help, my father spent the next 20 minutes showing them four different brands, the advantages of each and which seemed like the best fit for them. When confronted with making a choice, they looked at each other, hesitated, and said they just weren't ready to buy yet. My heart sank, but my father was unfazed. "That's fine," he assured them with a caring smile, "but could you help me understand what your concerns are?" One by one he addressed each one until finally they said they weren't sure it would fit in the space they had at home or whether they could afford it.

"I see," my father responded thoughtfully. "Why don't you finance it for two years at a very low interest rate and have us deliver it on Monday? If it doesn't fit or you change your mind, we will come pick it up, cancel your purchase and refund your entire deposit." He had addressed every one of their objections and they looked at each other as they contemplated his offer. The pregnant pause was exhilarating; though my father was very calm and relaxed, I loved the tension of whether they would buy or not. Finally, the husband cautiously responded. "OK, but only if we can really return it if we change our minds."

I felt a rush of excitement flow through me like I had just sunk the winning shot in a championship basketball game. It was the moment my father taught me one of the most invaluable lessons he'd ever share – that no is the first step to any sale. I was hooked on the rush of selling, but I just didn't know how I would do it myself. The thought of talking to strangers on my own was terrifying. After the new TV owners paid for their purchase and thanked us for our help, they turned as they walked out the door. "Good luck with your new career!" they shouted to me.

After they left I gave my father an enthusiastic hug. "That was fun!" I exclaimed, "Let's do it again!" He returned the hug, but kept to his word. "That was your only lesson," he said. "From now on you are on your own. I know you will become very good at selling," he assured me, placing a confident hand on my shoulder. "Remember, just ask the customers about themselves and what they are interested in, let them convince themselves they really need it and then overcome all their objections. Do that and they will almost always give you their money." He made it sound so simple!

"OK," I responded skeptically, "Most of that makes sense. But, come on, how do you make customers convince themselves they really need the TV if they are not even sure they are ready to buy it?" I said, with more conviction than I had expected. "That is a very good question. See, you are already becoming a good salesman!" He patted me on the back with an extra glitter in his eye. "You want to get the customer to see themselves using the TV and having fun, to bond with the idea of having one. Ask them questions like where they plan to put it, who they'll invite over to watch with and what shows they're most excited to see at home. You are trying to get them to create an emotional bond with the TV experience rather than focusing on the cost." That was the best selling lesson I ever had.

Though I was very nervous to try selling all by myself, after a while I became very comfortable and actually looked forward to my next unscripted encounter. It was much like learning to drive a car. The first time driving on a real road, I was very nervous when a car approached me in the opposite direction and relieved once it passed. But with each passing car, I became less and less nervous until I actually enjoyed seeing them whiz by. With selling, it took me several attempts before I really began enjoying the experience. Once I gained my confidence, I felt alive trying to build trust with strangers, helping them persuade themselves into a purchase that would leave them grateful and satisfied when we were through. With nearly every sale, I felt as though I had made a good friend, and lo and behold, many of my customers came back year after year to find me when they needed a new appliance.

My big breakthrough came when I realized that I wasn't trying to take customers' money, but rather supporting them in filling a need. Once they trusted me and we found the right fit for them, how to pay or finance their purchase was easy. Each customer presented a very different challenge and I never got bored. The fact that I earned commission on everything I sold made it even more exciting. Earning my own commission also taught me a great deal about how to motivate salespeople. There was no noticeable difference between the best brands of TVs we sold. However, I earned 7% commission on Sylvania and Magnavox TVs while getting only 1% on Zenith brand sets. Unsurprisingly, I sold only one Zenith TV my entire time working at my father's store, and that was just because the customer insisted.

Within a few weeks I started making much more money selling appliances than I received from my allowance. I felt so confident and grown up, fully earning my new status as an adult! While my Saturdays at the store became a bit more routine over the next five years, my love for selling and filling customer needs only grew deeper with time. It was so much more emotionally fulfilling for me to bond with customers than putting numbers and machinery together in my later years at Guido's. When we began growing the Italian ices business, I discovered that it was fairly easy to hire great operational and manufacturing executives to keep factories on point, but finding a talented "rainmaker" who could close multiple large sales was much more rare. And that's just exactly what my father was and I became.

I'm not sure if it was nature, nurture, or just my dogged persistence, but customers knew how much I cared about them and often allowed me to become a trusted advisor and good friend, helping them with more than just buying our products. Once someone knows how much you genuinely care, that you have their best interest in mind beyond your own self-serving goals, your words have more power. No matter what your profession, we all need to influence people in life. Whenever engaging a new customer, I always tried to connect heart to heart. I had done it in the food business, and now I was ready to do the same thing in the medical device industry.

When I walked through the front door after returning home from Florida, my one-year-old son ran as fast as his little legs would take him, jumping into the air and flying into my outstretched arms. I was gone for only two days, but I could have sworn he had grown. I hoped the time-consuming demands of starting a business wouldn't rob me of the day-to-day joys of watching my son grow up. While I couldn't control the amount of hours my new venture would require, I was able to control my approach to the time I did have with the family, and made a commitment to always be present and really enjoy every moment with my precious baby boy.

Ann gave me a big kiss and then told me that Neil had called. "If you're really interested in the latex glove business," she explained, "He said you should meet him at the Los Angeles airport tomorrow and fly with him to Malaysia." She soothingly stroked young Brett's back as she followed up. "By the way, why Malaysia, and where is it?"

Neil had selected Malaysia because it was the leading grower of natural raw latex at the time, and had the finest latex institute in the world with research and development expertise in close proximity. The low cost of raw goods and brilliant technical minds would be crucial to becoming a leader in the industry. Neither of us really knew where it was so we went downstairs and got out an atlas. We found Malaysia across the Pacific, nestled between Thailand and Singapore in Southeast Asia. "Well," she said nonchalantly, "At least the sales and marketing are U.S.-based. Fingers crossed that keeps you closer to home most of the time."

I called my parents and told them about Neil's phone call. Though things were unfolding much more quickly than anticipated, we decided I should waste no time and join Neil on his trip to Malaysia the next day. They wished me safe travels and reminded me to enjoy the trip. I promised to call them as soon as I learned enough to discuss. Then I went upstairs, packed my bags and braced myself for an adventure.

The next morning, I met Neil in the Malaysian Airlines lounge at the Los Angeles airport. I was both excited and apprehensive. This was my first foray outside North America, and when I walked into the airport, I actually believed I was flying straight into a jungle. "What on earth am I getting myself into?" I wondered over and over again. Opting to enjoy the ride, I decided to just sit back, observe and let Neil make all the decisions. The flight was very long – over 19 hours – but the service on Malaysian Airlines was impeccable! The flight attendants were stunning, dressed in beautifully ornate traditional Malaysian attire and their English was perfect. Later, I discovered that Malaysia had been a British colony and English was integrated into the education system and even used to argue cases in their legal system.

Given how little I knew about the medical device industry, I spent most of our flight mapping out what I needed to learn on this trip and came up with a short list of initial criteria to determine our odds for success in the industry, and whether we should invest our time and money:

1. Is the need for latex gloves big enough for another competitor?

2. Can we significantly differentiate our product from the existing gloves in the market?

3. Will large hospitals allow a small startup company with only one product to compete with the leaders in this market with multiple products?

4. Will there be enough time to get the company profitable before the glove shortage ends?

5. How much money will we need to get to cash-flow breakeven?

While nowhere near complete, this list would make a good start, I decided. I would also need to find out how gloves were made, how we could make them even better in the future and what our customers really needed. While it was no small task, I gave myself two to three weeks to thoroughly do my due diligence so my parents and I could make a decision when I returned home. When we finally arrived at our hotel in Kuala Lumpur, I was surprised to find a luxurious lobby beyond anything I had imagined. It was decorated with the finest marble and most elegant chandeliers I had ever seen. The place was buzzing with business people from around the globe, filled with excitement and opportunity.

The first two days were spent shadowing Neil and pounding coffee in meeting after meeting with people from all corners of the earth looking to buy latex gloves. While it took everything in me to fight the jet lag and stay awake, Neil looked alive with energy to spare, completely in his element as he stood strong and confident with everyone we met. Whether this was authentic, or exaggerated for my viewing, I could sense how much Neil loved this process and was energized in talking about his product. The last thing in the world I would've imagined was that he was out of money.

As we met potential customer after customer, it seemed like many of them knew even less about latex gloves than I did; we saw fishermen, restaurant owners and others who had no business experience at all, but smelled a get-rich-quick opportunity. They all seemed to have buyers who desperately needed gloves and plenty of money to spend on them. With such a massive shortfall to fill, due to the new latex glove regulations for American healthcare workers, customer demand was not a concern.

I truly believe that we get rewarded in direct proportion to the size of the needs we fill. When we fill small needs we receive small rewards and when we fill large needs we receive large rewards. I didn't know how long the glove shortage would last, but I saw this as an enormous, immediate opportunity and was eager to learn more. I envisioned us becoming the world's leading latex glove manufacturer with the best-quality gloves, but was also trying to figure out where the real demand would come from when the shortage finally disappeared. With companies desperately trying to ramp up the number of gloves produced, I figured quality would likely get sacrificed in the name of quantity.

After an exhausting but insightful few days of business meetings in Kuala Lumpur, we drove two hours north to Ipoh, where the infamous glove manufacturing machine resided. Neil had rented a warehouse and started building his machine, but ran out of money before he could complete it. He gave me a quick tour of his half-built treasure, enthusiastically explaining what steps were left and how our process would create softer, superior gloves. But with the machine still in progress, we had no proof of its capabilities – just his word.

Most startups have incomplete information, and we have to judge whether or not unproven promises will be delivered. I wasn't yet sold on our ability to produce a better glove, or that Neil's vision could differentiate us enough to create an advantage over the established competitors. A big part of our decision to invest would rely on our ability to quickly identify what our customers' future needs would be, and whether or not we would be able to fill them. Otherwise, we would just be meeting a temporary demand until the current glove shortage ended.

Clocking in as Malaysia's third-largest city with a population of over 500,000 inhabitants, Ipoh was not a small village like I had imagined, but rather a booming center of industry. Our first morning there, I decided to take a jog at 6 a.m. to tamper down my persistent jet lag. Though it was dark, I figured I would run along the road for a while and just turn around to run back. I enjoyed the soft silence before sunrise and found a familiar comfort in seeing English letters listed alongside the local Malay script on all the street signs. Just as I was beginning to get comfortable a half hour into my run, my mind began to wander. "What would happen if I were pulled over and kidnapped?" My pace quickening with mounting anxiety. "No one would know where I was or how to find me if I stumbled into trouble." As one of the only Westerners in town, I stuck out like a sore thumb, and had no way of knowing what type of neighborhood I was running through.

Having sufficiently spooked myself, I decided abruptly to turn around and head back to the hotel. But after 20 minutes, nothing looked familiar, and I realized I was totally and utterly lost. It was still relatively dark outside and most people had not yet awakened for business. I finally saw a young couple opening their shop and ran up to ask for directions. They did not speak a word of English, and though I felt safe, my cheeks flushed with embarrassment. Not only did I get lost, but also I did not know the name of the hotel I was staying at.

Through hand signals and charades, the couple finally understood I was looking for a hotel. They wisely walked me down a few storefronts to a back room where there was a woman who spoke perfect English. I described the hotel to the best of my memory and she said it must be the Casuarina Hotel – I had just taken a wrong turn. She gave me directions back, and after racing there, a tremendous sense of relief rushed over me the moment I finally spotted my hotel sign. That is one mistake I would never repeat!

After making it back to the hotel in one piece, I spent the next few days gathering an understanding of the latex glove production process. Neil and I started at the source, getting up at four in the morning to walk amongst quiet fields, down the carefully planted rows of long, lean latex trees. I watched as the young tree tappers skillfully climbed the narrow trunks, cutting small incisions into the soft bark, inserting plastic tubes with a sense of ease and efficiency. The milky white latex dripped and oozed, slowly filling the bucket hanging below. Once full, these buckets were collected and poured into a large vat along with a host of stabilizers and chemicals so they could be transported to neighboring collection centers, where they would be consolidated into larger batches with more chemicals and shipped out to make latex gloves. As I watched the men mix in the foul-smelling chemicals, I couldn't help but think that this couldn't be healthy rubbing up against nurses' skin day in and day out. It seemed strange to me that glove companies would put so many weird chemicals into something meant to protect the skin.

Back in my room at night, I reflected on what I had learned. Raw natural latex dripped out of trees just like maple syrup, but needed chemicals and stabilizers to be transported without spoiling. Then, shipments from a variety of small latex farmers were combined before dividing the vats of liquid latex into separate shipments, destined for either latex gloves or solid latex mats for tires.

One of the lessons I learned at Coca Cola was how difficult and expensive it was to change consumer behavior. But thanks to the universal precautions, healthcare workers were now required by law to wear gloves 10 hours a day instead of 10 minutes a day. With a drastic change in customer behavior already in place, I began to think long term about how this change would affect our users' needs and requirements.

My mind returned to the chemicals and preservatives used in the production process. It had been done this way for decades, but if I wore chemical-filled gloves ten hours a day, chances are my sensitive skin would break out in a rash. This had to be the case for at least some of the millions of healthcare workers as well. This was it! Removing the chemicals from our gloves seemed like the perfect way to differentiate ourselves from the competition. While all the major medical glove manufacturers were churning out as many gloves as fast as they could to protect healthcare workers from the AIDS virus, we would make the highest quality gloves to protect doctors and nurses from the glove itself. I just needed to figure out if we could do it.

The next day when I met Neil for breakfast, I asked how we could redesign the equipment to remove all the chemicals. "It's no problem," he replied without a thought, "But why would we want to do that? No one else is." After I explained my thought process, Neil noted that he was an engineer and didn't know much about the customer need, but if I thought it was important then we could add 100 feet of boiling water baths to the end of the machine design that would remove the chemicals from the gloves before shipping them. It was inexpensive to run, he explained, and wouldn't add much to the total cost of completing the machine. I liked the fact that Neil didn't question me when it came to customer needs, just like I wouldn't question him on whom to buy latex from or how to build the machines. Good signs we'll mesh well together, I thought, happy to see another positive indicator.

I didn't know whether other companies hadn't thought of this, or whether the high cost or extra space needed for retrofitting all their existing glove-making machines scared them away. Either way, I was thrilled that things seemed to be coming together! While I was initially concerned about my lack of expertise, being a newcomer to the industry seemed to be working in my favor, as I questioned every step of the process.

My mind was racing I was so excited. By making a fundamental change in the way latex gloves were manufactured and marketed, we could take a startup business and grow it into industry leadership, making a big difference in a very important healthcare industry. I knew it wouldn't be easy. We would need to hire many smart people who could learn fast, and hope that the current glove shortage would last long enough for us to establish enough financial stability to grow and compete with industry giants.

Big companies have lots of money, but much like a massive sea vessel, it takes them longer to maneuver and change direction. It would be a race against time, and the faster the marketplace was changing, the bigger advantage we would keep. Nimble and quick, we had to focus on getting so far ahead that by the time the big players turned around, we'd be too far ahead to catch. It was unclear how much the lessons I had learned at Guido's and Coca Cola would help me in the latex glove business, but this was such an exhilarating opportunity, I needed to at least take the next step.

Between customer meetings, supplier interviews and a rush to complete the glove machine, the next two weeks flew by. The more I learned about this opportunity, the more my gut told me we were onto something very special. A few days before my return to the states, I called my parents to explain what a great opportunity this was to make a difference in the world and tons of money all at once. "Don't worry about making lots of money," my father instructed. "The questions here are whether we can differentiate the product significantly and fast enough, how much money it will really take to get cash-flow breakeven, and if Neil is a good partner. Remember, create value and money is simply the score of how well you've satisfied your customers!"

We had always been a great team, and he'd identified two of the five questions I had originally asked myself on the flight over, right off the bat. It was obvious that the need for latex gloves was big enough. While I hoped this meant that large hospitals would be willing to buy latex gloves from a small startup without other products, I wouldn't know this for sure until we began selling into the market. And figuring out how long the latex shortage would last was another determination we'd have to sort out as we moved forward. "OK, boys," my mother jumped in, "Richard, let's just not make any commitments while you're there. We can discuss it once you're back so you aren't blinded by the excitement and novelty of the situation."

Next I called Ann, relaying the same story I'd shared with my parents, and letting her know I'd be back in three days. "I miss you and Brett so much and I can't wait to see you both!" We sent each other a shared hug at the exact same moment before I said good night. As I set down the receiver, a wave of homesickness rushed through me. The nonstop schedule and constant thrill of this new adventure had filled my every waking moment, but after hearing Ann's voice, three weeks' worth of emotion hit me in a moment. Suddenly, my heart felt heavy as a brick, sinking deep into my stomach as my throat constricted, and uneven shallow breaths shot quickly in and out with pangs of longing for my wife and young son.

While these emotional moments without the ones I loved most could feel overwhelming, I never felt guilty about leaving home for so long. I knew building a world-class company from scratch took personal involvement and great sacrifice, and I was extremely blessed to have a supportive partner always at my side in spirit. With Ann on board, I was ready to forgo the comforts of home and undertake the necessary time away from her and Brett for the purpose of shaping an entire medical industry. While there were obviously no guarantees of success, with my parents and Ann on my side, it was a gamble I was willing to take.

By the end of three weeks, I was bursting with excitement and dragging with exhaustion all at once. When I returned home and presented the opportunity to my parents again, they shared my enthusiasm. My father agreed right away to split the investment between the three of us, but my mother objected. She was not opposed to us investing in the new business, but she insisted I allow my brother and two sisters to invest as well. I was adamantly opposed. Though we all had ownership and worked in one way or another in Guido's, SafeSkin was different. Neil made it perfectly clear up front that he didn't want any other relatives working at SafeSkin, only allowing in my Uncle Bob after I explained that family relations were irrelevant; he was the best salesman I'd ever met, and I needed him.

I would be the only one doing all the work, travel, and sacrificing time away from my family. Since my siblings were going to do none of that, I challenged my mother, why should they receive the benefits of my hard work? "You are paid a good salary to work hard but receive equity for investing money," my mother sternly reminded me. "I'm sure you will be very successful, but if you do not share the financial rewards with your siblings, you will create an economic chasm affecting not only your own relationships, but those of the entire next generation of our family as well." If you ever met my mother you would realize it was senseless to argue with her; she was very moral and almost always correct. "I'm confident you'll make enough money for us all," she assured me, "Just don't be too greedy."

For a week I struggled each day and night trying to see her point of view, discussing it with Ann, but I still couldn't get myself to agree. It just wasn't fair. Quite torn up, I tried to take a step back and distance myself from the situation. I realized I had two choices. Either I agree with my mother and let my siblings invest alongside me or I stick with what I thought was fair and disappoint my mother. I was emotionally exhausted and though I still thought she was wrong, I decided the cost of creating a rift in the family was worse than the unfair plan she had presented. So I agreed to take her advice and allow her, my father and three siblings to buy into a share of my investment. In the end, she was absolutely right, as usual. I'm still very close with all my siblings, we travel on vacations together and the cousins have a beautifully tight-knit relationship. I was lucky to have a family culture established by my parents: stick together and always put our family unit first.

Letting go of things we do not agree with but decide to do anyway is a very important skill to hone as a young entrepreneur. Many decisions we have to make in life and business have no fair options, and after compromise or concession most people hang on and resent giving up what they believe is right, especially if it is something they think is rightfully theirs. I never found this type of pride-driven suffering to be worthwhile. Instead, I return to my favorite question: "Do I want to be right or do I want to be successful?" I put success before pride every time, allowing my goals to drive my decision-making thought process.

There are endless decisions to be made, and no way to get it right every time. But by coming to thoughtful conclusions and accepting all my decisions 100% once I make them, I let go of what could have been and don't suffer the regrets of the past that haunt so many people. Once I decided to take my mother's advice, not only did I accept it, but I fully embraced it and consciously tried to make my entire family feel part of the investment. Agreeing with my mother and inviting my siblings to invest alongside us was one of my best decisions in life.

CHAPTER 9

BACK IN THE GAME

By May of 1988, after only four months of retirement, all the paperwork was completed and I was back in business. The Jaffe family agreed to invest $1 million cash and $1 million of bonds as collateral for 45% of the company, as Neil originally proposed. Neil kept 45%, and his original investors together held 10%. I became president of SafeSkin USA, Neil remained President and CEO Safeskin Corp, and we were to be 50/50 partners operating the business. I was responsible for sales, marketing, and distribution, he oversaw engineering and manufacturing and we would share the finance responsibilities.

To be honest, I was pretty cocky about the amount of success I had already achieved by the age of 35. As ridiculous as it may sound, at the time I really believed anything we touched would turn to gold. Somehow, the memories of continuous near-bankruptcy and the incredible luck we had in exiting Guido's successfully seemed to suddenly slip away. Rose-tinted glasses fogged our view of the many useful warnings from our past.

Neil had planned to build only one latex glove machine to get started, but that clearly wasn't going to make a dent in meeting the massively growing demand. My father and I began discussing a much more aggressive growth strategy soon after the paperwork was finished. "Dad, from what I can see, the demand for latex gloves greatly exceeds what this one latex glove machine can produce. I can sell the year's production in a month or two – and that's a conservative estimate," I said matter-of-factly, "We will be just another small fish in a large pond working with one machine."

"Ah, I'm glad you brought it up," he agreed. "I was thinking the same thing. We'll need to build at least a dozen machines right away." That will cost a lot of money, I thought to myself. "We should start with four or five more machines immediately if we want to establish SafeSkin as a major player in the medical glove business," he went on. "How else will we be able to compete with industry giants if we don't have the capacity to supply the largest hospitals and distributors?"

Things were escalating quickly. "Maybe we take things a little slower, give me a chance to learn the business a little better before jumping in with both feet," I reasoned. But he didn't concern himself with my learning curve. "Either we are all in, or we shouldn't have bothered with this business in the first place," he insisted, waving off my concerns. "The market is exploding and we are in early; we have to find a way to be the fastest, best-quality latex glove company in the world. If we move fast enough," he continued with that familiar, mischievous twinkle in his eye, "The big guys will never be able to catch up!" We scheduled a call with Neil the next day before he went back to Malaysia to explain our ingenious accelerated growth plans.

After expressing how thrilled we were to be working together, my father opened the conversation by sharing his vision for the company with both Neil and me before launching into his sales pitch. "Neil, now that Richard and I see the size and immediacy of the latex glove opportunity here, we don't believe building one machine will be sufficient to survive." His tone was soft, yet urgent. "It may be fine in the short term while there is a large glove shortage and any product will fly off the shelves, but building a business in the long run will require both the best-quality gloves and enough quantity to be relevant to the major distributors and hospitals. To stay ahead of the curve, Richard and I think we should build 15 glove machines as quickly as you are capable." A heavy silence hung on the phone as we waited for Neil's response.

"I don't disagree with your thinking," Neil began slowly, as we could sense he was trying to assess his options. "We just don't have the money to do that with the amount you've invested," he said matter-of-factly, verbally tossing the ball in our court. "How many machines can you build with the money you have now and how much more money will it take to build the rest of the machines?" I jumped in, trying not to sound too eager. "The money we now have is only enough to buy the necessary land, pay the workers and finish the first machine. After that we will need a little more than $1 million per three machines. So that would be in the ballpark of $5 million more to build and operate an additional 14 machines," he concluded definitively.

Dear Lord, that was much more than either of us imagined. It felt like my heart stopped beating for a moment and I tried to catch my breath as my mind (and mouth) started racing. "Wow, that's a lot more than we were expecting," I blurted out. "Are you sure about those costs?" Though my father and I had the funds from the Coca Cola deal, neither of us were ready to put up that much cash. "Absolutely certain," Neil assured us without missing a beat.

We peppered Neil with all sorts of questions, both about how he would go about building all those machines and what else we could do to build them without another $5 million cash. Maybe Malaysian financing, given the hundreds, if not thousands, of jobs we'd be creating? But no matter which approach we took, things always ended with Neil insisting that our plan was only possible if we put in the cash needed.

Finally, afterabout 30 minutesofbackandforth, Neilconceded that he could possibly get the cash from a local Malaysian bank if we put up another $5 million in bonds as collateral. As dad and I sat there, a little stunned, we looked at each other and then my father finally told Neil we needed to talk about it and would call him back later that afternoon. "That's fine," Neil said, without the weight of the financing on his shoulders, "But I'm heading back to Malaysia in two days and need to know how to proceed."

As soon as we hung up, my father looked at me with a knowing twinkle in his eyes. "This is an excellent opportunity for us to get more equity and own a majority of the business! We don't need to put up the actual cash, we just need to find a bank to take our bonds as collateral. We can secure the bonds with Safeskin's equipment, inventory and receivables until the company makes enough money to pay off the loans," he confidently asserted.

Reading the overwhelm and nervousness on my face, my father assured me: "If anything bad were to happen, we could always sell the inventory, machinery and receivables to pay down the loans." I had very little experience with businesses actually failing, but I worried it wouldn't be as easy as he was making it sound. When I started to express my concern, my father tried to calm me. "Take a deep breath, this is all part of the excitement in creating a new company. Let me do the talking with Neil and you can just listen."

Later that afternoon we called Neil back to discuss our options. My father started by saying we needed to build the other 14 machines or it didn't make sense to complete the first one. "We will put up half the collateral necessary if you put up the other half," he baited Neil, but to no avail. "You know I don't have the money, otherwise, I wouldn't have taken you in as partners to begin with," he shot back. "You need to put up the full $5 million of collateral if you want to execute your plan." The negotiations were underway.

I sat on the edge of my front-row seat as my father continued. "We are not putting in more money for free. If we put in more money, we need to get more equity in the company" he insisted. "There is no way I am going to give up any more equity," Neil snapped, sounding insulted we would even ask him to think about it. "I am already down to 45%!" We were at a standstill, and it was the first true test of how we would resolve differences.

My father put the phone on mute and whispered, "Let him sleep on it and if he is as smart as we think, he will come back and accept it." He took the phone off mute and said to Neil in a thoughtful, coaching tone, "Sleep on it. Think about the downside of having a larger ownership in a small business that might not be able to survive in the long term versus a little smaller piece of a very large and successful business worth much more." We agreed to talk early the next morning the day before Neil was to fly out to Malaysia.

When my father and I got off the call, we discussed what we thought Neil's objections really were. Dad surmised that it was not only a matter of equity, but of ego as well. This company was Neil's baby, and he couldn't swallow the thought of us owning more of it than him. After thinking about his perspective, it made perfect sense. Neil started with visions of owning a small business, worked on it for over a year and saw himself as owning the whole thing with just a few friendly investors. He'd only met us a few months ago, and now we wanted to grow it into something huge and take majority ownership.

Though that is what happens when you run out of money, Neil wasn't ready to accept that fate yet. He had already convinced us to invest millions of dollars and now he was playing hardball and insisting we put in more money if we wanted to grow it faster. Since Neil saw my father as a tougher negotiator, my father and I agreed it was best if I opened the discussions the next day. Our goal was to get Neil on board and ensure we ended up with over 50% of the business so we could control our exit when the time was right to sell.

As we regrouped with Neil the next morning, I tried to reframe the situation with his priorities in mind. "Neil, let's take a step back here and make sure we are on the same page. You and I still have 50/50 decision-making authority in operating the company, and you are still CEO. If we put in more money, we need more equity. That's how business works and it is only fair. When we ultimately go public or sell the company, you'll still be the one to get all the accolades," I explained, assuring him that I agreed on what was rightfully his. "But if we don't do this, I'm concerned we won't grow fast or big enough to survive. Remember, you don't take percentages to the bank but rather dollars. You will be a much richer man when we finally sell the business if you allow us to own a slightly larger percent of the company and grow it into a much bigger pie!"

Neil now had a dilemma. He knew we were right, but this was his baby and he just couldn't get himself to give up more equity. Maybe it was recognition of his role, maybe it was his desire for a bigger payday or maybe he simply worried he'd miss his plane to Malaysia, but Neil didn't say no. "How much more equity do you want?" he asked reluctantly. Right then I knew he would ultimately agree. "For $5 million of additional collateral, we need another 10% of the company," I responded reflexively. This would bring us up to 55% with our original investment. My father and I hadn't discussed how exactly we would approach him since we thought it would take much more time for him to roll over, but it felt like the right number I could negotiate from without totally pissing him off.

"Under no circumstance will I give you more than 50% of the company," he quipped back furiously, "Take it or leave it!" I waited a moment for him to calm down. "That is not enough," I reasoned quietly and calmly, "We need at least 51% of the equity to protect our investment." I could almost feel him seething through the phone. "You only need 50.1% to protect your investment and that is all I am willing to give you. Take it or leave it right now or there is no deal." It was a perfect negotiation, as we had gotten exactly what we wanted and Neil felt like he won the negotiations bringing us down from 55% to 50.1%. At that point my father jumped in and said "Richard, Neil is right. Don't be greedy. It is a fair compromise and though neither side is happy, both can live with it. Think it over on the plane, travel safely and call us when you stop over in Los Angeles today to discuss the details."

After some last-minute financing details agreed to and only the paperwork to complete, Neil returned to Malaysia to find a bigger factory, complete the first machine and begin an additional four right away. Meanwhile, I engaged the public relations firm we had used at Guido's to promote our gloves. Given the massive shortage we were working with, I decided to go with a company I could trust – a company that knew me well rather than a company that knew the industry well. Then I looked up regional and national medical distributors and started cold-calling them one by one.

After I explained that we had a new startup producing high-quality latex gloves, every single distributor enthusiastically confirmed they would buy as many gloves as we could deliver. This seemed like it was going to be easier than I ever imagined!

After less than a month, I had completed all the tasks on my list and Neil invited me back to Malaysia, where he had bought a large, bankrupt rubber tire factory with several empty buildings and plenty of land. He completed our first glove machine and moved it over to our new factory and quickly got it into production. While also starting construction on the next four machines simultaneously, he was completely overwhelmed. Strategically, we made a very good decision to invest a little extra money into creating an agile production process. Most big glove companies built one large glove-making machine that could churn out 15 million gloves per month, which is the most cost effective to build and run. However, we decided to build five smaller machines that could make three million gloves per month each. This way we could make small, medium and large gloves all at the same time and, more importantly, if one machine broke down we could still keep the other four running.

On my flight back to Malaysia, I spent time thinking about what it was I wanted to create. I began by visualizing the outcome: SafeSkin becoming the industry leader by creating safer and more comfortable gloves that the nurses and doctors loved to wear. To achieve that dream, we could not be a small company. We would need to be willing to take risks and do things differently than our larger competitors. Entrepreneurs achieve visions not through meticulous analysis like those in finance, but rather through using deep-seated gut instincts and then surrounding themselves with smart people who can learn fast. I couldn't wait to get started!

Energized by the exciting road ahead, I was thrilled to be back in Malaysia. I was less thrilled, though, at the giant mess waiting for me. As I walked into the factory I was met by a sea of rejected gloves strewn across the floor and islands of unused boxes growing at an alarming rate. Workers were darting chaotically past – and often into – one another, and our quality-inspections process looked more like an elementary school glove-trashing contest than the efficient assembly line I was expecting. Clearly, some help was desperately needed.

We agreed that Neil would continue building the four remaining glove machines and I would oversee the glove production and hire additional workers. I thought I was done managing manufacturing, but I didn't mind the unexpected return

I was giddy to be back in business again. Before I returned, Neil had taken in a local Chinese partner and general manager named Mr. Toh to help him run the factory and build the machines. A thin man with a sharp black mustache and permanent scowl, Mr. Toh wore all black and carried a long sword on his belt at all times. Something about his presence left me quite unsettled. So I wasn't exactly jumping for joy when Neil explained that Mr. Toh would be reporting directly to me, but given how overworked he'd been, I figured I could suck it up.

After the first hectic week, I realized I was not going home for a while. I never imagined the energy and supervision necessary to accelerate the building process under such a tight time crunch. Though Neil had hired three shifts of construction engineers who were sprinting around the clock to get our new machinery built, welding the steel and assembling the chains into functioning glove machines still took time – a luxury we did not have. While we built our own factories at Guido's, it was always for future expansion and the seasonal nature of our products gave us a built-in lull. Now we had an overwhelming, constant demand halfway around the world that needed as much product as we could send yesterday. Neil and his crew were moving with ridiculous speed but we still couldn't make all our ends meet.

I called Ann and told her if she wanted to see me soon she would have to leave our now 15-month-old son with a relative and come visit me in Malaysia. I missed Ann dearly, plus she was a remarkably capable professional and would be an invaluable extra set of hands for whatever challenge we faced. At the moment, our biggest unhandled issue was getting a training manual written and translated. The current process, a brief verbal explanation to the workers by Mr. Toh, wasn't leading to great results. But I figured this was a conversation that could wait until Ann arrived. Overjoyed at her impending arrival, a few days later I was heading to the airport and just about bursting with anticipation. The business had been so busy that I hadn't had a chance to fully realize how much I missed her. I so badly wanted to share all this excitement with my best friend, for her to see it for herself. We locked eyes as she emerged out of customs, and as she ran and jumped into my arms, my heart just about exploded. I could feel a passionate excitement in my bones – one that existed only for her flooding my entire body. I smiled so hard my jaw hurt, and we kissed and savored the long, romantic embrace like newlyweds.

The next day, Ann joined me in the factory where we had a nice conversation with Neil and his wife, Jeannie, before taking a quick tour of our facilities. She then got straight to business, asking what she could do to help, and I gave her the lowdown on the training manuals. "Great!" she exclaimed, "Give me a day to look around and observe, and I'll start writing it tomorrow." It was a funny visual, watching this tiny Jewish lady following around the Malaysian supervisors, attempting to document a foreign process that was literally being described in Chinese. She never learned how to read another language, let alone write in characters. Yet somehow she found a way to understand and document the entire manufacturing process, capturing the instructions on how to mix the correct chemical/stabilizer balance, coordinate proper chain conveyor speed and oven temperatures, strip gloves off the glass formers and determine if they passed quality standards.

Ann was a great sport and didn't mind a challenge, but was less than thrilled that she was spending her days in 100 degree humid production areas while I interviewed potential workers in an air conditioned office. "How's that air conditioning treating you?" she baited with a strong dose of sass after recounting the frustrations of her day. I explained that it was only temporary and I'd be back on the factory floor once hiring was done, but focused more on letting her express her grievances.

Though Ann and I worked together at Guido's and Coca Cola, I never allowed her to work directly for me, knowing that was a Pandora's box of problems if we took our disagreements home. But, having no choice here, I decided to really focus on listening to her opinions and complaints, making sure each one was addressed. We committed to discussing all things that bothered her in a professional fashion, agreeing up front that if we disagreed after a full discussion, I would have to have the final say. There were a few small disagreements on how different things needed to be expressed but, despite the occasional eye-rolling, we never had a problem. It didn't hurt that, just like my mother, she was almost always right.

Honestly, I was glad that she saw how hard we were working so that once she returned home, she wouldn't think I was just traveling around Asia and having fun. After a grueling week, the manual was complete and we took a break from the overheated chaos of the factory for a two-day visit with Neil and Jeannie to our latex supplier's plantation near Singapore. It was a welcome change of scenery, and fun to explore someplace new and exotic together.

After Ann went back to San Diego, I stayed on in Malaysia for another eight weeks, only returning home for a quick mid-July trip to be the best man in my brother's wedding. Surprisingly, it only took a week at home before I was itching for the action of the Malaysian factory. After savoring that wonderful week walking with my wife on the beach, rolling around on the floor with my son and spending time with my mother and father, I was looking forward to my long journey back to Malaysia. The frenetic pace back there left no time for homesickness, and I knew it was only temporary. It was a challenging dynamic, and having a life partner who understood and supported me made all the difference; it was absolutely crucial to my emotional health and the business at large.

Neil decided that since he had been in Malaysia for several months on end, he would go back to the United States for a month when I arrived back in Malaysia. Prior to my return, Neil hired an extremely talented managing director, CM Lee, a world-class engineer who deserves much of the credit for SafeSkin's ultimate success. With a warm and welcoming smile that effortlessly pierced through his professional demeanor, CM had an incredible sense of ease about him, and just the experience and leadership we needed on the factory floor.

Starting out as a line supervisor, CM climbed the ranks throughout his 17 years at National Semiconductor, and was running two of their production facilities when Neil placed an ad for someone to run our factory. Beginning to feel like there wasn't anywhere further to grow at his organization, CM came across our ad in his local newspaper and was intrigued. He drove two hours down to Ipoh, and as Neil showed him around the factory CM felt an immediate connection with our story, and good chemistry with Neil. Equally excited about the idea of entering the exploding latex glove industry, CM determined this was just the type of change he was looking for. He returned home, gave his notice and came on board with SafeSkin a month later. After he joined, CM became much more than an executive hire. He elevated our entire manufacturing operations, and was a complete game-changer for the company.

Neil's last instruction to me before leaving for the U.S. was to fire our original Chinese partner, Mr. Toh, before CM began working. I didn't understand why Neil couldn't do it himself since he was the one who hired him, but Neil reminded me that they didn't have a good relationship and it would be best if I fired him. Though I had fired dozens of employees at Guido's over the years and learned how to be compassionate and direct, it still made me nervous. I had a sinking premonition that my conversation with Mr. Toh would not be pleasant.

Unsure of what to expect, I chose a small, quiet restaurant about 15 minutes away from the hotel to meet for dinner. It was the first time I had seen Mr. Toh outside of work. Trading in his dark work outfit for dark, torn street clothes, Mr. Toh donned his all too familiar scowl and long sword on his belt as he walked through the restaurant door. This is not going to go well, I thought to myself. I tried beginning with small talk, asking how his family was doing, but Mr. Toh was having none of it. "Why have you invited me here?" he demanded in an uncomfortably loud voice, already drawing the attention of our fellow diners.

I tried to explain as calmly and compassionately as I could that though we appreciated his help in getting the company started, we would be hiring a new general manager and therefore needed to relieve him of his responsibilities and buy back his shares. We would offer a generous exit package, I nervously continued, as Mr. Toh dug into me with quiet rage in his eyes. I held my breath and could feel my heartbeat reverberating throughout my body as he just continued to sit there, silently staring me down from across the table. I was beginning to understand why Neil refused to fire him.

"Mr. Toh, do you understand?" I quietly inquired, struggling to keep my voice steady. Nothing. He just kept staring right past me and I could sense the fury pumping through his veins. This is it, I thought. This is what happens right before I end up in a ditch somewhere. Just when I thought this staring contest from hell couldn't get any worse, Mr. Toh jumped up and, without breaking eye contact, withdrew his sword and pointed it at my neck in one swift motion. "You cannot do this to me," he threatened, holding his voice and sword steady. "I will kill you for this. Not tonight, but when you are not looking. You will be sorry!" Replacing his sword with an unsettling sense of speed and skill, Mr. Toh stormed out of the restaurant.

Stunned, I sat silently for God knows how long. Once I regained some blood flow and started breathing again, I began cursing Neil under my breath. Remembering my first death threat from the Orthodox box maker, I became oddly nostalgic for those scary days at Guido's. At least then I had Tony to take care of me. Now I was on my own in a foreign country with no one to turn to. What was I doing to attract these crazy threats? I nervously went back to my hotel room and immediately called Neil, frantically describing the terror of what had just occurred.

Neil seemed completely unfazed, and I realized that this was exactly what he expected but conveniently failed to mention. I was furious. "How the hell could you put me in such a dangerous situation like that without a word of warning?" I shouted into the receiver, pacing across my room. "Well," he said calmly, "I was worried that if I told you how Mr. Toh might react, you wouldn't go through with it." He wasn't wrong, but seemed unsettlingly comfortable with the fact that I could have been killed that night. In fact, he sounded positively chipper when assuring me I had handled things masterfully. Still, he agreed it was best to hire an armed bodyguard to accompany me for the next few weeks until he returned, just to be safe. Those were the scariest three weeks of my life.

Being driven to and from the factory each day, I feared disaster around every corner, constantly looking over my shoulder, half expecting to find Mr. Toh's menacing glare waiting for me. The scariest part of my commute was a two-lane road that crossed over an old set of railroad tracks about halfway between the factory and my hotel. When trains passed through, they would cause a 5-10 minute wait, spontaneously trapping us in traffic. Like a sitting duck just waiting for Mr. Toh's sword (or very possibly a hired hitman's bullet), I couldn't stop replaying Sonny's gruesome death scene from *The Godfather*: two cars pulling up on either side of a tollbooth stop and spray his vehicle with machine gun fire. Every morning as I left my hotel, and each evening as I packed up from work, I silently dreaded crossing those tracks, my own cruel form of Russian roulette.

I must admit that, while I pride myself on being rational and balanced, I was scared shitless. Every moment waiting at that railroad crossing I was consumed with panic. I knew I needed to figure out a way to keep my mind together, I just didn't know how. Talking myself out of it was useless. I found moments of peace in trying to focus on the tasks of the day, but it was a matter of seconds before the paralyzing fear barged back in. Every moment not focused on the present was filled with panic. Realizing that the terror would not serve me or keep me any safer, I redirected my mind to happier times walking down the beach with Ann and Brett. Mentally feeling the sand between my toes, I closed my eyes and visualized waves crashing on the beach as I kept a long and steady breath.

Fortunately, those next few weeks passed without incident and Neil finally returned. CM Lee would be starting in a few days, and the moment Neil showed up, I got myself back on a plane home as soon as humanly possible. Neil had created this problem and he could finish handling it, I thought. Finally able to breathe after boarding my familiar flight home, I anxiously pondered what I had gotten myself into.

Though I was still excited about the business opportunity, this passing drama made it clear that Neil and I did not have shared values. I could get over the fact that he had made such poor hiring decisions, and even that he asked me to fire Mr. Toh. But the fact that he saw nothing wrong with blindsiding me and had no remorse for tossing me into such a potentially dangerous situation without warning made me think that if push came to shove again, he would be willing to sacrifice my well-being for the company. Over time, I cooled off and realized it was not as big a deal as I was making it, but the sheer terror I felt for those few weeks was unlike anything I'd ever experienced. Not even the death threat from the Orthodox box maker came close.

This was the first time I questioned Neil, and wondered if it would happen again. I scolded myself that maybe I should have taken more time to learn about his background. Being partners in business is much like getting married; it is dependent on trust and communication, and we don't really know our partners until we actually live with them day in and day out. As I sat curled up in an airplane blanket, I vowed then and there to always be more thorough in due diligence of my future partner's character and values, not just the business opportunity. But, I didn't have long to mull over the future.

CHAPTER 10

THE GAMBLE

When I finally landed home, it was September 1988 and the demand for latex gloves was insatiable. All types of people were buying gloves overseas and selling them even before they arrived. We saw dentists, real estate salesmen, restaurant owners and non-business people, all putting up letters of credit just to get their hands on latex gloves. They had often completely sold out their inventory before the containers even arrived from Asia. As is often the case in situations of scarcity, there was a fair share of horror stories with over eager buyers getting burned. Some people put up letters of credit to unknown sources only to find bags of sand instead of gloves when their shipment arrived. Additionally, many of the gloves coming in from Asia were notoriously poor quality. Lousy conditions for the consumer, but great settings for us to enter the market.

Once CM Lee took over the factory, the quality and quantity of our gloves skyrocketed. He had been running a semiconductor factory before joining SafeSkin, and with his experience and attention to detail, he got our floors spotless and machines fine-tuned in no time. Things were already looking up when we got a tip on another big break. My father's friend Leonard, who had introduced us to Neil, offered to connect us with a lobbyist in Washington, D.C., who could help us land a multimillion-dollar government contract for latex gloves for the next calendar year. I'd never worked with government contracts before, but hearing stories of people getting burned and knowing that we'd be able to sell every glove we could make without the contract, I was hesitant.

However, both Neil and my father were excited at the prospect of such an important connection, and I agreed this could be a big one. Neil insisted that he should accompany Leonard to Washington, since they already had a relationship. I protested, already uncomfortable with Neil's recent judgment, pointing out that it made the most sense for the head of sales and marketing to be present. But after a conference call together, Leonard requested Neil to accompany him, explaining that it was more executive lobbying than selling. Despite the fact that I was running sales and marketing, Neil was still CEO and had previous experience lobbying. So I agreed to let Neil accompany Leonard to the first meeting and discuss next steps when he returned.

My father saw the frustration on my face as we hung up. "We are lucky Leonard brought us this opportunity," he reminded me, "It's really his meeting, so at the end of the day he can take whoever he chooses." Though I was not happy about the situation, I resigned myself to the fact that Neil would be going so I let it go. One of the greatest gifts I ever gave myself was an early practice of accepting the things I cannot change, which freed up my focus for the actions I can take to affect my goals.

After Neil attended the first meeting, we agreed he would attend several more over the next few weeks until we knew that the opportunity was real. He and Leonard had met with many government representatives familiar with the glove purchasing process, all of whom were very confident we would get the contract.

If we could meet all their requirements, the contract was ours, Neil announced with pride and excitement. Out of the loop and unclear on what this meant, I wasn't busting out the confetti quite yet, as we sat with my father to discuss the situation. We're taking a lot of risk without anything in writing, I pointed out. "Welcome to Washington," my father told me, agreeing with Neil that this was how lobbying works.

Longing for the 'Made in America' touch, the Congressional Buy America Act required the U.S. government to purchase all latex gloves from domestic producers. In the case of a shortage, waivers could be issued for overseas purchases, which is exactly what happened in 1988. With the shortage still holding strong, our contacts assured us this would continue through 1989 as well. This alone would have been fine, but we also needed to build and maintain a massive inventory of gloves held in warehouses across the country to prove our capability to supply the multimillion-dollar contract at stake.

I had worked tirelessly to establish a network of distributors ready to buy all our latex gloves as soon as they arrived, and they would not be happy to hear about delays on account of a government contract. But this was our moment, Neil and my father explained, an opportunity to establish SafeSkin as more than a supplier, but a leader in the latex glove business. The distributors will always be there, they reminded me, but the government latex glove contract only comes up once a year. So, as the odd man out on the opposite side as my father, I eventually acquiesced to their decision. Instead of an instant sellout, with at least 15 cents per glove, we stockpiled all of our supplies into five different warehouses across the country.

Though we had lots of great family time during that holiday season, I couldn't shake the nonstop thoughts of the government contract. Industry trends and news outlets projected that the glove shortage would continue well into 1989; however, we hadn't even reached the new year when a huge influx of gloves began arriving from Asia, causing prices to plummet quickly. The massive shortage was rapidly turning into a dangerous glove glut right before our eyes.

And still, we didn't know exactly when the government contract would be awarded. "Don't they realize it would be prudent for them to finalize the contract before 1989, given the amount of logistics such a large contract entails?" I angrily asked our team, fuming with anxious irritation. Neil and my father kept telling me to relax; this is the normal process, they insisted. But I knew there was no chance of quelling my anxiety until we had a signed contract. I tried to stay positive by jogging on the beach and meditating every day, which took a bit of the edge off, but nothing provided any lasting relief.

Noticing my unnatural edginess, Ann checked in to ask what was wrong. I unloaded about the massive pressure and insane stakes we were dealing with. "If anything goes wrong, it will be too massive, too late to fix it!" I lamented. Knowing there was nothing else I could do in the meantime, she repeated my core philosophies back to me, encouraging me to relax and accept the things I can't change. "Remember to breathe," she lovingly reminded me, "Whatever happens, you'll figure it out – you always do." Her irresistible smile still gave me butterflies, but couldn't erase the knots of worry in my belly. I wasn't so sure I would be able to find a way out if things went awry this time.

As we rang in the New Year, I sat with great hope but silent trepidation. CM Lee had our factories in tip-top shape, sprinting ahead at all-time-high production levels. Our warehouses in the states were beginning to fill up and we had dozens more ships full to the brim with latex gloves en route. All we needed was the signed government contract and our business would take off like a rocket ship.

On an otherwise sunny morning in early January 1989, I was anxiously planning the next trip to inform my potential distributors that we still didn't have any gloves for them when I got the call. Only, it wasn't the call I'd been praying for. Neil got both my father and me on the phone, and started off by saying something was terribly wrong. My heart sank and I began to sweat. "How long is the contract delayed?" I interrupted before he could finish. Inside I knew what he was about to say, but I just didn't want to hear it. He explained that either our Washington contacts were lying all along or the government decided not to give another year's waiver for the Buy America Act; either way the government contract was gone.

This whole risky plan to make SafeSkin take off would now drive us into the ground. Every muscle in my body revolted and I struggled to breathe as I felt the weight of my crumbling world crushing my very existence. Frantically grabbing at mental straws, I began cursing myself for ignoring that sinking feeling I'd had about this all along. Neil and my father went back and forth for another 15 minutes trying to determine how this could have happened, but I didn't hear a word they said. Every aspect of my being – my breath, my pulse, my mind – were on absolute overwhelm. It was one of the darkest moments of my business career to date.

We had dug ourselves into a hole and somehow my father, Uncle Bob and I needed to find a way to sell the millions of latex gloves sitting in our warehouses along with the millions more on their way. To finance the construction of the 14 additional machines, my family had initially put up an extra $5 million in tax-free bonds, purchased with proceeds from the Guido's sale to Coca Cola. When I asked about the risk of using our family savings as collateral, my father explained we should be plenty safe; the equipment, receivables and inventory would all be used as collateral before they could touch our bonds. But on top of this, I had personally guaranteed SafeSkin's bank loans in Malaysia; something I'd never done before and never have since.

In retrospect, we probably needed my personal guarantee to grow as fast as we did, but I just wish someone had explained to me that I was risking my home, my bank account and everything I owned if things fell apart. Once my father contended it was the best thing to do, I didn't bother doing much research before signing to personally guarantee the loan. But as I quickly learned, when things go wrong, assets often aren't even worth ten cents on the dollar. So it's not that you should never sign personally on a business loan, but you should certainly know a hell of a lot more than I did as to what it entails.

We were fighting fierce battles on every front. First, we needed to begin calling up medical distributors across the country and start selling off our massive inventory as quickly as possible. We didn't have the option of shutting down the factory to save money temporarily; if we did that, Neil explained, we would never get it staffed and started again. Instead, he promised to reduce production as much as he could while keeping a skeleton staff.

But market conditions weren't in our favor either. As more and more gloves from all over Asia entered the United States, prices had dropped from 15 cents per glove in November 1988 to just six cents per glove two months later. Now in early January, we had no idea how much further they would fall. Ultimately, it fell to 3.5 cents per glove in April, which was below our cost. Worse than that, as I started calling on hospitals and distributors, it didn't matter that they loved our quality; everyone had bought enough gloves to last two full years, and having paid by letters of credit, most of them couldn't even send the gloves back if they wanted to. So here we were with millions and millions of latex gloves, no salesmen besides my father, my uncle and myself, no distributors and no customers.

We had dug out of big holes before, but nothing like this. It became very clear that we were in way over our heads. And at the end of the day, all of this – the millions of dollars, tons of supplies and factory full of employees – fell on my shoulders, and mine alone. Less than a year ago I was carefree, money in the bank and the world at my feet. I replayed the year in my head over and over again, trying to pinpoint how it had all gone so terribly wrong so quickly. I had walked into this opportunity thinking I was an incredibly gifted executive, that somehow anything I touched would turn to gold. What made me think we were anything but extremely lucky to get out of the near-bankrupt situation at Guido's?

When things go well, I love socializing about the office and getting into good conversations with my team. But when truly epic crises arise, solemn solitude is the quickest way for me to assess my options. I retreat to my own mental cave to think through a variety of different options until I find something that might work. In fact, one of the best strategies I adopted was to explore the route I liked least, considering all the potential benefits, as well as the obvious downsides. It's something I got from my father. When looking through a logical lens, we often are limited, thinking in the box so to speak. But by bouncing through lots of ridiculous-sounding options, my mind would get increasingly creative, and that's when the most innovative ideas would come. Diving into most out-there ideas wasn't a one-stop answer to my problems, but rather a tool to help me get there. And once I'm onto a promising idea, I see that light at the end of the tunnel, commit my entire consciousness to running towards it, and hope to God it isn't the headlights of an oncoming freight train.

That being said, none of this was any type of flip-the-switch solution. I laid many a night in bed with Ann, releasing my fears and frustrations, questioning how I'd gotten us back into this situation again. But she's always been an incredible rock, more support than I could've ever hoped for in a life partner. She would remind me of all the blessings in our lives, recalling some of the wonderful memories we'd made so far and how incredibly lucky we were to have each other. She managed to shine light and laughter into my soul with precious sentimental moments, but I still couldn't forgive myself for allowing this to happen.

After a few weeks of self-induced suffering, I realized I wasn't getting anything done while wallowing in my problems. So, I decided then and there to pull myself up by my bootstraps, forgive myself for making the same mistake twice and focus every last ounce of my being on finding a solution. I needed to find new customers, any customers really, who would be willing to try our SafeSkin latex gloves. Not an easy task when the hospitals and distributors were being bombarded with huge volumes of low-cost, poor-quality gloves, and wouldn't even take my calls. On the rare occasion that I did get through, I was asked to call back in two years.

After many lengthy, late-night discussions with my father and Uncle Bob, we decided that if hospitals wouldn't get on the phone with us, we had to hire someone they would talk to. We researched and decided we needed to hire a network of medical brokers – people who sold 10-15 different medical products to hospitals and were paid on commission, since we couldn't afford to pay them a dime without a sale. Narrowing our pool further, we had to find successful brokerage companies that did not have products competing with our gloves and were willing to dedicate time to the difficult task of selling gloves in a highly saturated market. Not exactly a cakewalk.

Uncle Bob volunteered to find our knights in shining armor and, much to his credit, he quickly recruited two great broker networks that fit our needs, covering both coasts and most of the country in between. Highlighting the monetary benefit in selling high-quality gloves to existing customers after the shortage subsided, Uncle Bob convinced these brokers to take us on despite the massive glut we were sitting in. But even with 40 commissioned sales reps pushing our gloves, the rest of 1989 was extremely challenging.

Despite slowing down production as much as possible, we were still hemorrhaging money in order to keep the factory open. Burning through our Coca Cola payday, we were seeking out new ways to stay in business with unprecedented desperation. While we'd struggled with Guido's, I'd never had so much on the line, or a family facing the consequences if I lost it all. In this dark and trying period, it was my forever source of light that kept me afloat. Ann was there to listen and support me through each and every challenge. I knew that as long as we had each other, we would somehow make it through – even if I couldn't, for the life of me, imagine how.

Two things happened in the fall of 1989 that would eventually help turn the business around, and they came in the most unexpected of places. I was watching television with Ann's father, Charles, in their Las Vegas home, when an ad came on about a book called *Think and Grow Rich* by Napoleon Hill. Fran Tarkenton, the famous NFL quarterback, was explaining how this book changed his life, claiming that anyone could turn their misfortune into prosperity if they simply read the book and followed its instructions. Though it was quite the grand claim, I was willing to try anything at this point, and solemnly swore that I would do whatever it took to follow his instructions.

I was overjoyed when I saw the book in the airport bookstore on my way to Oregon the following week, and immediately read it cover to cover – underlining, internalizing and reading it again. It's easy to overlook or skimp on the importance of our mental state and the frameworks we use to see the world; it's not something we're taught in school, and there are no metrics or measurements to go by. However, it is one of the biggest factors for success, and with this book, I'd found detailed, tangible steps to build myself the mental foundation to get me there. It was my new secret weapon, and has stayed with me ever since.

It's all based on a simple yet powerful equation in life. Results = Intention x Mechanism. While I'd practiced calming my thoughts through meditation, here I learned to control them by focusing on concrete, written goals and measurements. So often when solving problems, we get hung up on the how and lose our fire and focus on the end result. However, Hill argues that when we have written, measurable results and 110% intention, the mechanism will appear. Everything else stems from a burning-white passion for the end results.

So how does this all actually work? First, we are instructed to write out affirmations detailing what we want to achieve in measurable terms, the value we will deliver, sacrifices we're willing to make and what specific date we want it by. Anyone following this strategy must repeat every day the affirmations first thing upon waking and last thing at night before falling asleep, encouraging the subconscious to repeat these affirmations throughout the tasks of the day and dreams of the night. This allows us to harness our intuition and subconscious, continually projecting our desires to the universe 24 hours a day, seven days a week.

Sure, there may have been some bold claims and unfamiliar talk about the power of the universe here. But I was so desperate at the time, I never bothered to question whether it would work or not. I did everything as instructed and allowed myself to be totally bought into this way of thinking.

By the time I returned home from Oregon, I had finished my

affirmations and was amazed at how they could create such a huge change in my energy. The book suggested choosing stretch goals that I could get passionate about. Nearing 1990, a time when we had virtually no sales, hope or money, and no clear way to keep the business afloat, I wrote the following affirmation:

By January 1, 1991, SafeSkin Corp will be selling eight containers per month (8 million gloves) and Richard and Ann will have $1 million in the bank. I believe deep within my heart that we will have these orders and security in our possession. My faith is so strong that I can see these orders and security right before my very eyes. I can reach out and touch them with my own hands. They are now awaiting transfer to us at the time, and in the proportion that we deliver the best-quality gloves and unparalleled customer service we intend to render in return for them.

Genie, I command you to repeat this statement 1,000 times per day, slowly with emotion and conviction so that my burning desire will be expressed through this auto-suggestion to inspire my subconscious to broadcast this message throughout the entire universe. From the heavens and beyond to the oceans and below, from the mountains and above to the deserts and beneath, every atom in every cell will reverberate with my burning desire and infinite intelligence will pick up on my burning desire and transmute my burning desires into a physical reality. Amen!

Though the book instructed me only to repeat my affirmations first thing in the morning when I awoke and last thing at night before I went to bed, I was repeating my affirmations several times a day. Desperation can be a handy tool when harnessed productively.

I printed a few copies and put one up on my bathroom mirror, in my office and on my desk at home. I even put a little red dot in the middle of my watch, creating a reminder for me to repeat my affirmation and visualize my success every time I checked the time.

You may think this sounds crazy, and that's fine. But I honestly believe that reading *Think and Grow Rich,* and following this framework, was one of the major reasons we were able to turn the company around. We follow endless frameworks, formulas and guidelines to get every aspect of our businesses running efficiently, yet far too often when it comes to the powerful minds and emotions driving the people who make it all happen, the exploration and organization stops. Often written off as fluffy or discounted due to man's inability to measure or prove it, strategies to control the mind and motivation are some of the most underutilized resources at our disposal as intelligent beings.

My religious commitment to this framework gave me hope when I couldn't see any in the environment around me. It helped relieve the constant fear of the catastrophic consequences if we ran out of money and had to shut down the company. We could no longer pay our bills and most of my days were spent convincing suppliers to continue working with us despite only being able to pay a portion of our current bills. While I couldn't eliminate my draining daily reality, or the very real fears of going bankrupt, reciting my affirmations afforded me a breath of fresh air. The paralyzing stress would always come crashing back, but I knew I didn't have to drown. I clung to this practice like a lifeboat, and slowly over time, my mental status quo began gradually improving. The periods of hope and focus grew longer, and the moments of crippling fear shrank in intensity and frequency. I continued reciting these affirmations multiple times a day for the next ten years, adjusting the size of my goals the first day of each year. The point of this practice was not to hit my targets, but to inspire hope and keep me focused on the big, audacious goals in front of me. Though I never achieved any of the annual goals I set, with time I far exceeded every expectation I had imagined.

Affirmations were the first big change that helped turn the business around. The second occurred on our flight home from that same fateful weekend visiting Ann's family in Las Vegas. I happened to look over as Ann was flipping through one of her magazines and spotted an advertisement for hypoallergenic makeup. "That's it!" I thought, nearly jumping out of my airplane seat as a lightbulb went off in my head. Why not call our gloves hypoallergenic?! I had spent so many hours racking my brain how we could differentiate SafeSkin latex gloves from all the chemical-filled competitors overwhelming the market. This was just the answer we were looking for! Though it would not alleviate the current glove gut, here was my marketing angle for when the market dried up and hospitals' inventories were depleted again.

I couldn't wait to get back to the office the next day and file with the FDA for a hypoallergenic claim.

About 30 days after we submitted our first FDA application, we received a notice in the mail denying our application. Opening that letter felt like watching my new beloved puppy getting hit by a car. Dejected and perplexed, I gave myself an evening to cool down, and called up the FDA in the morning to figure out how to get the hypoallergenic claim. No such category existed, I was told in a cold and matter-of-fact manner. When I pushed to get direction on what I could do, I was told the only option was resubmit my application. It did nothing to solve the problem and didn't make any sense to me, but without any other alternative I instructed my assistant to resubmit the same application the next day.

Another 30 days went by, only to end in another maddening

rejection letter from the FDA. But something caught my eye. This time, a different reviewer signed the rejection. Feeling we were onto something, I instructed my assistant to resubmit the same application again, but this time she protested. How could I expect a different result if I wasn't changing anything, she challenged. "It's our only option!" I insisted, after explaining my initial call and the different reviewer on this rejection, "We just have to keep our fingers crossed for a new reviewer who will say yes."

Another 30 days went by, and another rejection came in, this time by a third inspector. Distraught but determined, I instructed my assistant to resubmit the same application one final time. I knew deep in my heart that a hypoallergenic claim was our best angle; it was critical to our success, if not survival. But this time, she refused. "Insanity is doing the exact same thing over and over again and expecting a different result," she insisted, exasperated and completely bewildered by my behavior. Having been so focused on the end result of our approval, I hadn't noticed her growing frustration and was caught by surprise.

"You can resubmit that application immediately, or find another job," I fired back, with uncharacteristic intensity. Desperately grasping at straws, I knew this was our only hope to significantly differentiate SafeSkin gloves from other brands. This was life or death. But in that moment, I hadn't communicated the big picture I was looking at, and she didn't feel the gravity of our situation. All she saw was her boss, stubborn as a bull, clearly at his edge. Startled, she quickly resubmitted the same forms one more time.

Believe it or not, this time the Hail Mary worked. Thirty days later we received a notice from the FDA approving our claim, thereby allowing us to market our latex gloves as hypoallergenic. So often in business it's that trait, the dogged ability to continue pushing forward past the point where most people would quit, that separates success and failure. I was extremely lucky to have landed in front of a reviewer who said yes, but it took three no's to get there. So many people quit after working so hard for so long, right before the big breakthrough would have come. We never know if or when that big break will happen; the only certainty is that it never will if we give up too quickly.

CHAPTER 11

FIGHTING ON

Despite the improvement in my perspective, and FDA approval under our belt, the business continued deteriorating through the first half of 1990. Even with our new medical brokers, sales were low. The monthly bills to keep the Malaysian factories running at bare minimum were quickly burning through the last of the money my family had received in our sale to Coca Cola. It was an endless daily battle, trying to sell any gloves we could on one front, and fighting off calls to pay our bills on another.

I did my best to stay positive, repeating my affirmations with religious conviction, but as the chances of survival grew slimmer, I felt the dark grip of depression creeping back in. Regular family walks on the beach and nonstop words of love and support from Ann served as a constant stream of uplifting energy, but it was getting harder to maintain any semblance of positivity when left alone with my mind. Sitting in this unwelcome fog, every action demanded double the effort, and the once-bright rays of hope and happiness grew increasingly dull. I hadn't known this unsettling feeling since my early days at Guido's, but once I recognized it for what it was, I committed to doing everything in my power to fight it.

"You are not a victim," I reminded myself, mentally pointing to all the wonderful things in my life rather than the terrifying truth of our near-bankruptcy. My only really bright spot came in March, when Ann delivered our beautiful baby girl, Charly. No matter how difficult the day had been, all I had to do was hold her in my arms and her love pierced through that mental fog, however thick.

The love I felt for my son was infinite, and I knew we would grow up to become best friends, but no words can describe the depth of love between a father and daughter. Charly stole my heart the moment she came into this world, before I even had the chance to gaze into her big, brown eyes. I knew this love had changed me, and would keep me wrapped around her beautiful little fingers for all of my days. With it, I felt a newfound urge to provide all the tools she needed to achieve her dreams.

During the quiet nighttime moments throughout Charly's first few months of life, I'd hold her close to my chest whenever she awoke, connecting heart to heart as I rocked her back and forth to sleep. In those moments, nothing else existed. I focused on sending all the love in the world into her beautiful little being, and I swear, I felt her consoling love come right back in return. "Don't worry, Daddy, everything will work out fine!" I imagined her saying. I wanted so badly to believe her, and in those brief moments, I actually did. Exhausted as I was, I was still determined to fight my way out.

With our hypoallergenic claim, I had a new story for all the customers who had rejected us, a reason for them to get on the phone and buy our latex gloves. The same distributors and hospital providers who wouldn't call me back before, suddenly started listening when I wasn't selling them anything, but rather offering to let them try out our new FDA-approved hypoallergenic gloves. It was something new, something the industry hadn't seen before. Slowly, doors began opening.

One of my deepest beliefs in business is that our customers have all our answers. "Listen to the customer and pretend they have all our money," I used to tell our salespeople. "All we have to do is give them what they want and they will give us all our money back." I was determined to find out what our customers really wanted, and what they would pay for.

Once we were finally allowed to visit the hospitals and medical distributors for a demo of our new hypoallergenic latex gloves, we asked how they liked them, if they would consider purchasing SafeSkin gloves for their personnel as inventories depleted and whether there were any improvements we could incorporate for them. Though sales remained minimal for the first few months, many hospitals started running low on inventory and expressed interest in ordering gloves later that year. With this, we received valuable product feedback; though everyone loved the SafeSkin hypoallergenic latex gloves, many commented they would prefer gloves with less powder.

At the time, powder was used to slide the gloves off the porcelain formers in production and onto user's hands. We'd never gotten this feedback before, but I took it back to CM Lee and our engineers in Malaysia to see if they could develop a powder-free version. They asked why we needed to remove all the powder since no one else was doing it. "The customer is always right, and our customers want less powder," I explained. "If we're the first ones to give them what they want, we will have a big head start. We'll succeed by filling their needs earlier and better than anyone else."

"You are the customer expert, Richard, so I trust your judgment," CM conceded. "It will not be easy to develop a new process like this, but we will do everything in our power to ensure we are successful as quickly as possible. It may take a long time but we won't let you down!" CM had always lived up to the expectations he set, so when he spoke with complete confidence I was almost certain he would succeed. That feeling never faded over the next several months as our engineers worked tirelessly to develop a powder-free glove. Meanwhile, we kept trying to sell the powdered ones still sitting in our warehouses.

Neither of us made much progress for months. That is until one morning when CM called with a particularly chipper tone to his voice and exciting news to share. "We have discovered that the only way to make a powder-free glove is to alter the latex chemistry on the surface of the glove," he began. "It's been a very challenging process, but after months of phone calls and experiments we have found a way to apply a chlorination process whereby we can treat the entire surface of the gloves on the inside and outside!" CM announced, beaming with pride.

"That is great news, fantastic work!" I congratulated him. "When can we start selling them?" I asked, imagining the excitement on our customers' faces as they tried on their first pair of powder-free gloves. "Not so quickly," he cautioned. "It's not that simple. We've developed the process, but the chlorination solution is so strong it chewed up a half dozen washing machines along the way. We've designed custom washing machines with stainless steel and high-speed jets that can stand up to the rigors of the process without breaking down."

"Amazing, you are on fire!" I exclaimed, grateful to have his talent and expertise on our team. "Ah yes, thank you – but I'm not done yet," CM said, pausing my praise. "The most challenging part of this process is figuring out how to completely remove this new solution from inside the fingers of the gloves after we've soaked them. But our team has managed to custom design a state-of-the-art Cyclone dryer that can remove the liquid from inside the gloves. We're the only ones in the world with a machine like this; it looks like the Apollo spacecraft." CM's smile shined through the phone as he spoke. I was thrilled to hear the joy he got in solving the vast array of problems we threw his way, and even more excited about the solutions he came up with.

"We've actually had these machines for a while, but couldn't get a repeatable process," he admitted. "But just this week, we've confirmed a new process that can consistently deliver powder-free gloves meeting our specifications! We can't make too many yet, but once you confirm how many you can sell we can scale up to meet anticipated demand. I will overnight samples of the powder-free gloves that passed our quality-control audit and we believe can be reproduced consistently. I suggest you submit them to the FDA for a hypoallergenic claim since they were made the same way as our powdered gloves, just with an additional process at the end to remove the powder."

I just about jumped for joy. "This is incredible, CM, fantastic work! I will submit them to the FDA, and you figure out a way to manufacture as many powder-free gloves as you can. I promise you, we can sell many more gloves than you can ever produce," I challenged him with a twinkle in my eye. "Richard, given enough time, we can make millions of powder-free gloves each month," he retorted back, laughing off my challenge. "There is no way you can sell them all!" We were like little schoolboys scheming up a playground wager. "Wanna bet?" I baited him, "CM, our sales team can sell tens of millions of powder-free gloves each month. There's no way you guys could keep up with us." I could hear his smile, as we shared a verbal handshake. "I accept your challenge may the most talented team win!" We broke out laughing, appreciating that in some ways we'd never grow up.

Following CM's advice, we went through the same process of applying to the FDA with the previous hypoallergenic approval attached. Much to our delight (and relief), we got an FDA approval on our very first try just 30 days later!

Though we had received the FDA approval for our hypoallergenic claim for both the powdered and powder-free gloves, we still weren't selling much yet, and SafeSkin was completely out of money. With our family funds entirely invested in the company and Malaysian banks breathing down our necks, the daily financial pressures to pay our bills and the bank were almost unbearable. Then one fall day in 1990, I received a notice in the mail from Standard Charter Bank in Malaysia that they were foreclosing on the factory and my personal guarantee was being called to cover the loans if we didn't pay them off immediately. I knew things were bad, but I never imagined it would come to this.

Theoretically, this was never supposed to happen. Initially, my father and I were only investing an additional $5 million of bonds as collateral to build 15 machines, not putting our entire family savings at stake. However, as time went on the company faced the continuous conundrum of needing more money or going out of business. Neil had none, so we continued to lend the company money each quarter until we drained every last penny from our family savings. When making an investment, it is incredibly important to determine your absolute limit, draw a line in the sand and stick to it. I don't regret anything, as we managed to make it out the other end by the skin of our teeth; but make no mistake, we were most certainly the lucky 1%. Ninety-nine out of 100 people in this situation lose everything. And in this moment, that's exactly what I thought was happening to us.

I sat Ann down and explained everything to her. Though she knew things were going poorly, this was a massive shock for her. These are the moments where people's true colors shine, and it showed me what an incredible woman I had married. She took a second to take in the situation and process the magnitude of what

I'd just said. "Our first priority is maintaining our health," she began, still shaken by her father's sudden death less than a year earlier. "As long as we're together we'll make it through." Awestruck by her incredible response, I smiled and let the power of the moment envelope us; gazes locked, eyes welling, we were grateful and petrified, holding onto each other for dear life. I knew I could survive anything with her by my side.

After a few deep breaths and a long, lingering embrace, Ann dove straight into practicalities. "Can they take away our house?" she asked, her trembling voice betraying the fear of this new unknown. I wasn't sure about much, having never thought through the precarious situation I was in. "I think so, but only if my name is on the title to the house." Since our house was in joint ownership at the time, we agreed to transfer it into her name alone as quickly as possible. Nervous and uncertain of the legalities, we checked in with a few local lawyers who informed us that claims on personal guarantees could go back 90 days on assets sales or transfers. So we had no idea if our plan would protect us from foreclosure, but it would certainly make it more difficult for the Malaysian bank to take away the roof over our children's heads.

Ann was always one of those women who instinctively thrived under crisis. Eyes on the prize, she continued focusing on solutions, offering to go back to work as well. I gave her a big squeeze and kiss on the forehead. While I appreciated the support, she had worked as a registered dietician and school foodservice director, and we had a toddler and infant at home. "Honey, you can make at most $70,000 per year, I owe $10 million! You take care of Brett and Charly and let me figure out how to get us out of this mess."

With two children to care for, the stakes of my entrepreneurial games got a whole lot higher. This was one of the lowest points of my business career, and it took a massive mental toll. That creeping mental fog I'd been fighting off devolved into a full-on hurricane, and it shook me to my core. I tried to stay strong in front of my wife and employees, but I could barely keep the mask up, and the moment I was alone I collapsed into tears. Doubting every ability I'd once prided myself on, it was as if I'd suddenly discovered that I was a fraud; I'd just gotten lucky and cocky the first time around, and now my family would be paying the price.

I did my best to redirect my thoughts, pointing my mind to past obstacles overcome. The numerous near-broke winters at Guido's, duels with a financial partner trying to put us out of business and a myriad of crises for the company that all pre-dated our eventual success at Guido's. Plus, if I could pull myself out of that dark hole as a lonely, overburdened 22-year-old straight out of college, I could do it again now, I reminded myself. It was not necessarily seeing exactly what to do and executing it that I prided myself on, but rather my ability to focus on the things that I could control, with an unstoppable persistence to carry on. And while many people find themselves alone in these gut-wrenching situations, I was part of an incredible family and team who would be by my side for the long haul, through thick and thin. All things considered, I have things pretty good, I concluded with a momentary smile.

"Exactly," my inner critic would butt in, derailing my positive train of thought, "You didn't have a family then. You could be an irresponsible 20-something, but now you're a horrible husband and failure of a father, making your beautiful family pay for your mistakes!" In these moments, not even young Charly could cure my pity party, and it was an endless game of mental ping-pong trying to keep my mind above water.

But all I needed was the little spurts of fresh air to keep me hanging on. Thus began my mantra: "If I do not like the way I feel, I need to change the way I think!" I repeated it to myself as often as I could, and added in regular morning jogs on the beach near our Del Mar home, another great escape and healthy tool for the darkness I was fighting.

Though I found solace in repeating my affirmations several times a day, it didn't seem to be impacting the reality of our business situation. My misery had plenty of company with Neil, who shared my sense of panic and despair, as well as my father, who was constantly searching for a way to make me feel better. But in these stressed-out times, we all knew that the only way we could save the business was to sell our way out of it, and that fell directly on my shoulders alone.

While our business reality wasn't changing quickly, it finally dawned on me that I needed to change the way I measured success if I wanted to stay sane. My new measure, I decided, would be the ability to get up each morning for a jog on the beach, and simply witness the waves crashing. I knew that if I could get up every day, start with a healthy habit and a small success under my belt, I'd continue to do my best and eventually things would change.

When life is going well, it is easy to stay positive. However, everyone faces their own obstacles, and the key is figuring out how to keep a positive mental attitude while persevering through the hard times. "This too shall pass," my wise grandmother Rose used to knowingly assure me, using the old Jewish saying her parents had repeated during much tougher times of anti-Semitic violence in their native Poland. I'd been consumed with my problems, but as an immigrant, widow and young single mother of three, she'd seen far more hardship than I could ever imagine. If she could keep her head up, I thought to myself, I could too. I just needed to keep my head afloat long enough to be around when the tide turned, and ride the wave of positive energy to success.

All of these practices really began to benefit my mental state of mind. One night, when I was feeling particularly low, Ann and I had made a commitment to attend a friend's 40th birthday party. "Why don't we stay home and just play with the kids tonight instead of going to the party?" I suggested, in absolutely no mood to socialize or hold adult conversation. But Ann recognized that wallowing alone in our sorrows wouldn't help.

"I understand how disappointed and scared you are. I am too," she confided, as she held my hand in hers. "But many of your close friends will be there, and it will be good to feel their love and support. If you don't want to share the details, then don't bring it up. But at the very least, let's show up, see how you feel and just follow your heart!" she lovingly encouraged me. She was right, as usual. Since many of my friends already knew the business challenges I was facing, I decided to share the news of our foreclosure and personal guarantee notices. When surrounded by trusted friends, it actually felt better not having to hide our predicament. Though I was embarrassed and scared, I decided to try to put on a strong, positive face and will myself through the party.

My friends began to ask how I could keep such a good attitude when I was about to lose everything. I pointed to my amazing family and support at home, and that if I needed to, I had the ability to recreate everything if we eventually lost our house and savings. I certainly didn't want to start all over, I assured them, but if I had to I would. I'd gotten myself to the place where I could say this with confidence to the people around me, a huge step forward from where I'd been, even if I only believed it a fraction of the time. Forcing myself to fake it and keeping a positive attitude without hiding from the problem was a hugely helpful step in keeping my head above water.

When I got really low, my father would try to cheer me up, assuring me not to worry, as he had been through worse (though he wouldn't tell me when). But at least I had my hands on the wheel of what was happening. I can't imagine the sense of helplessness he must have felt in having to watch and wait without being able to take action himself. And when he had his lows as well, I would step in to remind him that this too shall pass. While he never acknowledged it out loud, I was able to hear the lack of hope in his voice; his energy and tone would fade so far, he was barely audible. "We have to remember, this is only temporary, Dad!" I would remind us both enthusiastically. "How many times in the past at Guido's did we think we were going out of business and we fought hard and found a way to pull through? We always survive. We will do the same here!" I am not sure that I actually believed what I was saying, but I knew it was what he needed to hear. I actually felt much better for a while when I was helping him stay positive. Fortunately, when one of us lost our hope, the other was right there to pick him up. Together, we pushed through the end of 1990.

Foreclosure notices are not usually so sudden and I couldn't understand why Neil had not told me how bad things were with the bank. When I finally got in touch with him in Malaysia to ask how this had happened, he explained that the number-two executive at the bank in charge of our account hated him. He didn't know why, but he distrusted Neil from the moment they met. Neil had a meeting scheduled in three days to convince them to hold off on the foreclosure notices on the factory and my personal guarantee, but he wasn't very optimistic about our chances. I did not know anyone at the bank, as Neil had handled all the communications and relationships, but either way, this was now my problem and I needed to figure a way out. "Who do I know in Malaysia," I asked myself, "Who could help us secure at least another 30-day grace period so we can shop our loan to another local bank?"

In times of crisis, I've learned to slow down and focus only on the solution, not the problem. Suddenly, it hit me; I belonged to the Young Presidents Organization (YPO), a global association of presidents from many different types of medium- and large-size companies. "Of course!" I exclaimed to myself, "Why hadn't I thought of this before?!" I decided to look up a Malaysian YPO'er to see if I could get some help. Most YPO'ers will return calls from fellow members; I was just praying that would prove true here.

I pulled out the directory, turned to the Malaysian chapter and randomly dialed the head of a large international accounting firm. I left a message with his secretary with my name and YPO affiliation, asking for him to call me back for an urgent question. Much to my delight, the bank chairman returned my call the very next day. I explained the situation and asked if he knew any executives at Standard Charter Bank. He suggested I call a different Malaysian YPO'er who was now the Chairman of Price Waterhouse, but who used to be the chairman of that bank. I thanked him for his time and rapid response and called the YPO'er he suggested.

Even more surprisingly, the chairman took my call immediately. I reviewed the situation with him, and explained that I was only looking for an additional 30 days to move our account to another bank. A little bewildered as to why they were so adamant about shutting us down immediately, I asked whether he still knew anyone at the bank who might be able to help us. Though he knew many senior executives, he said he couldn't promise anything. But he assured me he would make a call and see what he could do. I never heard back from him again.

At the end of the week, however, I received a furious call from Neil demanding to know what in the world had I done. I hadn't a clue what he was talking about. He explained he had his meeting at the bank with the executive handling our account, who'd yelled at him for 30 minutes straight, "ripping him a new asshole." Apparently, he did not appreciate us going over his head. In the end, however, he gave Neil an additional 30 days, and promised that after that, he would be there personally to shut us down. I didn't know why Neil was so upset. Regardless of the bank executive's profane tirade, my YPO contact helped buy us another month, I pointed out. And he had better get working immediately to find another local bank to take over our loan.

Not knowing if the company would be foreclosed on, combined with visions of losing our home, made sleeping practically impossible. The exhaustion made everything worse. I repeated my affirmations religiously, but as soon as I finished the last word, the stress came bounding back every time. Neil said he was making some progress, but we wouldn't know anything for sure until a bank board actually met to approve us. As we approached the last few days of our grace period, I tried not to show to my wife and employees the unbearable anxiety and fear that poisoned my every moment.

On the last day of our extension, I was just finishing dinner at home with Ann, Brett and Charly, when the phone rang. I knew it was Neil. I looked at Ann with trepidation on my face and walked over to the phone slowly, holding my breath as I picked up the receiver to hear my verdict. "We got it! We were approved by the new bank!" he blurted out. I couldn't believe my ears.

"Are there any contingencies or is this a final approval?" I asked, thinking it was too good to be true. "It is a final approval. The HSBC Bank bought out the original loan from Standard Charter Bank and actually gave us a better deal and longer terms," he explained, sounding as if he was walking on air. "CM called in every last favor and somehow used his personal contacts – we're still alive! Please share the good news with your father and let him know!" With this, CM and my local YPO brother became immortalized in my mind, my Malaysian heroes.

I let out a sigh of relief and turned to Ann to shoot her the thumbs up, beaming ear to ear. As soon as Neil finished giving me all the details of the new bank deal, I hung up the phone and let out another big scream. I ran over to Ann and picked her up with the biggest bear hug I could, before grabbing both Brett and little Charly as the four of us danced around the room. The kids had no idea why we were dancing, but they giggled and shouted along with us, loving the goofy celebratory boogie and getting swung in circles around the room.

As soon as we put Brett and Charly to bed, I went into my office to call CM. As soon as I heard his voice on the other end of the phone, chills flowed through my body. "CM! Neil told me about the new bank approval; there are no words to express how grateful I am for this incredible achievement – thank you," my eyes welled, as waves of relief and emotion began to hit. "How on earth did you pull this off?"

In his very modest and low-key way, CM acted like it was no big deal. "In the two years I have been in Ipoh, I have gotten involved in the local community and made some very good friends," he casually explained. "One of them was an executive at the local branch of HSBC. He had mentioned wanting to expand their local business, so when Standard Charter wanted out, I told him there was an immediate opportunity to take over our business if they could move fast enough. I made a presentation illustrating what a good opportunity it is to gain a local, long-term customer given how our business is turning around. So he called headquarters, and once he got approval to look at us, he managed to push it through." CM paused thoughtfully for a moment. "We were very lucky he was able to move so quickly."

If it was possible to hug someone through the phone, I would have. "Lucky he was able to move quickly, but more so lucky to have you on our team," I assured him. "You've saved more than this company; you've kept a roof over my children's heads, and saved my family from intense financial hardship. I am forever grateful." In surviving these type of harrowing moments together, CM and I developed an incredibly deep bond; we became like family. Despite rarely getting to see him, my children grew up knowing CM as their trusted uncle across the Pacific.

CM wishing Ann a happy 40th birthday during a family trip and company party in Thailand.

Once the relief and excitement of our survival had passed, it was back to our not-so-rosy reality. Though we had dodged a big bullet with the foreclosure and personal guarantee notices, without additional glove sales we would be facing the same fate within the next year. We had unloaded most of our glove inventory for whatever low price we could find just to stay afloat, and it was next to impossible to sell the stock we had left. We still faced daily concerns about being able to pay our truckers and suppliers. And with money and inventory running low, I worried that even if we did get glove orders, we wouldn't be able to make them. This would be a good problem to have, I decided, and kept my glass half full as I looked for ways to sell what gloves we had left.

CHAPTER 12

CLIMBING OUT

The following week, I was laboring over our marketing strategy when I got a call from our New York glove broker with our next big break. *The Medical Laboratory Observer* (MLO) magazine had just published the results of an independent study by Hoffman La Roche comparing five brands of gloves, and SafeSkin gloves significantly and consistently outperformed all the other gloves across the board. Our failure rate was only 3.9% (below the FDA's 4% limit), while all the other gloves tested with 15% to almost 50% pinholes upon arrival. I nearly jumped out of my skin. I knew we were the best latex glove, I just never had concrete proof. Now we had to figure out how to use the study to our advantage, and fast.

Over the next several days, articles about the study also started appearing in newspapers such as *The Miami Herald, The Long Island Newsday, the Los Angeles Times* and others throughout the entire country. We needed to ride this newfound media wave, so I called my father to brainstorm how to best take advantage of this great public relations opportunity. We quickly agreed that I should put together a package with our literature, the newspaper articles and the MLO glove study, and start mailing them to every medical distributor and hospital we had ever called on. I would then follow up with a phone call asking if they had received my letter with the article, and offer to get them a spot towards the front of the line to get gloves shipped directly from our factory.

This was so important that I needed to make every call myself. "Take the rest of today to write up a script of what you want to say to each potential customer you're going to call, and think through all the objections they may have," my father instructed me. I had not heard him so calm and forceful for a long time. The powerful tone of his voice gave me great confidence. "I know what their first objection will be," I responded, having become an expert at getting shut down by these distributors, "They don't need any more gloves at this time."

"Yes," my father said, "But your job is to overcome their objection by convincing them to trust you and take a chance on you personally. Guarantee them that the hospitals will need the gloves. Let them know that there is no risk on their side because you'll allow them to return the unsold gloves if they can't sell them." I breathed a sigh of relief; there was a light at the end of the tunnel for the first time in awhile. I needed to find a way for distributors to trust me personally, even though we had zero orders for these gloves that no one needed yet.

I spent the rest of the day working on my pitch, practicing it with my father over and over again. That night I got the first good night's sleep since I could remember. The next morning I awoke confident and poised, excited to leap into action. I ate a good breakfast, kissed Ann and the kids goodbye and headed into the office for a groundbreaking day. Sitting back into my chair, I set a large glass of water at my side and told my assistant not to interrupt me for the next three hours unless it was a customer returning my call. Before picking up the receiver, I closed my eyes to briefly meditate and visualize our customers thanking me for calling, exclaiming that of course they would buy our gloves now that there was demand for them. Slowly, I opened my eyes and dialed the first potential customer on the list.

After getting through to the person who'd received my package and engaging in some personal small talk, I explained that while we were out of domestic inventory due to a surge in demand, we could ship directly from our Malaysian factory to their warehouses if they purchased a container (one thousand cases). If they couldn't sell them, I went on, we'd be happy to take all the gloves back.

It was a crazy idea to try to get strangers to buy one thousand cases off the bat, but we were desperate and had to try anything that might possibly work. Despite my best efforts, I received rejection after rejection. With overstocked warehouses, distributors insisted that they didn't want to buy ten cases, let alone one thousand. When I continued persisting, the exasperated voice on the other line assured me that they wouldn't buy our gloves unless we sold to the hospital first; then they would only order whatever the hospital ordered. No one wanted to hold inventory of unsold gloves while they still had so many sitting in their warehouses. Dejected but not defeated, I kept calling down my list, hoping to convince someone to place an order.

Finally, late in the afternoon, I got a break when Ben, the owner of United Medical in Dallas, took my call. I think he only took it because he liked me. I'd visited him a few times, we'd gotten lunch together and he had always said he'd love to help me (but still had too many other gloves to sell first). When I inquired about the literature package I'd sent over, he confirmed that he'd seen it and congratulated me on such great public relations attention. I could feel a genuine sense of care and affection in his voice, and for the first time I felt like I had a real opportunity to close a sale. Though my heart was pounding faster and faster, and my mind was searching for a way to ask for an order, I knew I hadn't talked about his family or business needs enough to pitch him yet.

After a few minutes of small talk about his wife and kids, I asked if he was still trying to grow his hospital business. "Of course!" he responded. "We are always looking to grow our business, but it's getting harder and harder each year." This was it, my perfect chance to ask for an order. "I have a new way for you to grow your business and give your hospitals what they want. Since the glove study came out, hospitals from all over the country are calling us to find out where they can get our hypoallergenic gloves," I opened, with a voice much more sure than I really was. "I have no more gloves in our U.S. warehouses and customer orders backing up, but for you I can push your order to the front of the line and ship a container directly from our Malaysian factory right to your warehouse in Dallas."

My palms were sweating profusely as I held my breath and waited for his response; I hadn't been this nervous since my first encounters at my father's appliance store 20 years prior. "How many cases of gloves are on a container?" he inquired, not seeming upset at my request. "A 20-foot container is one thousand cases, and a 40-foot container holds two thousand," I quickly responded. "But I can only squeeze out enough gloves for a 20-foot container at this time unless you absolutely insist on the larger container," I conceded, assuring him, "As soon as you sell those out I can ship you another 20-foot container."

This was the moment of truth. I felt like I had asked for the order just at the right time and given him a choice, not a yes or no option. This was one of the reasons I loved selling: immediate feedback on whether I did a good job or not. After what seemed like an eternity, Ben started laughing. It was not the reaction I was hoping for, and I worried I'd blown it. "Young man," he began, in his smooth, Southern drawl. "I don't need 10 cases of gloves at this time, what makes you think I would buy a thousand cases?" He paused, giving me space for an answer, but I figured I'd just let him continue on. "Nevertheless," he eventually said with a smile in his voice, "I like your balls and style so I will agree to buy a 20-foot container of gloves from you, so long as you promise to take back whatever we can't sell 90 days after we receive them." One thousand cases equates to one million gloves, or approximately $45,000.

At the time I was so shocked that I couldn't tell if I misheard him. Was he for real? I decided to take him at his word, and while my heart was jumping for joy inside my chest, my phone voice was all business. "It's a deal! Great decision, sir, you won't be sorry, I promise you that." I responded as calmly as I could. I looked around for someone to share the good news with as I hung up the phone, and ran out of my office to hug the first person I could find.

When I finally calmed down, I picked up the phone and called my father and let out another big scream when I heard his voice. "Calm down," he laughed, "You did good. Now we have to figure out a way to get enough money to buy the latex for all the gloves you just sold!" I never thought about that. I was so focused on selling a container of gloves that I forgot we had sold for a loss or given away trial orders of all of our latex gloves these past two years just to stay afloat.

Our warehouses were empty, the factory practically shut down and we had no money. This is why our original bank wanted to close us down. While we finally had a purchase order, most lending institutions would only lend on an actual invoice after shipments had been sent out. So onto the next challenge: where to find the cash to buy the latex needed to make a million gloves.

With the help of our accountant, Stanley, we found a factoring company that would lend us the money before shipment, with a lofty interest rate of 15%. I'm sure this was a favor that Stanley called in, but all that mattered was that, after a lot of paperwork, they gave us the money we needed.

While this first win was elating, after two days of nonstop phone calls, no one else would even remotely consider making a purchase. Even my greatest sales pitch couldn't change the fact that distributors didn't need gloves until they had orders from the hospitals. Desperate but refusing to accept no, I finally decided to shift gears and take my customers' direction to reach out directly to hospitals for initial purchase orders.

Much to my delight and surprise, several of the hospitals were beginning to run down their existing inventory and could soon try out small orders of our hypoallergenic latex gloves. Once I had a small trial order from any hospital, the next step was to convince their distributors to order a much larger one a million-glove container. We began by preempting their objections, guaranteeing distributors we would take back any gloves the hospitals didn't use. Combining this with unrelenting persistence, we began receiving one order, then another and another. It was hard work and often took several calls to the same buyer, but I had found a sales pitch that worked.

Several months later, our distribution manager, Gene, came walking into my small office with a smile on his face; he actually received more orders for gloves that day than trucking companies calling him for payment on our past-due bills. It was in that moment, somewhere in the middle of 1991, that I knew we'd turned the corner. I finally saw a light at the end of the tunnel. If we kept working hard, I genuinely believed we might just have a way out of this big mess.

That night when I returned home, I shared my exciting new revelations with Ann. "Beyond just surviving," I gushed with newfound enthusiasm, "We may actually make it big!" As I wrestled with the kids in our nightly ritual of cuddles and hugs, a wave of optimism engulfed me. How quickly things had changed! Ann even jumped into the dog-pile and rolled around on the floor with us. While I always did my best to hide my stress from Charly and Brett, they always seemed to pick up on my particularly joyful energy. They giggled and laughed as I tickled them silly, while Ann and I shared a loving smile, never missing an opportunity to feel grateful for our blessings.

As anticipated, our brokers started receiving more and more trial orders, and containers finally began arriving from Malaysia. However, as our gloves made their way to hospitals around the country, complaints began rolling in. We hadn't commercialized our powder-free gloves yet, and it seemed that our original, hypoallergenic gloves were loaded with too much powder. So much that, apparently, the excess powder was floating into the air andgetting all over the hospitals. Atthesame time, our distributors had more orders than inventory and were demanding more gloves immediately. It was amazing how quickly it had turned from a crisis of no demand to a crisis of not enough supply.

I found myself at a defining crossroad. Our very first value is to exceed customer expectation, which we clearly weren't meeting, but we also needed cash to stay in business. I couldn't afford to send the gloves back to our low-cost workers in Malaysia to remove the excess powder: that was a fact. But it just wasn't right to ship customers any gloves with too much powder. While it would benefit our cash flow and keep us afloat in the short term, it would do so at the expense of our reputation, and that was not the kind of company we wanted to build.

When facing a crisis, creating a speedy but thoughtful response to contain the problem and prevent it from growing comes first. Then we deal with the immediate symptom pressing on our doorstep. Neil notified the factory and established new specifications to contain the problem from growing, but we needed to find a solution for all the gloves with excess powder sitting in our Los Angeles warehouse, as well as those currently being shipped across the Pacific. I struggled to find a solution but couldn't come up with one. As usual, I called my father for advice. "I agree with you wholeheartedly," he began after I updated him on the situation and my strong stance against selling any more over-powdered gloves, "You only get one chance to make a good first impression and that is how hospitals will remember you forever. Let me ask you a question about the excess powder," he said. "What would you do if your shirts had too much powder?"

"I guess I would just throw them in my dryer and then clean the filter when I was done," I responded, not seeing why he was taking me off topic with so much to do. After a long silence, he connected the dots, "Then why don't you do the same thing for the gloves?"

I had never thought about that option. "Great idea, Dad!" I thanked him, my mind taking off at a mile a minute. "All we have to do is buy a half dozen commercial dryers, rent some warehouse space with electrical outlets near the port of Los Angeles, hire some day labor and send a few of our office staff to help supervise and monitor the acceptable powder level!" I blurted out, happy to see a new solution come together so quickly. All we need to do, I figured, was turn off the heat to the dryers to avoid damaging the gloves and just spin them until the excess powder was removed.

It took about two days to procure six commercial dryers, locate warehouse space near the port, install the necessary electrical wiring and make arrangements to move the gloves to our new location, one container at a time. A team of six workers then emptied each box of gloves into the dryers, turned them on long enough to remove the excess powder and then repacked one hundred gloves back into each box, ten boxes per case, before sending them back to our local warehouse for shipment. After several trial batches, we figured out how long to spin them, and lost surprisingly few gloves in the process. Our biggest issue was the filters; though we cleaned them continuously, there was so much powder getting removed that the dryers eventually broke down after a month and had to be discarded. Luckily for us, those overworked dryers lasted just long enough for us to get by until the lower-powder gloves began landing ashore.

For about 30 days we continued this process, which ate away all of our profits, and led to constant complaining from our distributors who needed more gloves yesterday. Our salespeople, who bore the brunt of the distributor complaints, advocated fiercely for us to keep shipping the over-powdered gloves.

"Powdery gloves are better than no gloves!" they insisted. Neil was worried we wouldn't withstand the financial burden of these extra expenses combined with no income for another month while we removed the powder. But he supported my decision once I made it, and defended it whenever salespeople called him to object.

Eventually, after 60 days of delays, our distributors and hospital customers were very satisfied with the quality of the gloves and customer service they received. I was proud to live by my values, and incredibly lucky that it was only a 60-day stretch; much longer would have possibly meant going out of business. With the over-powdered fiasco behind us, the rest of 1991 was a continuous sprint to fill all the orders we were receiving.

CHAPTER 13

SPEEDING UP

It was unbelievable to me that just a year ago we were struggling to make our bank payments, and now we had made over a million dollars – $400,000 of profits in June of 1992 alone – and we were forecasting to rake in over 10 million dollars by New Year's. Our cash crunch was all but over and our challenges quickly switched to increasing production and managing our salesforce directly to accelerate our growth. CM Lee and his team were building new machines and cranking up the factory production level to an all-time high, and I hired four regional sales managers to supervise the brokerage network until we could afford to hire our own salesforce.

While all this was happening, a disturbing trend started showing up in the hospitals. Hundreds of healthcare workers began breaking out in rashes from using other brands that had not removed the chemicals from their gloves. Dozens of nurses had gone into anaphylactic shock and were forced to contemplate leaving the healthcare field. My original premise about my own skin breaking out in a rash was coming true for others.

At the same time, nurses having adverse reactions to powdered gloves tested our hypoallergenic, powder-free gloves and were able to get through their workday rash free. When I asked the factory to significantly increase the amount of powder-free gloves, CM Lee said they could only make about a million gloves a month to get started but that they would ramp up as quickly as possible once we proved it was needed.

"CM, I am telling you we need all the powder-free gloves you can make. What will it take to ramp up?" I asked with a bit more force than usual. "It will take quite a bit of time and money," he warned. "We will need more space and equipment, and still have to build effluent treatment ponds, as well as more washers and cyclone dryers. This also requires a huge hiring increase to get enough workers to turn the gloves over. Making gloves powder-free is an offline process – every single glove needs to be washed and turned inside out by hand – so it takes time to ramp up, but we can start as soon as you say go."

"CM, listen carefully. Not only am I saying go, I am saying go as fast as you possibly can. Whatever you can make, we can sell. I already bet you that I can sell more powder-free gloves than you can ever make," I chided, appealing to his competitive nature. He had been a national squash player for Malaysia in his younger days and had never lost his competitive spirit. "I will hold you to it!" he challenged back, smiling as he spoke. His combination of kindness and professionalism, and tendency to always take on a challenge with a smile, were only a few of the reasons I grew to love him like a brother.

While the glut of powdered gloves on the market had faded away, there was still ample supply and prices remained depressed, with less than a 10% margin. Since we could only make a limited amount, I decided to introduce the powder-free gloves at double the price of our powdered gloves and sell them for 8 cents each (close to 70% margins). When customers questioned the high price, I explained that it cost more to make them. As I had learned at Coca Cola, we can always reduce the price of a new product, but it was extremely difficult to raise prices after a new product has already been introduced. Plus, I knew that buyers like to receive big discounts, so if I priced it high enough I could always give them a 25% or 30% discount and still maintain a good profit margin.

Though we knew our customers wanted less powder, we never anticipated the truly incredible depth of their desire and their eventual willingness to pay more for such a product. To say we hit the nail on the head for our customer need would be a gross understatement. Not only did we sell all one million gloves the first month after our double-the-price roll out, and two million gloves the second month, but we also ended up running the factories 24 hours a day, seven days a week, 365 days a year for eight years and still couldn't keep up!

It wasn't easy maintaining our massive growth. Purchasing agents at hospitals hated us, as we cost them far more money than they had budgeted. They loved the glove-gut prices and budgeted for those low costs moving forward. They did everything they could not to let our powder-free gloves into their hospitals. But as our four new sales managers began riding along with our brokers to learn more about their customers and territories, they found that the salespeople who were really successful in introducing our powder-free gloves got around purchasing agents by going straight to the lab technicians, providing free trials and receiving overwhelming support in return. Labs often had their ownbudgets for purchasing products in small amounts. Once in the lab, word of our powder-free gloves spread like wildfire throughout the hospitals. Nurses from all over the hospital would visit the labs to trial our powder-free gloves, and before long most of the nurses on the main hospital floors were stealing our powder-free gloves from the labs and demanding them from their purchasing agents. While this worked for most of the hospitals where one of our brokers had close ties, the incentive just wasn't there for the rest of the broker network, who had dozens of other products to sell and wouldn't risk pissing off their purchasing agents. Unsurprisingly, they were not as diligent and it was at this time that we decided to fire our broker network and hire a dozen of our own direct sales teams who would be selling SafeSkin gloves exclusively.

It was a very challenging time for me, as these brokers had become friends; they had taken a chance on us, supporting us when no one else would. But this is what our business needed to keep growing, and we had to do what was right for the business. While it was still hard to dismiss people I cared about, at least our amazing growth gave me the ability to feel good about our goodbye. They had earned a great deal of commission on SafeSkin products, and we gave the brokerage team six months' notice as well as an unusually hefty bonus as a thank you.

Now, with some great SafeSkin sales successes under their belts, our four regional managers were ready to breed their own teams of superstars, the absolute best salespeople in the medical device industry, who would work their asses off to make as much money as possible. When I sat down with our managers to hash out criteria, they were even stricter than me. We didn't have time to teach people how to sell, our new hires needed to be able to learn the virtues of our hypoallergenic powdered and powder-free latex gloves and hit the ground running. This meant going after our competitors' top salespeople, specifically those with several years' experience who consistently ranked in the top 10% of their current salesforce.

"Great," I agreed, "Who doesn't want a salesforce like that? But how do we get the best people to leave their companies?" The entire team laughed and told me not to worry. Here I got a friendly reminder that life is all about incentives. Most large companies cap the amount of commission their best people can make. If we developed a pay structure that provided our salespeople unlimited commission, allowing us to all get rich together, we would have no problem. Plus, we had the secret weapon of the potential stock option. When we went public, our sales team had the opportunity to make some serious money on top of the limitless commission. It all went back to simple lessons I learned in my father's appliance store selling TVs – or rather, in the noncommissioned TVs I didn't sell – where the incentives go, the energy flows.

It sounded so simple I was bewildered as to why big companies would sabotage their own growth with restricted pay plans. But that was not my problem; our sales managers were right, and we were ready to lure the best and brightest to send our growth numbers through the roof. I had each manager report back with their final three choices in each of the 12 regions we created. Often, they would reach back into their former companies and pull out the best salespeople or call on top performers from competitors they hated going up against.

Within a few weeks we hired one of the greatest sales teams I've ever worked with, or the "dirty dozen" as they affectionately dubbed themselves. I also promoted one of the sales managers, Judy Grimes, to be the Vice President of Sales. An incredibly talented young lady with the 'x' factor to make it rain, Judy commanded every room she entered. With good looks and a powerful presence, when she talked, everyone listened. She was tough, and put in the time and effort on her end to ensure each of our salespeople around the globe could answer every objection they faced. Occasionally her intensity could rub people the wrong way, but she insisted on putting the customer first and I always respected her for that.

We were not without our differences, but I quickly learned that if Judy was given a clearly defined goal and the space to do things her way, she'd knock it out of the park every time. If, on the other hand, I tried to have her do things my way, the details would always drag us down. Everyone needs to be managed differently; Judy was so strong-minded that she needed goals articulating the outcome, not direction how to do it. That only works when dealing with talented executives we can trust, and lucky for us she was both! For the next four years that Judy was with us, she and her sales team blew us away, never missing a quarterly sales forecast no matter how aggressive it was. We eventually hired over 60 sales reps across the United States and Europe.

In three years, we'd gone from a small, nearly bankrupt startup in 1990, to a recognizable threat going head-to-head with glove manufacturing giants like Baxter International, J & J and Smith and Nephew. The more business we stole from them, the more buzz we got about us. As purchasing agents realized they couldn't keep our powder-free gloves out of their hospitals, they began pushing for a mix of our powdered and powder-free gloves throughout the hospital to keep their costs down. This gave a much welcomed boost to our powdered glove business as well.

Back at home, Brett was charging through kindergarten with what seemed to be superhuman energy, Charly had grown into a breathtaking and beautifully kind 3-year-old, and in March 1993 Ann gave birth to our incredible firecracker of a daughter Maxi the baby of the family. The joy of watching our children grow was unlike anything I had ever experienced: heart-expanding, awe-inspiring and at times outright mind-boggling. There was nothing quite like the pitter-patter of hearing my little gems rushing to meet me when I walked through the door, and the love of my life waiting with a smile and a kiss. It was a love beyond anything I'd imagined growing up and it continued fueling my drive to make SafeSkin a success.

While not always a favorite activity amongst the kids, I cherish our color-coordinated family photos throughout the years.

As we entered the summer of 1993, the business was expanding at a breakneck pace. The hypoallergenic powdered and powder-free latex glove business had taken off just as the glove glut ended and another shortage began. As projected, our revenues had grown to $34 million in 1992, and we were forecasting $57 million for the current year. Production capacity was completely maxed out in Malaysia, and though our wages were low beyond the American imagination, the factory wage had increased by more than 60% over our four years of business. Much of this bump resulted from the expansion of the Malaysian semiconductor industry, which shot up the demand for quality labor. With Malaysia's rising wages and our restricted capacity, Neil and CM determined we needed to expand to a new factory in a lower-cost country and would require additional capital to do so.

So it was off to the races, and Neil and CM searched for new factory sites across Vietnam, Indonesia, Thailand and Burma (now Myanmar). It was all pretty foreign to me, but after an exhaustive search they came back confident that southern Thailand was by far our best option. The site was a three-hour drive from our Malaysian factory and the two had negotiated with the Thai authorities for a 10 year tax-free status. And with a strong, consistent source of latex, this location had the lowest risk for interruption of supply.

Now that we had a plan and location in place, we needed to figure out how to raise the capital necessary to build the new factory. A few weeks after scouting for factories, Neil returned stateside, and my father and I flew down to Florida to go over his findings and discuss how we would finance this next step. It basically came down to borrowing more money from the banks or going public. While we had successfully taken Guido's public, back then we had only been raising $4 million through a much smaller and less sophisticated broker network. It would take a lot more work to bring SafeSkin public, as we were a highly visible international medical device company trying to raise $30 million and would be working with top-tier firms to do so.

While business was going great, I was hesitant in our sales forecasting abilities – at least not in the accuracy an IPO would require. So I started with the banks, musing about a $25 million loan from Asian or American institutions. Clearly, my father and Neil were on a different wavelength. They immediately shifted the conversation to a public offering with such ease and agreement, as if it were a foregone conclusion. Like the agreement had happened without me. "A good friend of mine has a son at Alex Brown (major investment bank in Baltimore)," my father said, quickly moving into action, "And they've agreed to meet with us next week!" So the agreement definitely happened without me. While they were probably right, I didn't like being left out of the loop.

Sensing my disappointment, my father quickly assured me that they didn't want to distract me from all the sales challenges at hand. The faster we grew, the harder our competitors came after us. There were plenty of pricing challenges from budget-conscious customers threatening to switch brands, along with personnel issues as we continued turning over the weakest 10% of our salesforce. Dad and Neil's consideration and assurances were all well and good, but we all knew that most of the work presenting for the IPO would fall on my shoulders. Our success would hinge on our ability to convince the bankers that we had a stable and consistent revenue and profit stream, and I was the one responsible for them.

After a busy week of mostly ignored sunshine, we left the Florida office and flew up to Baltimore to interview the team at Alex Brown. Though I had been through this process nine years earlier, this time was completely different. As a significantly more successful company, we were meeting with first tier investment bankers that had greater resources, intellect and rigor. It was an exciting and slightly intimidating challenge. And I was ready to dive in.

As we arrived, my father's connection was ready and waiting to greet us. After some polite introductions, he explained that since he was in the financial services sector, we'd be meeting with the medical device team who would determine whether we fit their standards to go public. They were amazed at our rapid growth and blown away by our nearly 70% gross margins. "Unbelievable for a commodity business!" one of their bankers marveled. I politely tried my best to explain that we were not a commodity; our hypoallergenic claim and powder-free process differentiated us from all other glove companies. But I didn't quite get through to them.

"All the other large glove companies had a host of medical products," another banker said, "Why is it that they don't just bundle them into a package and insist hospitals buy their gloves in order to purchase the rest of their products?" In this moment it became clear to me that we were dealing with financial analysts and not business operators. Just because something makes financial sense doesn't mean that's how business will be run. While selling in a bundle is efficient, when a hospital, or any business for that matter, wants a product, they'll find a way to buy it.

Despite the minor difference in perspectives, the meeting ended on a remarkably positive note as they praised us for our incredible growth story. We could expect to hear back in about a week. As the three of us headed back to the airport, Neil heading off for Florida and my father and I returning to California, we all agreed that we liked the Alex Brown team very much, and would happily have them take us public. Not that I spent much time thinking about it – the next week flew by as I caught up with a myriad of sales and logistic issues that had piled up while I was gone.

At home things were no calmer. Every time I left for several days, Brett and Charly would sprint into my arms the moment I came through the front door, hanging off me like a jungle gym as I slowly made my way to Maxi and Ann. While she was too young to crawl, let alone talk, every time I picked up Maxi to hold her, it was like she told me through her eyes that she noticed these absences and didn't like them one bit. I felt so blessed yet so torn about my busy travel schedule. I just prayed that the sacrifice would be worth it, not just for the company I was building but for the future security and welfare of our family. When I finally got to give Ann a hug and kiss, I knew I was the luckiest man in the world!

Later the following week, I noticed my assistant had penciled in a lunchtime call with Neil and my father titled *IPO Update*. Without wasting much time with pleasantries, my dad explained we'd heard back from Alex Brown and they'd decided not to take us public. Though they liked us and the story very much, they felt that disclosing our "obscene" 70% margins in the IPO process would put a target on our backs; all our larger competitors and medical device companies not yet in the glove business would see our margins and flood the market with powder-free gloves at lower prices, eventually driving our margins down to the 20-25% industry average. I was shocked. Our own success was derailing our efforts to raise the money we needed to expand? It didn't make sense. In the end, their IPO doomsday forecasts never materialized; we ended up maintaining 60% margins for the next five years. But that didn't help us here.

Determined and confident they were making a mistake, we agreed that Neil and Dad would search out other top-tier investment banks while I stayed focused on the sales, marketing and distribution. Neil was not without growing pains on the manufacturing side, but CM Lee was completely capable of handling most of them with minimal direction. We needed to move quickly to secure our ideal factory site in Thailand, and Neil and my father wasted no time setting up multiple meetings with a host of top-tier investment banks within a week. When I saw how easy it was to get the meetings, I knew we would convince at least one of them to take us public.

We used the objections from our first meeting to tweak our presentation for other firms, explaining upfront why we were not a commodity, identifying how we could maintain our margins and illustrating how the glove market was exploding with ample growth opportunities. Each meeting went better than the last, and the three of us could sense we were on a roll. After an action-packed week, we agreed that Smith Barney seemed like the best choice. As excited as we were for them to represent us, they were even more excited about bringing us public. Their one requirement was that we include a second investment bank to co-promote the IPO, and after meeting with Montgomery Securities, a small boutique firm in San Francisco, we enthusiastically agreed.

Once all the details were agreed upon, Smith Barney put together a schedule that would require us to meet our June forecasts, prepare our roadshow over the summer and start making presentations after Labor Day. Neil tried to push them to complete the IPO before the summer, since we needed the cash to buy the land in Thailand yesterday, but to no avail. They wanted the June quarter financials to get the best price they could, and suggested we borrow the money from a local bank and pay it back with the proceeds from the IPO. We decided to put off expanding in Thailand until after going public.

As we continued our explosive growth throughout 1993, things were crazy in the best way possible. The factories were maxing out production, our rockstar salesforce was expanding and bringing in tons of new sales with them, and we were frequently outgrowing our office spaces. It was hard to believe that less than three years earlier, I was transferring the deed of our house into Ann's name and gazing into baby Charly's eyes for a sense of relief from the constant, agonizing worry over how to pay our bills.

We had come remarkably far and learned a great deal in those three years. One of the best lessons I learned during this more recent "good crazy" period was how to hire an epic team and get out of the way. Putting together a management team that was more experienced than I in each of their own specialties allowed me to measure their performance rather than manage their activities, freeing me up to focus on our strategy and future challenges as well as large customer visits. Though each of them were experts in their own area, I was the one with the full picture, constantly verbalizing our vision and goals, directing each piece and giving constant feedback to everyone, keeping them informed about where we were headed.

In order to keep the pieces of this moving puzzle going in the right direction, having a right-hand man was key. Or in my case, a right-hand woman. In July 1993, as business was exploding, I needed to hire a new executive assistant who could keep up with me. Usually when interviewing, I have some intuition within the first 15-20 seconds on how I feel about someone, and the chemistry either builds or falls from there. But rarely have I felt the instant connection I experienced when Maripat walked through the door. A sharply dressed woman with incredible people skills, Maripat had a uniquely powerful sense of poise and self-confidence. She spoke not about what she could do, but rather how she would gather a deep understanding of how my mind and business operated in order to maximize the amount of work she could take off my plate.

I hired her on the spot, and as promised, she picked things up with remarkable speed, making many decisions on her own while still recognizing when something should be pushed through to me. Often times, I would purposely dawdle around before meeting a potential hire, leaving them to talk to Maripat and then asking for her input after the candidate left. She was almost always spot on. Maripat became a close confidant and key advisor, and stood at my side through thick and thin for the next seven years.

I must admit, however, that I did hire a few executives whose performance disappointed me, and I spent most of my management time with them. Sometimes it was that we just hired the wrong people who weren't able to see changes coming, manage other people well or solve complex problems by themselves. They missed deadlines and commitments that affected all the other areas. Other times, we hired people who were right for the job at the time, but the needs of the company quickly outgrew their capabilities with 100% growth year over year, eventually requiring that we replace them. Though I always felt loyal to our employees, I knew by now that it was more important to do the right thing for the company.

Though we had dealt with this a little bit at Guido's and in the early years of SafeSkin, as our business was exploding we needed to continually get the wrong people off the bus and the right people into the correct seats or it would quickly drag us down. Everyone makes mistakes in hiring; it is an imperfect process requiring decisions based on limited information. The really successful companies train well, measure performance, give feedback and replace the non-performers quickly.

Hiring the right people and creating a culture of trust, integrity and open communication is absolutely essential for a fast-growth company. We were very lucky to have hired many incredibly smart and dedicated people who believed in and fit into our caring but performance culture, where people legitimately loved coming to work, cared about the people they worked with and, most importantly, thrived off creating value for our customers.

THE IPO ROLLER COASTER

All was well as June rolled in. We had plenty of orders and were right on target to hit our financial forecasts for the second quarter. That is, until I received an urgent call from our customs importer. Apparently Connie, our West Coast sales representative, had found out that the Sony TV factory in San Diego needed low-cost latex gloves and organized a shipment of rejected gloves with pinholes (industrial C grade) to be sent to our Los Angeles warehouse before making their way to Sony. In actuality, it was quite creative to find a channel to distribute rejected gloves that were currently getting trashed. What Connie didn't realize was that U.S. Customs required all gloves on medical-grade shipments to have fewer than 4% pinholes. Unfortunately for us, the factory workers had loaded some of the C grade gloves onto a medical container, separating them only by a plastic divider.

As is their policy, Customs randomly selected imported containers to inspect and it just so happened that they chose our mixed medical/non-medical glove container to sample upon arrival. When they took glove samples from throughout our container, we were considerably over the 4% limit. Our Customs importer, Mark, went back and forth with Customs, trying to explain the difference between medical-grade and industrial-grade gloves and providing the paperwork that designated some of the gloves as industrial rather than medical, which therefore should not be subject to the same limitations. But none of it made any difference.

After two days of arguing, our team had gotten nowhere and called me to explain the situation. "We've never failed an inspection," I exclaimed, "Didn't you explain that this shipment was separated by a plastic divider into medical and non-medical gloves?" Mark assured me he did. "They didn't want to listen," he said. "I even called the assistant port supervisor, but he cut me off and refused to even let me explain. It felt like one of your big competitors got to him; we're being stonewalled," Mark concluded. "There's nothing we can do right now but wait until five consecutive shipments pass inspection. Only then will SafeSkin be removed from the official hold list, which will go out this week. What's worse is that all SafeSkin shipments of gloves at the port will be held until we're off the hold list." Holy. Shit. I couldn't believe this was happening.

This was incredible in the absolute worst sense of the word. Without getting our containers released in the next 10 days there was no way we could hit our forecasted revenues, which would completely jeopardize our public offering. "How long will it take for them to inspect the next five containers?" I pushed impatiently. "That's an even bigger problem," Mark said. "There's massive delays and personnel shortages at the moment, so they said they won't get to us for another four or five weeks," he admitted apologetically. "BULLSHIT," I exclaimed instinctively, "Someone needs to be able to expedite our inspections. Who is in charge of customs at the port?" I demanded, as the adrenaline sent my heartbeat pounding and my mind into overdrive. Without a speedy solution our IPO was in jeopardy. And without the IPO, our funding for the new factory would vanish, as would the growth of our company.

Mark gave me the name, phone number and address of the U.S. Customs supervisor at the port, but warned me there was nothing else I could do. He had been through inspection holds like this before and not once had anyone been successful in pushing Customs faster than they were willing to go. I thanked him for the information and called my father as soon as I hung up the phone. I was fuming. "Can you believe all of our gloves are on hold for at least a month?! Unless we can convince them to inspect five new containers this week, it will be impossible to hit our forecasted revenues."

Dad knew the ramifications before I even finished talking, and went straight into crisis mode. "Get in your car and drive directly to the supervisor's office. Do not leave until he agrees to inspect your containers immediately. Offer to pay overtime, move the containers to another warehouse, whatever it takes. Just get it done!" he insisted, as if I had some magical power.

"It is not that easy!" I protested. "Of course it is not easy!" he fired back sternly, "But we have no choice. We've come too far and survived too many challenges to lose it all now. I don't care if you need to sleep at his office, just figure out what it will take and get it done. You are the only one who can save us and I know you can do it, so just go!"

I had never heard him so insistent or certain I could figure something out. While focused for sure, Dad was usually much softer and would ask me how I would handle a situation before sending me off. But this wasn't business as usual. If we didn't get the containers released in time to ship by the end of the month, our public offering was probably off the table and our outright survival would be at stake. His obstinate certainty was just what I needed to hear. Underneath his forceful tone of voice, I knew he must have been scared as hell. But I found some confidence in his strength and he was right – failure was not an option.

When I called Ann to explain the situation, she agreed with my father's plan completely. She threw together a snack for the road and said she had one more thing upstairs for my trip. As I followed her into the bedroom, she turned around and playfully knocked me onto the bed. Jumping on top of me, she gave me a long, deep kiss and teasing slap on the shoulder. "Now go get those containers released like I know you can. I have another surprise for you when you come back, so hurry up!" I hopped into the car, grinning ear to ear, and raced up the coast to get to the port before it closed. The whole ride up I couldn't stop laughing to myself about what a great motivator Ann was. I was so lucky to have my best friend as my wife, mother of my children and number one cheerleader.

Though it didn't take long to get there, it took two hours to finally find the correct office. I rushed through the door just as the executive assistant was packing up to leave. I tried to catch my breath and charm her while explaining the situation and insisting on meeting with the most senior executive in charge. She didn't even look up or pause from packing up as she let me know I should either call or come back tomorrow.

I tried my best to make friends and get her on my side while continuing to make my case, but she was having none of it. "I cannot leave until you are out of this office and I have a very important meeting to go to right now!" she snapped. "Well I am not leaving until I meet with him," I calmly insisted, "I have strict instructions to sleep in his office if I need to, but not to return until I see him. So what do we do now?" If looks could kill I'd be dead. "If you do not leave immediately I will call port security and have you removed from the premises," her anger rose as she began to shout, "I promise you I will never put your call through to him in the future, and you will not see him!" This was not going well.

I remained calm and decided not to do or say anything. I just sat in silence staring at the wall. Clearly she didn't know what to do. But after a few minutes of excruciating awkwardness, she broke the silence. "OK. I tried to warn you!" she snapped as she picked up the phone. "Hello, yes, I need security in the supervisor's office right away!" I laughed to myself as she slammed down the phone; at least I was in the right office! Flying by the seat of my pants, I had no idea what I would do when security showed up. I just crossed my fingers for better luck with security than I'd had with the secretary.

As the door opened my heart leaped into my throat. "Supervisor Casey!" the secretary exclaimed in surprise. I just about burst with joy as she continued on, "This gentleman doesn't have an appointment and he refuses to leave. I called security and they are on their way." He looked at me with a quizzical but kind smile. "What seems to be the problem, Mr...?"

"Jaffe," I quickly responded, as I jumped up to shake his hand, "I only need five minutes of your time, but it is life or death for my company so please allow me to explain." I tried to find a balance of respectable professionalism, with a hint of the absolute desperation I was in. He turned to his assistant, "Nancy, you can leave, but just call security and cancel their visit. They have enough to do without us creating more problems for them. I will take it from here." She shot me the most disdainful scowl I've ever seen, but followed Supervisor Casey's orders as I followed him into his office.

My mind was racing, trying to figure out how to create a personal relationship with him in a very limited amount of time before asking him for one of the biggest favors of my life. But before I had a chance to say a word, he gestured to the chair across his desk. "Please sit down and call me Bill!" For such a busy man with so much responsibility to show me such kindness was a complete surprise. "What seems to be such a problem that you had to drive here and almost get arrested, Mr. Jaffe?" he inquired with an amused smile on his face. "Please call me Richard," I began, trying to match his inviting, friendly tone. He nodded.

I explained the entire situation, how there was a mistake but not a violation of the Customs requirement, and asked if he could just take our gloves off the hold list. "The code is very clear and once on the Customs hold list," he patiently explained, "Whether fair or not, you cannot be released without five consecutive containers passing inspection. If one of those five does not pass, then you'll need to pass 10 consecutive inspections to be taken off the list. Also," he continued, "If any medical gloves are on a shipment then the entire shipment is determined to be medical-grade gloves." There were so many containers of poor-quality gloves pouring in from around the world, Supervisor Casey explained, that his team began inspecting every latex glove container that arrived in their port, hence the massive delay in inspections.

I took a moment to empathize with his enormous challenges before gently insisting that there must be a way to find a solution that could keep us in business without upsetting his protocol. Ten minutes of fruitless pleading later, he looked down at his watch. "I need to leave now," he began, with a newfound hint of frustration. "The only possible solution is for you to rent a warehouse inside the Customs zone, move your five containers there with my approval, hire one of three inspectors I give you and have all five containers pass their inspection. Only when they file their inspection report will I have you removed from the Customs hold list, and only then can you begin shipping again."

My heart practically jumped for joy as he continued, "There is nothing I can do to stop your name from being published on the weekly hold list this Friday." Who cared about the damn list, we were still in business! I don't know why he was being so nice to me. Maybe it was dealing with aggressive union representatives all day, maybe he is just an obscenely kind man, but either way, I thanked him profusely and quickly asked for the names and numbers I needed.

I practically danced out the door before driving directly to my parents' house. My father beamed as I relayed what had transpired, clapped me on the back and exclaimed without a hint of surprise, "I knew you would figure it out! You always do." I wish I had as much confidence in my ability as he did. It never seemed to be anything specific I was doing, rather an enormous amount of luck that came my way. But either way, my only worry left was whether the next five containers would pass inspection, or if there could be more than one container with grade C gloves on it.

Since Malaysia was 16 hours ahead of Pacific time, I called CM immediately to verify that only one container had non-medical grade gloves. "Yes, there was only one mixed container," he assured me before apologizing immensely for the mix-up. He had given instructions to ship the non-medical grade gloves on a separate container, but some eager warehouse manager had combined them with a medical shipment in an attempt to get them there faster. "Don't worry Richard, this will not happen again, and I can assure you there will be no problems with any other shipment inspections."

It took about a week to arrange shipping five containers to a warehouse in the Customs zone and another week to get them all inspected. Despite CM's assurances, I was unbelievably nervous for those two weeks until we received the final notice that all five containers had passed inspection, and we were officially removed from the hold list. We sprinted through the last 10 days of the second quarter and were able to ship all the necessary orders to meet our forecasted projections. With another daunting crisis behind us, I turned my attention to getting our company ready for our public offering later that year.

With all business functions running smoothly and a superstar sales team in place, we decided to hold our first sales meeting that summer. This way, our salespeople from around the country could meet each other and share success stories. We still didn't have enough money for anything elaborate, so we rented space at a modest inn in San Diego for our meeting, followed by a company picnic. As much fun and excitement all the new salespeople had meeting each other, it was Brett and Charly who stole the show.

A rambunctious six-year-old, Brett was having a blast throwing around a football and playing tag with all the guys, while adorable little Charly was playing coy and stealing hearts while being passed around from salesperson to salesperson. I don't think her feet ever hit the ground. At four months old, Maxi was living the dream, spending the day sleeping and feeding. Everyone was so excited to be a part of such a special team and there was an electricity in the air that we were all part of something very special about to make waves in the medical device industry.

The factory was running around the clock and I was handling constant emergency calls from Asia, often in the middle of the night. Our sales and office personnel were growing by the week, our large distributors were asking to see me in person and it felt like even if I cloned myself, there wouldn't be enough of me to go around. Little Maxi was still waking up several times a night and there were no sacred moments of silence to be had. So when my father told me we needed to spend a week in New York working with the Smith Barney team on our road show, I was overjoyed. A silent hotel room all to myself? Dreamy.

After kissing Ann and the kids goodbye, I headed off to the airport. Going public was much easier than I anticipated this time around, and the week in New York flew by. The Smith Barney IPO presentations team took notes as Neil, Dad and I took turns explaining our history, products and the finances. I would be the only one to present, they informed us, since most of the questions would focus on strategy and continued sales growth. I couldn't tell if Neil was disappointed, relieved, or both. Either way, Neil agreed that the only goal was to raise the necessary funds for the Thailand factories to support our expansion. As we wrapped up that Friday afternoon, the Smith Barney team thanked us for our time and patience, letting us know we could expect the initial presentation within a week. After a highly productive week, I flew home confident and much more rested.

By Labor Day, business was still growing rapidly, our executive team had expanded and everyone was excited about the public offering. Every employee would receive stock options after 90 days of employment, and with a personal stake in the game, everyone was abuzz about how we would do. The salesforce was especially motivated, as we had promised a 5,000 share stock option award to the number one salesperson for the year. With CM handling all the manufacturing issues and Judy responsible for sales and marketing, Neil, Dad and I were freed up to focus on the IPO.

We still hadn't agreed on a final price with the senior executives at Smith Barney. We told them we needed at least $25 million after expenses to buy the land in Thailand and build our new factory, and were not willing to sell more than 20% of the company. To our surprise, they agreed without hesitation and said it shouldn't be a problem; they just needed to bounce it off a few customers after Labor Day to confirm.

So in mid-September, Neil, Dad and I flew to New York to hammer out the final details of our IPO. It was thrilling, and a little surreal, talking to investment bankers about our success when just three years earlier I'd been fighting off foreclosure notices and clinging to my affirmations for dear life. Now Smith Barney was valuing our company at almost $150 million. It was a moment to savor.

Though I had lived the business and knew our history inside out, I was having trouble getting up in front of a room with the Smith Barney executives to practice the presentation they put together for me. Drained to my core, I couldn't read the presentation with even a remote sense of enthusiasm. Every time I attempted to lift my energy, I forgot my words. My talk was littered with awkward pauses, stuttering and an overall sense of insecurity. While I crushed the question-and-answer portion, the prepared presentation was a trainwreck. I didn't understand what was happening – I usually loved this kind of stuff!

I was completely petrified. What if I choked and no one bought the IPO? What if they liked the story but didn't like me? After all the insanity we'd survived, the idea of my inexplicable stage fright causing SafeSkin's demise was just too much. It was like being a terrified teenager stuck with the high stakes of an IPO; not a combination I would recommend.

Catching the insecurity in my eyes, my dad pulled me aside on one of the breaks. "Listen son, you will do great," he promised, putting his arm around my shoulder. "You know this stuff inside and out. The story will sell itself. The financial numbers are great. Just remember that all the investors are buying is your enthusiasm in the business. If you believe in the business, and I know you do, they will believe in you." He gave me a big squeeze and some paternal assurance. "All you need is a good night's sleep and a microphone and you'll be fine!" I don't know if he believed his pep talk, or was simply trying to move my mind in the right direction, but I chose to buy into it. It's not like I had any other alternative.

It didn't exactly prove to be a quick fix. When the senior Smith Barney executive came in that night to listen to my final presentation, he suggested postponing next morning's roadshow until I was ready. The prep team quickly came to my defense, promising him I'd be fine. This was not their first rodeo and they had worked with plenty of presenters like me before, they assured him. They'd only scheduled one presentation with some friendly investors the first day to give me some practice and were sure that I knew my stuff. Once I had a room full of live investors I would find my voice, they said with an impressive amount of certainty. I envied their enthusiasm.

However, as I listened to the affirmations of my abilities and willed myself to believe them, I could sense the smallest bead of excitement begin to grow. That night, I followed my father's advice for a good night's sleep, began my morning with meditation and some confident affirmations, and told myself I would do the best I could. I detached my mind from anything past that. Talking in front of a crowd has always been fun, I reminded myself.

The next morning, I walked into a small ballroom at a Manhattan hotel, along with 50 or 60 investors clad in expensive suits. After one of the Smith Barney bankers introduced me, I slowly walked up to the podium, quietly repeating to myself, "I am excited! I am excited! I am excited!" As I took the stage, the last thing I saw before looking down at my notes was the concerned face of the senior Smith Barney executive who had advised that we postpone the road show, hovering in the rear doorway. I took a deep breath, let go of all my concerns and brought myself completely to the present moment. I don't know if it was the adrenaline pumping through my veins, my laser-sharp focus or a combination of the two, but as I looked up I was suddenly imbued with a massive wave of confidence. Looking across the audience, my enthusiasm reverberated throughout the room with every word.

I led the investors through our unlikely journey, explaining how we had grown with the customers' overwhelming demand for our hypoallergenic powdered and powder-free gloves while maintaining the highest price and the lowest manufacturing costs in the industry, allowing us to sustain such incredibly high margins. I was having so much fun that I stepped out from behind the podium and continued telling the story from memory. Without reading from a script, I exuded a natural sense of passion and conviction. I was in the zone, what some in modern psychology refer to as "flow," and there couldn't have been a better time for me to hit my stride. The investors were investing in me; all I had to do was gain their trust and respect.

Throughout the 40-minute presentation you could have heard a pin drop on the floor. The investors were hanging on my every word, and I was having so much fun, I didn't want it to end.

As I concluded with the final slide, I looked to the rear doorway as the Smith Barney executive shot me a wink and thumbs up. It was one of the greatest rushes of my life! As we breezed through the question-and-answer period, I was confident and direct, with an immediate answer for each and every question. When we wrapped up the presentation, the investors closed the session with an enthusiastic standing ovation.

My father practically tackled me as I walked off the stage, pulling me into the biggest bear hug. "You were great!" he cried, "I knew you could do it!" Neil gave me a high five, and you could practically feel the relief pouring out from the Smith Barney presentation team. "You were great!" the team leader congratulated me, "I knew you would be fine once you had a real audience, but you truly blew them away. Absolutely nailed it!" I thanked her and gave her a big hug. "Seriously though, thank you," I said. "I could not have done it without your direction and support!"

As we headed back to the hotel, I was relieved and excited. I couldn't wait to call Ann and share the success of the day. "It was incredible," I gushed, "I totally nailed it. All my fear and trepidation evaporated as soon as I walked up to the stage. It was like an energy source from the universe came through my body, and I was just the vessel delivering the message. This crazy 'in the zone' high I had only ever known playing basketball. It felt so incredible, I didn't want it to end!"

She let me have my moment, as I went on and on before interjecting. "That is wonderful! I knew you could do it. Does that mean you sold the entire public offering?" she questioned. "No. This was only the first meeting, but if the others go as well as this one, I'm sure we will be oversold. I can't wait to get up and tell the story again tomorrow!" How quickly my perspective had changed from fear to exhilaration.

The next two weeks were a whirlwind, as we knocked out four or five meetings a day in addition to lunch presentations. I continued to hit on all cylinders, matching my first performance at each and every meeting. We hit New York, Boston, Philadelphia, Chicago, Minneapolis and Kansas City all in the first week alone. Then we circled back to New York, Boston and Philadelphia for those who couldn't catch us the first time, and added in Baltimore for good measure. By the time our roadshow wrapped up, we were oversold; the bankers had two to three times more orders than stock to sell. We tried convincing them to raise the offering price, but they insisted on keeping the price low so their customers could make more money as the stock went up. We would get the money we needed to build the new factory, they reminded us, no need to be greedy. After arguing for a day or two, we finally relented and ended up selling 2.9 million shares at $12 per share, for $30 million after expenses.

As I sat on the surreal flight home, trying to let the reality of it all sink in, I reflected on the craziness of the past few years and how incredibly lucky we were to have gotten here. Things can change so quickly when it comes to making money. In *Think and Grow Rich*, Napoleon Hill compared accumulating money to swimming in a river. Grinding through a startup can often feel like swimming upstream. It's demanding and exhausting, and just when we feel like we can't survive another breath, we hit the crest of the river and start cruising downstream. Money starts flowing so quickly that we ask ourselves, "Where has this money been all this time? How is it so easy now when it was so hard for so long?"

CM Lee guides our board members through our Thai factories.

As we entered 1994, I was less concerned with why the tide had shifted, and more focused on riding the wave of success. Powder-free gloves were becoming the fastest growing category of the latex glove market, growing by an astounding 200% from 1993 to 1994 alone, and SafeSkin represented 96% of the powder-free market. Business was booming with sales exceeding $57 million, and profits coming in at nearly $12 million. Between this and the proceeds of our public offering, we were able to pay down all our debt, return my guarantees along with all the loans and collateral from my family, break ground on new state-of-the-art glove factories in Thailand and expand our salesforce. We introduced several new powder-free latex gloves and our salespeople were on fire, especially with the incentive of stock options now for the top five salespeople of the year.

By this point, we had begun building an incredible culture that truly felt like family. As many of us started having kids around a similar time, families throughout the company vacationed together and built bonds that remain close to this day. Since everyone received stock options, when the company did well, we all did well, adding to our kids' college funds and creating the ability to invest in experiences for our families.

We had also created a new awareness in hospitals of the benefits of powder-free gloves. Our sales team educated lead nurses on the dangers of extended exposure to powdered gloves, leaving them with colorful brochures to share amongst their colleagues. We also displayed at dozens of local and national hospital shows, where nurses could try on our new hypoallergenic, powder-free gloves, their reactions on display for all to see. And they absolutely loved them! Now privy to the possibility of glove protection without powder covering equipment and drying out nurses' skin, hospitals began demanding our powder-free gloves. The unsolicited queries began rolling in from hospitals and distributors alike.

We were shipping millions of latex exam gloves a month by the start of the year, and had entered the lucrative sterile-surgical-glove market with our novel Supra-textured surgical gloves. Though lower in volume, sterile surgical gloves were our highest-margin product and established SafeSkin as a complete player in the glove industry. While weather was rarely a concern for me in sunny San Diego, all of that changed in the spring of 1995. Asia's latex-growing regions experienced the most intense rainfall in memory, continuing strong throughout the summer months as well.

Unfortunately for us, when it rained the tree tappers couldn't extract latex from trees, and the supply of raw latex dwindled just as increasing automobile sales drove up demand for latex rubber tires. With this, raw latex prices skyrocketed to their highest level in 60 years. If we didn't raise our prices, we would lose serious money. While this is something we could possibly weather as a private company, we didn't have wiggle room with public shareholders to answer to. So, as usual, I called my father to discuss our plans.

After I explained the situation, he mulled things over for a minute. "Do you have a choice to raise your prices or not?" he inquired. "No," I said emphatically, "Latex costs are going up not only for us, but for all our competitors. The difference is they have other products to absorb losses, while we only sell gloves." I nervously strummed my fingers along my office windowsill as I waited for his answer. "Well then, it's simple: your only challenge is to get Judy [vice president of Sales] to convince you how to do it. She knows how to execute the price increase much better than you do, so find a way to have it be her idea." My father made everything sound so easy.

I was less convinced, and spent the next few nights tossing and turning. We were already the highest-priced glove in the market and needed a 20% price increase to offset the majority of the increasing latex costs. How the hell were we going to raise our prices by that much and keep growing the business? I knew Judy would be less than thrilled; she and her salesforce were compensated based on cases sold, and a price increase usually meant a reduction in sales. But based on the profit promises we made to Wall Street when we went public, keeping our current prices just wasn't an option. Dad's words of advice kept ringing in my ears: make it her decision and let her convince you how to do it. "Simple," I thought to myself, "Yeah, simple when you're not the one doing it."

The next day I called Judy into my office expecting a struggle. When she sat down I spent a little time catching up on family and life before getting down to business. "Everything is running so smoothly! Customers love us, we've got amazing momentum with the sales team," she glowed, "So tell me why on earth do you look like someone just killed your favorite pet?" Guess I didn't have much of a poker face here. I took a deep breath and explained. "Unprecedented monsoon rains have hit all latex suppliers in Asia and our cost of latex has doubled. We're talking about the highest latex prices in 60 years. I'm working to negotiate lower prices, but we're having trouble getting enough latex to make our forecasts. It seems like either we pay these higher prices or we don't get enough latex to produce all the gloves we need."

The excited smile on her face quickly changed to a calculating frown. "What does this mean for our customers?" she asked. "We need at least a 20% price increase within 30 days," I quietly replied. "Twenty percent in 30 days?!" she howled as she stood up and paced the room, "Are you kidding me?" I could see her mind racing through the details of it all, and how our customers would respond. "I have done 5%, and even 10% price increases before, but never 20%. Are you sure we need that much?" she pushed back.

I nodded affirmatively, and she quickly understood our predicament. "Is this part of the commitment we made to our investors when we went public?" she asked, much more calmly this time. "Yes, but more importantly, it is the right thing to do for our business. Our competitors will have to follow suit at some point, so we are better off as leaders in the market educating our customers why this is necessary," I explained. "Once you explain the details and they check your facts, they will eventually accept it, even if they don't like it." Much to my surprise and delight, Judy didn't hesitate or question me for a moment. "I will be back to you tomorrow with a plan on how we'll execute a 20% price increase without losing any business!" she promised, "And I'll come with a list of which customers we'll need you to speak with directly." What a weight off my chest! Moments of crisis and hardship are when we can truly gauge the capabilities of staff and colleagues, and in this moment I could not feel more grateful to have Judy by my side.

The next day she presented a detailed plan exactly as I had requested, with a small caveat that every customer have an opportunity to place one reasonably sized order at current pricing before the price increase went into effect. Though we definitely got a considerable amount of push back, our salesforce executed the plan perfectly, even managing to pick up some new business at existing prices before the price hike went into effect. While our profits took a hit from the pricing pressure, revenues for the year grew to $117 million, and *Forbes Magazine* rated us America's best small company of 1995, based on five-year return on equity. While the business charged ahead, we were beginning to hear rumblings throughout the industry that many nurses were breaking out with rashes from extended exposure to latex. No one knew if it was an allergic reaction to the chemicals and proteins in the gloves, or the actual latex itself. With a customer-centric focus throughout the company, our customer-facing teams made sure this news was passed on. Although our powder-free glove had pretty much denatured the allergenic-inducing protein in latex, meaning the reactions weren't happening with our gloves, there was still this nagging fear of latex-made products.

Prioritizing this urgent customer need, our senior executives tasked our research and development team to create a comfortable and cost-effective alternative to the latex glove. After a variety of unsuccessful attempts, our team developed a medical-exam glove made from nitrile, a petroleum-based derivative. After we introduced the purple nitrile glove, it quickly became the gold standard in the industry and accounts for more than half of the gloves used in hospitals in the United States.

This incredible innovation started with a very serious problem, one that continued to haunt us. But the key to our success wasn't in avoiding undue blame. Yes, as a hypoallergenic product our gloves weren't the root of these reactions. But there was a budding problem in the industry, and our success was in addressing it early – quickly skating towards where the puck was going to be.

CHAPTER 15

NEW EXPANSIONS

Though I was still enjoying running a successful public company, it was about this time I realized I needed to start planting the seeds for our eventual sale. Business was still good, but it was getting harder and harder to keep growing revenue and profits at expected rates with only gloves. And with a rising number of lower-cost, lower-quality, powder-free gloves entering the market, hospitals were putting the pressure on us to slash our prices. Planting the seed early would enable me to have an educated buyer that trusted me and understood our organization when the time was right.

So beginning in 1995 and continuing every year, I made it a point at annual industry conventions to spend time with John Metz, the president of Kimberly-Clark Medical, the leading gown manufacturer. With noncompeting products and all of the same customers, we shared our thoughts on the challenges of the medical industry, bemoaning distributors' rising power and subsequent demand for more marketing dollars and greater rebates for themselves. But most of our conversation centered on the common needs of our customers and distributors, and every year I reinforced my belief that our joint customers wanted to buy gloves, masks and gowns together from one source.

For the rest of 1996, the accolades kept on coming as we became the clear leader of the latex exam glove market, climbing up to 24% market share. Baxter Healthcare, our top competitor, had dropped to 18%. By the end of 1996, revenues had grown to $150 million and our stock price had almost tripled from our IPO three years prior. While all this success was great, we were concerned that our stock price had risen so high that it would deter some smaller investors from buying it. So in November, we announced a two-for-one stock split of our common shares to get more shares in the market at a lower price, just one week after the company's addition to the Standard and Poor's *SmallCap 600*.

Business was good, but I still never strayed from my habit of visiting our largest customers to ask how things were going, and if they had any needs that weren't being met. Throughout these conversations, one repeating theme became clear – our customers wanted to buy their gloves, masks and gowns as one bundle from the same company. Ease and convenience.

By 1997, I was actively planting the seed that Kimberly-Clark should buy the entire SafeSkin company some day. John immediately picked up on my intent, and while he congratulated me on a job well done, gloves were just a commodity in his eyes and he couldn't justify paying over a billion dollars for a commodity company. By that time, SafeSkin's valuation had climbed to over two billion dollars. I pointedly disagreed, pointing out that commodities didn't carry margins in excess of 60%. Either way, he heard my message loud and clear and, unbeknownst to him, I learned the highest price he might someday consider paying for SafeSkin! The next year, Kimberly-Clark bought Technol, the leading mask manufacturer, so I knew there was a good chance that we were probably next.

While SafeSkin continued growing at a breakneck pace, things at home were about to get even more hectic. Ann came home floating through the doorway one evening and proudly announced, "You are looking at the newest president of the San Diego Jewish Academy!" She bounced around the kitchen practically bursting with excitement. While Ann had always been involved at our children's elementary school, I had no idea of her ambitions to lead it. I shared my surprise and enthusiasm for her new role, inquiring how long she'd been thinking about it.

"It's something I've wanted to do for a while, but I didn't want to bother you when SafeSkin was struggling so badly. Now that things are going well, I figured I could take some more time out for this – is that OK with you?" Her sparkling brown eyes melted my heart as only her gaze could. "In terms of timing, in another two years it would be ideal," I admitted honestly, "But you've made more sacrifices for me than I could ever ask for, so I'll find a way to be at home a bit more. We'll make it work! My only advice is that you've got two years to make an impact, so pick one major project to accomplish, one legacy to leave. But first, tell me more about the school you're about to lead!" I placed my full presence and focus on my beautiful, ambitious wife with genuine curiosity. The school was doing great, she bragged. Renting space from two different synagogues, they had classes from kindergarten through 8th grade and served 500 students from around the county. Though the facilities weren't great, with tiny classrooms and parking lots for playgrounds, the teachers were top-notch and there was a waiting-list to get in. Serving on the board of one of the synagogues, I knew their rent was going up considerably the next year. "Honey, is your rent going up?" I inquired. "Yes," she replied with a quizzical look in her eyes. "Are your other expenses going up?" I continued. "Yes," her brow furrowed. "Are your teacher salaries rising?" I gently asked, sensing her displeasure. "Yes," she snapped, clearly impatient with this line of questioning. "And can you increase your enrollment or raise the tuition?" I finally asked. "No, absolutely not!" she agitatedly fired back.

"Where is this questioning going? I thought you were happy for me!" she accused, feeling attacked when she was expecting congratulations and support. "I am," I assured her, giving her a loving squeeze. "I just want to point out that your expenses are rising rapidly and you can't raise your revenues, so without some sort of action, it's just a matter of time before the school goes broke. Think things over, and then let's talk about what you can do about it." Her anger dissipated and the color drained from her face, as she wisely recognized the predicament the school was in. The next week, Ann sat me down to talk about the school.

She had decided on the legacy she wanted to leave. "It all made so much sense what you pointed out last week, and I would have never seen it myself. The only sustainable solution is to build our own campus. By combining the two locations, we can consolidate the overhead and provide a lasting home of Jewish education for all of San Diego!" I was taken aback. While the current situation wasn't tenable, I never imagined Ann would think this big. Just as I was trying to figure out the best way to tell her it was too big an undertaking for her alone, she interrupted my thoughts. "I know I can't do it alone, so if you'll buy the land, arrange the financing and raise all the money, I will do all the building and hiring necessary to leave a wonderful legacy for the both of us!"

I looked in awe at the beautifully intelligent woman I married. She figured out exactly what was needed and knew I couldn't refuse her request to leave a legacy together. But with the responsibility of running a public company, I knew this was a bigger undertaking than she let on. "How many acres are we looking at, and how much money do we need to raise?" I asked, knowing that I already was sucked into agreeing. "We only need six to eight acres and 12 to 14 million dollars. We've already scoped out a piece of land across from the Jewish Community Center; it's really no big deal!" she assured me with a confident smile on her face. "That shouldn't be too big a challenge with all the philanthropic people we know in town," I acquiesced, "Let me look into it." Ann didn't ask for much, and I knew resisting that adorable smile was useless so I accepted my fate without a second thought. "I love you so much!" she shouted with glee as she jumped into my arms, giving me a big hug and kiss.

The land she had found was no longer on the market, but she didn't miss a beat, assuring me she would put together a committee to explore other options. One month later, after an exhaustive search, there was only one piece of land that fit their requirements. "It's a combination of two parcels, one owned by a Holocaust survivor and the other by a real estate company," she said, as if it were already bought. "That's great, how big is it?" I inquired. "A bit bigger than we'd initially scoped." Her tone of voice did not bode well. "How much bigger?" I asked cautiously, with a preemptive wince. "It's a combined 42 acres, but I'm told we have to leave 25% as open land." My heart sank; I had already agreed to front the money for the land. "And this is the absolute only option?" I asked. "It's the only one," she assured me. I reminded myself of the unending sacrifices Ann had made over the years and mentally accepted the newfound magnitude of this undertaking.

After weeks of negotiations, I had no problem securing an option on the smaller parcel from the holocaust survivor, who was excited to see a Jewish day school on his property. Negotiating for the second piece of land was not nearly as smooth. Not by a long shot. It was owned by a company in Orange County called Greystone, run by a man with the name of Jon Jaffe, though no relation to me. My assistant, Maripat, booked an appointment, and the following week I made the hour drive north to see him.

With smart, yet casual attire and handsome looks to go with it, Jon was the picture of poise and confidence. Extremely cordial, he listened attentively to my request to buy the property for our school before politely assuring me he would never sell me the land. It was his first real estate deal in San Diego County and he was not about to give up this incredible show piece, complete with an ocean view. Despite all my best efforts, Jon kindly showed me the door and asked never to hear from me about this property again. While dejected at having to disappoint Ann, I understood his position, and quite frankly, would have done the same. Back at home, once we finished dinner and put the kids to sleep, I sat Ann down to break the bad news to her.

The exuberant energy dancing across her face made starting the conversation that much harder. "I tried everything I could," I assured her, "But he has plans for 45 high-end homes there and insisted that nothing is going to deter him. It looks like it's time to find a plan B." The color drained from her face, but her resolution stayed strong. "There is no plan B, Richard. We scoured the entire county and that is the only location that will work. This was only your first no, and I know you better than to accept that." She had been my closest friend and confidant through much larger obstacles, and knew how to speak my language. "If you do one thing for me throughout the rest of our lives, BUY THAT LAND! I don't care what it takes!" She was nearly in tears as she pleaded. My heart broke in seeing her so deeply dismayed, but how could I tell her she was asking for the impossible? I jumped next to her, holding her in a tight embrace as I assured her I would try again. "But you should still work on a backup plan," I warned, "Just in case."

For the next few days, Maripat tried to make another appointment for me to see Jon, but to no avail. After a few tries, his assistant pleaded with Maripat to stop calling. She had been instructed not to give me an appointment, and nothing Maripat did or said would change that. Jon wasn't the top of the food chain, I realized after a few days of thought, and it was worth a try to see if I could go over his head. As it turned out, Greystone was owned by Lennar, a large, public, home-builder company headquartered in Miami, and Jon reported to its president, Stuart Miller. I called up my good YPO friend Alan, who was active in the Miami business world, to explain my situation and see if he could help get me an appointment to talk to Stuart.

"Not only do I know Stuart," he happily informed me, "But he is a good friend – our families even vacation together! He is pretty consumed with a divorce right now, but I'm sure I could get you a call." Jaffe luck strikes again! "Fantastic, thank you so much, Alan. Please arrange for him to call me this week at his convenience." I would keep my fingers crossed, hoping I could pull off another miracle.

I had to travel to visit customers the rest of the week, but left specific instructions for Maripat to see if I could visit Stuart at his office in Miami next week, and if he refused, to get me a phone call with him on Sunday. Two days later, Stuart called my office and spoke with Maripat. "Mr. Miller, it is so kind of you to call," she greeted him. "Mr. Jaffe is traveling this week, but is giving a speech in Chicago next week and would love to stop by and see you on his way home. Are you available next Wednesday?" He chuckled, "Tell Mr. Jaffe that Miami is not on the way back from Chicago, and I only agreed to this phone call as a favor for Alan. There is less than a 1% chance he can buy the property, so tell him it would be wise not to waste his time."

Maripat listened respectfully and happily replied, "Congratulations, Mr. Miller, you just sold that property to him!" She was an incredibly smart and ballsy woman, part of why we got along so well. "You didn't hear me correctly, young lady, I said less than 1% chance he could buy it." Stuart insisted. "No I heard you correctly," she assured him, "You just don't know Richard at all. If there is even a 1% chance to buy the land, he will make a deal. If a meeting won't work, will you at least talk to him by phone this Sunday?" she inquired, just as I had instructed. "Of course. Have him call me at 10 a.m. sharp my time, and I will give him 10 minutes maximum." Maripat had done her job. Now it was my turn to figure out how to get Stuart to help me buy the land.

I sat down early Sunday morning with a strong cup of coffee, racking my brain about how I could convince Stuart to help me. Nothing came to mind. As the clock inched closer towards my appointment, I figured my best shot was to find a way to connect heart to heart, and then just ask for help. Asking good questions and listening was my strategy, but with only 10 minutes I had to find a way to create a connection quickly so he would agree to extend the conversation. As the clock struck seven, I picked up the phone and dialed Stuart.

"Good morning! Stuart speaking," a deep and kind voice greeted me. "Hi Stuart, this is Richard Jaffe, Alan's good friend. Thank you so much for taking the time to speak with me, especially on a Sunday morning." I responded, matching his warm tone. "Ah, any friend of Alan is a friend of mine," he said, "But I hate to inform you that there is not much I can do to help you." He cut straight to the chase; this was going to be more difficult than I thought. "Jon Jaffe runs our California operations, and he can do whatever he wants to do. He doesn't miss his financial projections, and I don't get involved in how he runs the business. We are a public company, so you know how it goes," he stated matter-of-factly. "Given all this, what would you like me to do?"

I took the next five minutes quickly summarizing why we

needed to buy the land for the school, that there was no other acceptable land nearby and that I was willing to pay market price for it. Nothing seemed to move Stuart. Time was running out, so I decided to pivot and play on his heart strings, hoping his divorce proceedings hadn't hardened him. "Stuart, I've been married 13 years to an angel of a woman. She is the president of our local Jewish day school, and it is her heart and soul. When I told her we had to find another property to build the school on, she broke down crying (I exaggerate a little) and told me, 'If you do anything for me for the rest of our lives, buy that land!' That is why I am calling you asking for help." Then I shut up, and just waited for his response. An uneasy silence settled over the phone line, but I was determined not to talk first.

Finally Stuart responded. "Despite my divorce, I still believe in the power and beauty of marriage," he began, "I will do something for you that I have never done for anyone before. I will call Jon Jaffe and instruct him to meet with you again. After that you are on your own. He can give you the land for free, charge you as much as he wants or not sell it to you at all. He has the final say on all properties in California and regardless of what he decides to do with you, he still has to meet his forecasted projections."

I didn't know what to say. That was exactly what I wanted to get out of the call. "Stuart, thank you so much. That is all I could ever ask from you. We really do appreciate it. I hope I can repay your kindness some day!" I thanked him. "Good luck with your school and good luck with your marriage. It sounds like you will need it for both!" he kiddingly remarked. Stunned but ecstatic, I sat back to appreciate what just happened. Alan's friendship was crucial, and I was incredibly grateful my appeal to Stuart's emotional side worked. Now I had to figure out how to convince Jon to sell me the land for a reasonable price.

The next day, Maripat called the Greystone offices and was greeted warmly by Jon's assistant, who promptly asked when I would like to come in. Stuart was good to his word. I was booked in for Wednesday morning, and spent the whole ride up struggling to determine the best way to approach Jon. He was a businessman first and Jewish second, so I was hoping he would have a soft spot for a Jewish day school as long as he got paid enough to make his financial projections. My challenge was to get him to accept the lowest possible price for the land he said he'd never sell.

I knew it would take more than one meeting; I just had to find a way to get the negotiations started. When I entered Jon's office, he greeted me with a smile. "Good morning, Richard. I have to give you credit. You are creatively persistent. Not many people could have gotten back in front of me, but I'm sorry to say you are still wasting your time – I am not selling you that land. It is my San Diego showpiece, my launching pad into that market." "Good morning to you too, Jon, and thank you for agreeing to see me again though I know you really didn't want to," I smiled in return. "That's not true," he objected. "I enjoyed our last meeting and would happily see you anytime you like; I just won't sell you the piece of land you are requesting. What don't you understand about the word no?" he teased. "Jon, you are going to be selling me that piece of property so we may as well start talking about it," I said, game face on. "How can you be so sure?" he asked, perplexed by my undying confidence. "Let me explain," I began, "You already told me you plan to build 45 luxury homes on that site. If I offered to pay you full price today for all 45 homes, would you sell me the land?" I asked, knowing the answer I'd receive.

"That's a ridiculous question – you would never do that!" he countered. "But if I were willing to pay that price, would you sell me the land?" I pressed. "I guess so, but what does that have to do with our discussion?" he asked with a quizzical look on his face. "This proves that there is a number somewhere between full price and zero that I can buy the land for. So let's start talking about the deductions – risks of permitting, time to build and sell, cost of money – that would make it worth your while to take a lower price from me today!"

He paused, slowly conceding to my logic. "You are right. There probably is a number I will accept. But if you are so smart, tell me how we get to a fair number that you are willing to pay," he challenged, realizing he was already sucked into the negotiations. "My suggestion is that you run your pro forma numbers for the project as if you were buying the land, not selling it, discount it at a reasonable interest rate for getting paid today instead of several years from now, reduce it again for the risk assessment and let me know what current value of the project you come up with," I shared, matter-of-factly. "Then we can start talking about a deal." He looked up at me with a newfound sense of respect. "That makes a lot of sense. Shouldn't be too hard for my team to run the numbers. I'll have them sent to you by the end of the week. Make an appointment to come back next week and we'll go from there." I did a mental victory dance as he continued, "Is there anything else I can help you with today? I'm heading in to back-to-back meetings and have an important phone call with Stuart. I will send him your regards," he kidded me as he showed me the door. "Thank you and I will see you next week!" I chided as I just about skipped out of his office with an extra bounce in my step.

I was floating on air the whole ride back to my office. While I had no idea what the calculations would come to, I knew the first round was sure to be way too high. But I gave myself a moment to bask in the pride of finishing the meeting with hope still intact. When I explained everything to Ann at home that night, she was over the moon. "I knew you could do it, I knew you would come through!" she exclaimed, jumping up and down. "Calm down, honey. We've got a long way to go, and we may be millions of dollars apart. I'll have a better idea when I get his calculations next week, but for now at least it's not dead." Before I could finish my last words she came bounding into my arms for a massive hug, squeezing me as tight as she could.

"I know you. Jon doesn't stand a chance negotiating with you!" she sang as she danced around the room. "Promise me you won't say anything to anyone until the deal is officially done," I demanded, trying to look stern faced. "I promise, but it doesn't matter since I already know the outcome. Hurry up, will you?" she chided. Somehow, I knew it wasn't going to be as easy as she thought.

The next few days flew by with SafeSkin customer visits and sales meetings to attend. Though buying the land was very important, I couldn't let it distract me from the massive responsibilities of running SafeSkin. Monday morning when I came into the office, Maripat welcomed me and said Jon Jaffe's office would be sending over the papers shortly. An uneasy feeling started forming in my stomach. And as I flipped through the pages my concerns were confirmed: he'd sent over a $9.5 million asking price.

I almost choked as I thumbed back through the document. They had taken all the highest possible values for themselves and it was nowhere near fair. I instructed Maripat to make me an appointment for Wednesday morning, and this time I was mad. Either Jon didn't give them instructions to use fair numbers, he told them to get the highest value possible or he was being cute starting the negotiations as high as he could, knowing I would hammer him down. Either way, the chances of agreement weren't looking good. I was willing to pay up to $7 million if necessary, but I was much more comfortable with a price of $6.5 million. I made up my mind to give it my best shot and if we couldn't cut a deal, Ann would have to find a way to work something else out. There had to be more reasonably priced land in San Diego the school could use.

Wednesday morning I drove up to Jon's office once more, confident but concerned. I had a feeling it would either be decided that morning or not at all. Jon greeted me with his familiar smile and open arms. Despite my recent frustrations, I had come to like him very much and meeting with him felt like talking with an old friend – something extremely rare in negotiations. "Good morning, Richard. I am really pressed for time so can we get right down to business? Did you get our calculations and are you in agreement on the price?"

He really did get right to the point. "Yes and no," I replied, diving right in. "I received them, but all your calculations were way too high. I asked you to look at it as if you were buying the land, not selling it. Your interest rate of money was unreasonable, your cap rate was way off and you didn't discount anything for the risk you are taking with the coastal commission and planning board." I was going to make him acknowledge each unfair calculation. "What about the value of the money today versus several years from now if you have to permit and go through the building process? Let's go over the numbers together and come up with a win/win for both of us," I implored.

That was my best shot. A suspenseful silence hung in the air, one reminiscent of that first customer back in my father's appliance store, debating whether or not to buy the TV. But this time Jon agreed quickly. He called in Todd, his top executive who had run the calculations, and we spent the next hour going over assumption by assumption. After we finally agreed on drastic changes to most of the unfair projections, Todd left the room, returning 10 minutes later with revised numbers. Much to both our surprise, the calculations came to $6.8 million dollars for the property. Jon looked stunned. "Are you sure these numbers are correct?" he sternly inquired. "Yes," Todd confirmed without hesitation, "These are in line with the lower forecast we had put together for you." Jon thanked Todd for his help, and it was back to just us.

He slowly turned to me and I thought he was going to kick me out. "This price is much lower than I had intended," he began in an accusatory tone, "But I am willing to sell you the land just as we agreed. Are you willing to pay this amount?" he asked, rather unpleased but resigned. I was already ecstatic but decided to take one more shot. Jon had a kind heart and his kids went to a local Jewish day school, so I decided to see if I could push him just once more. "I agree to the value of the property. It seems completely fair but I've got one last request."

I took a deep breath and continued, "I need you to deduct $500K as a donation to Jewish education for the children of San Diego. The school can't afford your price, but they really need the land. How about we pay $6.3 million and you have the honor of doing a wonderful *mitzvah* (good deed) in giving our children the opportunity to flourish in a permanent campus, just like yours are today?" I asked with an open heart, hoping that bringing in Jewish children would move him. He looked back at me, astonished. I hadn't thought this through in the slightest, but followed my gut. Trying for $6 million seemed like too big a stretch, but $6.3 million was right at the edge of reasonable.

Just when I thought the suspense would kill me, he finally responded. "That is a big ask. Let me think about it and call you over the weekend." He kept my gaze as he shook my hand goodbye. I sensed his resistance, but if there wasn't something in him that knew it was right, he would've turned me down on the spot. I thanked him profusely and reminded him what an incredible legacy he would be leaving.

The whole ride home I was beaming. Worst case scenario, he refused to deduct another penny and I got a price I could live with. I couldn't wait to get home to share the good news with Ann. When I walked through the door, three wild, screaming kids jumped on me as I avoided any elbows to the face on the bottom of the dogpile. "OK all three of you get up right away and go wash your hands for dinner," Ann shouted at them as they giggled and used me like a personal jungle gym. "Listen to your mother right away," I instructed, putting on my not-so-stern tone. When it came to parenting, I generally got to play the good cop. "I'm commercial, your mother is domestic," I reminded the kids whenever they came to me about rules and permission, usually after their mother had said no.

As soon as they left the room, she went straight in for the update. "How did it go with Jon? Do we have the property?" I stood up and gave her a big squeeze. "It went very well, he was more than reasonable and will call back with his answer this weekend. We'll know within a week, you just have to be patient," I cautioned her, not wanting to set high expectations in case Jon changed his mind. The next few days my thoughts of the property dissipated during the day as I ran from meeting to meeting, but it was the only thing Ann wanted to talk about when I got home at night.

Jon called me back that weekend while I was at a family barbecue. "Richard! It's Jon. Is this a good time to talk?" I quickly gathered my thoughts and asked for a minute to find a quiet space. "Ah, much better," I commented as I closed the door behind me. "I can hear you now. What have you decided?"

"Well, first I have to say you've got some pretty big balls asking for a half-million dollar donation after negotiating the price down over two million dollars," he exclaimed, leaving space for a response. But I decided that I had done all my selling in his office and was better off letting him talk. That nervous excitement of a big sale began fluttering about my stomach, but I bit my tongue and waited. Finally, when he realized I wasn't going to say anything, he surprised me. "Richard, I would be proud to make a $500,000 donation to your school. You are going to have to raise a lot more money to build it, but based on our interactions I have no doubt you'll be able to achieve it. I will have our attorneys draw up the papers and send them to you next week."

I couldn't believe my ears! It took everything in me not to start jumping up and down right then. "Jon, you are a gentleman and a *mensch* (person of integrity and noble character). I can't thank you enough, my wife thanks you too! You are truly incredible – enjoy the rest of your weekend!" I hung up, ran into the other room, picked up Ann and swung her around as I shouted, "We got the land! We got the land!" There were plenty of bumps in the road still ahead, but with Ann's leadership, a generous donation from my parents and incredibly hard work by dozens of dedicated volunteers, the new campus opened its doors in September 2000. Unfortunately, the future was not as bright for SafeSkin.

THE FALL

As SafeSkin continued to grow rapidly throughout 1997, our sales skyrocketed even without enough gloves to expand past our current customers. Organizations wanted our powder-free gloves so much, they were willing to get on a waiting-list that might take nine months to deliver. I always operated under the premise that we had a revenue crisis and kept pushing our salesforce forward, signing up new customers to be ready and waiting for our gloves once the new machines came online. Demand for powder-free latex gloves exploded and grew even larger than we had forecasted. That is when we strayed from one of our original manufacturing principles.

From the very beginning, we had always built numerous smaller, flexible machines, improving efficiency with each generation. Though more expensive and less efficient than a large machine, we were experts in building them and if one machine broke down – which they often did – we could still produce gloves on the others. But with the billions of gloves we were now churning out each year and rising pressure to lower our prices, Neil and CM wanted to build one massive, state-of-the-art, glove-manufacturing machine that would drastically increase our efficiency. It didn't make any sense to me. Any potential hiccup in production would delay our deliveries, opening the door for our competitors to swoop in. They'd been aggressively trying to steal away our new and existing customers with everything they could. Given the competitive landscape, I explained, the risk just didn't seem worth it.

But they had almost finished designing a cutting-edge machine – the Grand Master. Clocking in at two stories high and the length of a football field, it could produce a million gloves per day at a significantly lower cost than our smaller machines. Neil and CM were ecstatic about the design and efficiency, and committed to have it up and running in early 1998, just after the last batch of the smaller machines they were currently building would be finished. "Neil, I don't think you understand the size of the demand we're creating," I warned. "We already have sold all the production off the new, smaller machines and if the Grand Master is delayed even just a little while, it will allow our competitors to fill those orders instead of us."

"Don't worry about a disruption in supply," Neil assured me, "On the contrary, this will increase our glove production faster than building more smaller machines would." But I just wasn't sold. "CM, do you agree?" I asked pointedly. He paused thoughtfully, "There is no guarantee when designing and building a new machine, but I am highly confident that Neil is correct and this is the right thing to do." I wasn't sure if I felt better or worse after CM's response. At this point, they then walked me through the design and answered every question with facts and confidence. Unbeknownst to me, they had also already ordered the initial steel to get started.

The following morning I called my father and explained the situation to get his take. "I understand your trepidation and I don't want you to slow down selling, but manufacturing is Neil's final decision. Just like he deferred to you on final sales and marketing decisions, I think you need to trust him and CM to deliver in their area of expertise," he said. "But we have zero, I mean absolutely zero margin for error," I pointed out. "They're amazing at what they do, but what they do is build smaller glove machines. I don't like throwing all these unknowns in here."

I seemed to be the odd man out, so after voicing my protests, I begrudgingly agreed to stay out of the manufacturing decisions. Neil, CM and their teams started building the Grand Master, and I went back to focusing on our salesforce and taking care of our customers. As revenues climbed to record levels, the SafeSkin stock price continued to soar. In early 1998, the SafeSkin board announced another two-for-one stock split to lower the stock price a second time. With ambitious growth projections and customers lined up to buy all the gloves we could make, it was perfect timing for our new Grand Master to get in the game.

On the day of Grand Master's big launch, I nervously waited for Neil's call with an update on how things went. But it never came. Another day went by, still nothing. With my anxiety mounting, I decided to check in. When I called the factory and asked for Neil, the operator informed me he had been on the floor with CM working all night and would call me later. Shit, I thought, this isn't good. I didn't realize how *not* good things were until Neil finally called me back the next day. "What problem could be so big that you couldn't even call me back?" I barked before he even had a chance to talk. "Well good morning to you too! The reason I didn't call you back is because we have not been able to start up yet," he calmly explained.

"We haven't been able to synchronize the long, continuous chain with all the motors on the machine, and some of them keep shutting down. It's only a matter of time until we figure it out, but I can't give you a definitive estimate of when that might be." His even tone didn't damper the panic his words engendered. "We're running at full capacity in both Thailand and Malaysia, and that is all the gloves you can count on until further notice." I felt like I'd been punched in the gut. With the sales team on full blast, we could only last a week or two without the Grand Master up and running before having to decide which customers to stop serving. For the next two weeks we had daily updates, but nothing changed. Neil and CM brought in chain advisors and experts from around the world, but no one could figure out how to keep the machine moving. I was lamenting our preventable fiasco to my father one evening, when he gently cut off my wallowing. "If your problem is in Thailand, why don't you just go there and get it fixed?" I hadn't thought of that. I didn't know if I could add anything useful, but I definitely wasn't helping being in the U.S.

That night as we lay awake in bed talking, I explained the situation to Ann. As usual, she and my father agreed. "What is the downside of going to the source of your problem and seeing if you could help? A fresh perspective can sometimes be quite helpful, and at the very least you'll get a first-hand understanding of the problem." I thought long and hard about what she said and realized she was right. "What are you hesitating about?" she asked.

"Thailand is so far away and I have so many challenges here in the U.S. and customers to talk to," I explained. "I was just trying to figure out how I could resolve this without flying all the way over there. But you are right, I need to get to the source of the issue and understand what it will take and how long it might be before we're up and running. Every day counts!" The next day, I packed a week's worth of clothes and hopped on a flight to Thailand.

Heading straight from the airport to the factory, I was greeted by an exhausted Neil and CM. They walked me through the machine with great detail, along with all the fixes they had tried. There didn't seem to be a quick answer, and the more they talked, the larger the problem seemed. CM assured me that engineering-wise it should work, so it was just a matter of time until the fine-tuning and motor synchronization kicked in. They would get things running as soon as possible, he promised, but still couldn't provide a projection date of when that might be.

After two days of watching and listening to all the so-called experts suggesting different methods to try, I realized I was not contributing in the slightest, so I returned to the U.S. to devise a plan on how we'd communicate this with our customers. Somehow we needed to convince our new customers to continue waiting on us until the Grand Master was up and running.

The problem was, we had done such a good job educating our customers about the virtues of powder-free gloves that they felt compelled to try our competitors' versions in the meantime. While they agreed these were not as good as ours, they were still more desirable than powdered ones. The demand we had created for the SafeSkin powder-free gloves was now being filled by the lower-quality, lower-priced competitors' products. It was my worst fears come true.

With all the continued financial pressure hospitals were facing, I knew it would be very difficult to convince them to go back to our higher-cost gloves after months of huge savings on acceptable replacements. But we didn't just sit around waiting for our glove supply to come back. Instead, we put together an aggressive sales plan to attack the problem immediately, and try to hold on to our existing customers. To every customer whose shipment we delayed, we offered a 20% discount for their first 90 days after re-engaging. We made frequent visits to our major customers, focusing on maintaining the relationships we had built. Despite shipping out the powder-free gloves from our traditional, smaller machines, we were never able to fill our customers' orders completely, and hoped they'd replace the difference with SafeSkin powdered gloves. Though it worked for a month or two, without being able to tell them exactly when more powder-free gloves would be available, we slowly began losing customers week by week.

Though not having enough money to pay our bills in the past was exceedingly stressful, so was not having enough gloves to supply to our current customers. Seeing all the hard work and major hospital glove conversions that our salespeople had accomplished start to crumble before my very eyes was beyond disheartening. With long hours and a heavy heart, I needed to find some way to put balance back into my life. When I finally was able to go home, Ann and I would take long walks on the beach, holding hands and talking about the kids, the house – anything but the business. Her love and affection was like a warm spring shower washing away the day's worries and fears. But by the next morning, the phone calls resumed and pressure was back on.

Our powerful salesforce was distraught too. They had worked so hard to acquire and maintain these accounts. Their commission checks, which had been growing monthly, leveled off. To keep them motivated I had continual conference calls with each region, assuring our teams that this challenge was only temporary, using the personal relationships I'd built to ask for patience. I reached out to a few of the original "dirty dozen" salespeople, hoping they could convince the newer salespeople to be patient and ride out the shortage situation, but they too were hungry for answers.

I decided to maintain the sales commission payments at the level they had achieved before our supply shortage to boost morale. But the lack of supply wasn't even the biggest issue; it was not knowing when our shortage would end. Without Judy at the helm of sales (she'd left the year before), I found myself totally immersed in the details. Even once we did have powder-free gloves flowing again, I knew that many of the customers we had set up to buy them would not be waiting for us. The aura we had created in the industry, that SafeSkin was far and away the best powder-free glove, was quickly being dispelled by our competitors. Hospitals could save tens of thousands of dollars each month by switching to their powder-free gloves, and lower quality became acceptable when it came with such massive savings.

Six months after the original startup date for the Grand Master, Neil, CM and their team of consultants finally figured out how to synchronize the chain and motors, and the gloves started flowing even faster than originally forecasted. However, they didn't begin filling our warehouses until September and by then, the damage was done. While most customers we had managed to continue supplying stayed with us, many newer customers switched to competitor brands. With commitments through the end of the year, the few that were willing to switch back would only do so after the new year if we could offer a better deal. I had seen the problem coming, but it was one of those situations where there was not much else we could have done without a time machine.

Celebrations of momentary relief, as the Grand Master was completed in the spring of 1998.

With the stress of finding enough gloves to supply our customers quickly dwindling, I could see the pendulum was about to swing drastically in the opposite direction. With the Grand Master in full gear, our capacity exceeded 500 million gloves per month and oversupply was a real threat. It would not be easy to find enough customers to buy the tidal wave of gloves coming our way given how many customers we had lost. As Ann and I continued our regular walks on the beach, I shared my concerns with her and, as usual, she managed to ask the most insightful questions.

Taking my mind off the problem and onto future solutions, she was an invaluable sounding board and deserves a great deal of credit for helping me think through many of our greatest challenges. At the end of every walk, we would stop, wrap our arms around each other and take some time to watch the waves crash on the beach, giving thanks for how lucky we were. Rather than forgetting about the hard times, we used the memory of foreclosure and personal-guarantee notices to maintain a sense of gratitude. With a good dose of perspective and my best friend by my side, all the troubles in life couldn't bog me down.

Though our stock price continued to rise with our revenues, and we had somewhat tempered growth expectations, the pressure to find new customers was intensifying each month. We devised several special promotions to entice large hospital purchases and managed to reel in a decent amount of new customers scheduled to switch at the new year. The year ended on an optimistic note as our manufacturing challenges were finally behind us and our warehouses and distributors were stocked with powder-free gloves. We just needed to turn the sales faucet back on and convince hospitals that SafeSkin powder-free gloves were the only gloves they needed. We knew it wouldn't be easy, and needed something to rejuvenate the sales team.

We decided to take the entire sales and marketing team, 75 strong, to our Thailand factories for the early February sales meeting. While there were concerns about putting the sales team on pause for 10 days, we felt witnessing the production process firsthand would send them home with the excitement and passion needed to recapture our sales momentum. Many of the salespeople had never been to Asia, and this trip was aimed at cementing the team's camaraderie and loyalty, which had been under strain with all the delays. Whether eating together at Thai restaurants, getting up at 4 a.m. to watch the tree tappers extract latex from the trees or just witnessing the gloves being made from start to finish, having the team experience the excitement of our factories and beauty of Asian culture was inspiring.

One of the free afternoons while I played golf with most of the team, Ann joined a dozen or so SafeSkin staff members for a maritime adventure around Phang-Nga Bay, with turquoise water and tropical Thai weather like something from a postcard. Lying back as their Thai guides paddled away, the group was awestruck by the natural beauty of the deep sea caves, intricate limestone formations and jungle terrain of the surrounding islands. That night, as they gushed to the rest of the group about the incredible highlights of the day, many said it was one of the most amazing experiences of their lives, after the birth of their children.

The trip was a rousing success and everyone came back in the middle of February fired up and ready to rock our customers with new promotions and marketing plans to grow the business. But when we sat down with our finance and logistics team, it turned out that almost all of the promised new business never materialized. Our competitors had slashed prices even lower earlier in the year. New hospitals refused to start buying SafeSkin gloves and existing customers were calling for us to lower our prices or lose their business.

This was not just a bump in the road, but a major catastrophe. Our own warehouses were overflowing with gloves, and when new customers did not start buying, distributors ended up with more inventory than they needed. Though orders had slowed down in January, they virtually stopped in early February. At that point distributors were not sharing their inventory numbers with us or any other glove manufacturer. However, after several calls to senior executives at our largest distributors expressing the urgency of the situation, all of them agreed to disclose how much SafeSkin gloves they had in stock.

It took us about a week to get accurate inventory numbers from our distributors, and once we did it became crystal clear that we couldn't possibly hit our forecasted revenue or profits for the first quarter of 1999. If and when a company misses its forecasted financial projections, stocks almost always plummet. Private crises are easier to handle, but such a public failure would destroy our trust with investors, employees and customers as well. As the reality sunk in, my head began pounding and my stomach became queasy as my mind began to race. How had I become so disconnected with our customers? We were much bigger and more visible than ever before, and it is the CEO's job to see around corners, predict unforeseen challenges that others can't see, and have plans in place to avoid or resolve them. And here I was, blindsided.

I sat alone in my office for a while, not knowing what to do. Dave, our CFO, jolted me out of my stupor, reminding me that as a public company we needed to make a public statement notifying all Wall Street investors simultaneously that we would miss our forecasted projections for the first time. Completely distraught, I called my father and Neil to explain the gravity of the situation and decide on a plan of action. "Can't you just lower your prices, sell your way out of this and worry about profits later?" my father asked in disbelief. "It is not humanly possible to sell enough gloves to empty our distributors' warehouses and enable them to start buying before the end of this quarter," I gloomily assured them.

Neil's voice began to shake as the gravity of the situation sunk in. "Richard, I understand the situation, but is there anything else we can try?" he pleaded. "No!" I almost cried, "There's no way, that's what I'm trying to tell you." Once I convinced him, Neil quickly sprang into action. "Then get on the phone with our public relations firm, have them write a press release and prepare us for the nastiness that's coming our way." Neil's experience and ability to accept and keep moving without throwing himself a pity party helped pull me out of mine.

We spent the next three days locked in a conference room trying to figure out what to say and how to explain this major disappointment in our revenues and earnings. Somehow, word started buzzing around Wall Street that something was amiss and we began getting numerous phone calls from long-time investors inquiring about the situation. We were instructed not to answer any of them so we could notify everyone at the same time. The voicemails became more and more irate each day. Investors had been very nice to us as long as the stock price kept rising, but as soon as they feared losing a lot of money, they turned on us in a heartbeat.

While I'd weathered rough times in the past, I'd never done it in the spotlight. Now everything was about to be so public, and I felt totally vulnerable and exposed. For three days I couldn't eat, I couldn't sleep; I wanted nothing more than to shut the curtains and remain in the fetal position. But I knew that these most anxiety-inducing, paralyzing moments were the most important times to maintain healthy habits, no matter how much I hated it. So I undertook the increasingly monumental task of getting out of bed early every morning and went running along the beach. I meditated, said my affirmations and shared my anxieties with Ann.

It took an enormous amount of effort and was by no means a magic cure. However, when I forced myself to engage in these healthy habits, I managed to find moments of relief, small periods where I managed to escape my overwhelming reality by being completely present in the current moment. This reprieve was far too short lived, as the stark reality of disclosing our failure and the shitstorm that would come with it quickly barged back into my brain, but when I felt like I was drowning, those breaths of fresh air gave me just enough hope to keep me afloat.

We had called in an expert management consultant who specialized in public companies facing huge unexpected losses. I had to be honest with myself, our investors and our employees about how we had promised to deliver more sales and profits but did not achieve our commitment. Our consultant began by assuring us that we weren't the first public company to massively miss a financial forecast, nor would we be the last. He helped us prepare a script for our press conference then pulled me aside. "This is serious, but it's not the end of the world," he sternly reminded me. "Stop feeling sorry for yourself and deal with the facts. This happened, you can't change that, so tell the truth and move on! Everything else will work out over time."

His little scolding woke me up from my brooding, and was just what I needed. I reminded myself of my old mantra from dark times past: "If I do not like the way I feel, change the way I think!" Then it hit me. I was thinking all wrong. All my thoughts dwelled on past mistakes and fear of the future, reliving how I could have prevented our massive undersupply and loss of customers, and worrying constantly about investors' anger. I had to figure out how to live in the present, to just focus on dealing honestly with our mistakes, and winning back the customers we lost. Easier said than done, but at least I had a plan I believed in. We still had the best powder-free latex gloves, world-class manufacturing factories, the best salesforce in the industry and an amazing company. We were about to significantly disappoint our investors, that was a fact. I always believed that disappointment is just a gap in expectations, so we needed to recalibrate their expectations and then find a way to rebuild their trust. It would take some time, but I started feeling stronger and stronger as I focused on the honest fight to win back their confidence.

The morning of our press conference, I was nervous but mentally prepared. We announced that our revenues would be considerably lower than expected and earnings would break even, a far cry from the significant profits forecasted. It wasn't easy and I got battered with all types of nasty names and accusations. But with intense preparation, I came armed with all the answers I'd need, my mental guard up. No matter how antagonistic a question, I thanked each investor for their query, remaining calm and unemotional as I answered every one to a T. Still, no one was satisfied and beneath my professional exterior I felt absolutely awful. The stock market is always a gamble, I reminded myself. While many of these investors had made millions of dollars on the SafeSkin stock over the previous five years, they had trusted us with their money and we let them down. Accept the things you cannot change.

As soon as the news hit the street, the stock price dropped like a lead balloon – to no one's surprise. Within the week the company valuation had dropped over 60%, from a high of $2.5 billion just a few months prior to below $1 billion dollars in the days after the announcement. Though the stock price dropped faster and further than I expected, I knew it was out of my control. I decided to focus all of my energy and attention on our customers and employees, passing off investor inquiries to my CFO and treasurer. Maintaining our current business took my full and undivided attention, as competitors had begun telling customers we were going out of business in attempts to convince them to switch brands before it was too late. It was an incredibly trying time.

By this point I could recognize that these periods when I wanted to avoid the world and ignore my regular practices were the most important times to stick to them. My morning jogs on the beach reminded me of pulling through even more difficult times, and daily meditations provided much needed peace and calm. I always made an effort to leave work at the door when spending time with my wife and kids, and their hugs and affection reminded me that no matter what happened at work, I always had an incredibly loving place to come home to. They were my solace. The rest of my days were filled with crazy activity and everyone wanted a piece of me. However, any time I felt myself slipping back into playing the victim role, I caught myself and fought to control my thoughts, focusing only on the desired outcome and letting go of anything that would not help me get there. It was a constant battle, yet I knew this was the key to maintaining the stamina to survive so many crises over the years.

Keeping my positive frame of mind was the one fight I could not afford to lose.

CHAPTER 17

ONE LAST CHANCE

After the hellish press conference, we called an emergency board meeting to discuss the gravity of the situation and what we were planning to do to fix it. Several members questioned our ability to regain the trust of all of our investors and customers. We weren't getting berated; they applauded Neil and me for building the company valuation much higher than anyone expected, then opened a discussion on whether this was the right time to sell. While it wasn't a shocking suggestion, I was so focused on fixing the company I had not even considered selling it.

Immediately I resisted and resented the suggestion. Though I knew it would take a long time and a lot of hard work to rebuild the value of the company, I'd dug my way out of worse. As the different board members took turns sharing their thoughts, my mind wandered back to when my father and I first realized it was time to sell Guido's. The hurt, disappointment and despair of selling our first baby were eventually replaced with liberty and financial freedom after the sale. Was this the same situation? Still, even with my internal questioning, I couldn't bring myself to agree that this was the best time to sell.

When it finally came around to Neil and me to share our

thoughts, Neil jumped right in. To my surprise, he agreed strongly that there was no other choice but to sell the company and the sooner the better. As I began to protest, one of the other board members gently interrupted and asked me point blank, "Do you expect to hit our new financial forecasts for the next two quarters?" I took a deep breath and pondered the magnitude of the question. My mind began racing and seeing all the challenges we had directly in front of us. "Possibly," I slowly began, "But more than likely not." The room went silent and a dark cloud seemed to fill it. "Then that is basis to determine the best next move," he pointed out, "Try to sell the company in the next few months before you lose even more value."

My heart sank into my stomach as I realized he was right. At first I took it personally and fought back the tears. I felt like a failure. I wanted a chance to rebuild our great company and sell it on the best of terms, but by the end of the board meeting it was apparent that continuing as an independent company would be extremely difficult. Though SafeSkin gloves were still the best, competition was catching up to us and prices were only going to decrease. As a one-product company we had nothing else to soften the price decline. After another hour of discussion, the board concluded it was time to find a strategic buyer to purchase the company. They instructed me to interview several leading investment bankers and let them know which one I wanted to hire.

It had been almost a year since I had last seen John Metz. Kimberly-Clark had since bought Technol, the leading mask company, and I called him to catch up. "I read about your disappointing earnings call. It must be very challenging times for you," he said with a tone of compassion. "Yes," I sighed thoughtfully, "These are trying times, but filled with promising opportunities. The board has instructed me to hire an investment banker to review our options. If you have any interest in revisiting our conversation about acquiring a glove company, this is the perfect time to strike a deal."

There was dead silence on the other side of the phone. I decided to wait and let him make the next move. "I hadn't been thinking about that," he said with a hint of genuine surprise in his voice, "But let me discuss it with my bosses and get back to you next week." That was the exact response I was hoping for. "Don't wait too long, John. Things are moving very quickly, and a few extra days could be the difference between the ability to negotiate a mutually agreeable price, and getting stuck in a bidding war. Our customers have already told you they want to buy SafeSkin gloves with your gowns and masks. All we have to do is agree on a price."

"It's not that easy," he assured me, laughing at my predictable persistence, "But let me take the first step and see if we have any interest." When I hung up the phone I felt relieved. There was something about a sales process that really got my juices flowing. I had already accepted the fact that the end of SafeSkin was in sight, so now my responsibility was to get the very best price I could for our investors. I was actually at peace with it all and agreed that the time was right to sell. I just didn't know who else would buy SafeSkin if John came back and said Kimberly-Clark wasn't interested.

The obstacles to selling the company were growing by the day. In addition to our monumental task of earning back Wall Street's trust after missing a financial forecast, the entire glove industry was struggling across the board. Earnings were down and after poor-quality imports had caused many nurses and patients to break out in rashes, a class-action lawsuit was filed against all major glove companies in the United States, SafeSkin included. The plaintiffs claimed that all the glove companies knew latex proteins would cause an allergic reaction over time. Although we had a strong defense with our hypoallergenic processing and claim, that didn't prevent us from being named in over 300 lawsuits. I wasn't worried about the lawsuits themselves, but rather their ability to scare potential buyers away.

We wasted no time in getting moving on the sale. We quickly selected Morgan Stanley as our investment banker and flew their team to our San Diego office. After a lengthy discussion, they decided to hold an auction, allowing us to find multiple interested bidders and maximize the sale price of the company. Morgan Stanley quickly contacted all the major players in the medical industry and set up the auction process, but not a single company showed interest. I couldn't believe it. Things were even worse than I imagined.

At that moment I realized that I would have to sell the company and not rely on Morgan Stanley to sell it for us. I picked up the phone and called John Metz. I hadn't heard back from him in over a week, and though I was hoping for him to call me back, I couldn't wait any longer. After some brief small talk I cut to the chase. "John, I thought you were going to call me back after you spoke with your bosses?" I tried not to sound too needy. "Indeed, but they just got back in town yesterday," he began, as I held my breath, knowing this was the only hope I had. "They agreed that they have interest in SafeSkin, but instructed me to wait another quarter or two to see if you would get back and start hitting your quarterly financial numbers again."

Not quite the answer I was hoping for, but at least it wasn't a death sentence. We were still in jeopardy of missing our financial forecasts next quarter if everything didn't go smoothly; I had to figure out a way to get the process started. "John, SafeSkin will not be available in another quarter or two. We're reaching out to several other large glove and medical device companies that we'd be a perfect fit for," I warned. "Why don't we have our teams start the due diligence process and gather all the information you need, so that when your bosses are ready you have already completed the work? It won't take too much time or expense. You just did it with Technol last year, and you know our business almost as well as we do."

I was so happy I'd started the conversation with John years ago, and just prayed that it would reap rewards. "You know your distributors and hospitals want to buy SafeSkin gloves with Kimberly-Clark gowns and Technol masks. All you have to do is check our facts and agree on a price. SafeSkin public valuation has dropped to under a billion dollars. It could be a great deal for you!"

"I agree it would be good for Kimberly-Clark if we could cut a deal," John began, "But I must warn you, they have several reservations about purchasing SafeSkin, especially the mass of current lawsuits and concerns that missing your forecast might indicate a larger underlying problem." I knew these would be a headache. "John, every major glove manufacturer has been named in these lawsuits. Our gloves are hypoallergenic and powder-free. There's plenty of science proving ours never caused rashes, and we've got a huge amount of insurance to cover whatever costs are awarded," I insisted.

"OK, OK," he relented, "Let me get permission to look at the synergies between our two companies and see if we can set up meetings for next week to start the due diligence process." My heart just about leapt out of my chest with joy. "Thanks, John," I said, trying hard to hide my excitement. "I know you'll be pleasantly surprised at what you see." I hung up the phone and let out a massive sigh. We were still alive! Just keep moving, I reminded myself, just keep pushing this forward.

John got permission to begin the due diligence process, but couldn't touch price negotiations. I was thrilled. I knew the more time and money they spent looking at a deal, and the more emotionally involved they became, the better our chances were to get a deal done. We spent the next few weeks with our executive due diligence teams sharing information about customers, manufacturing, inventory, insurance, personnel and especially financial records and projections. Everything was just as we had promised, and even better than they expected. They seemed satisfied with our science and insurance regarding the lawsuits, and agreed it shouldn't hold things up.

Then, right after the due diligence was complete, John called and said he wanted to meet with me for lunch without our teams at the Rancho Valencia Hotel in Del Mar. I got extremely nervous. Maybe he's going to make his pitch for our company, I thought. But the uncertainty was daunting. Morgan Stanley had still failed to generate any other potential buyers, so all our eggs were in the Kimberly-Clark basket. I showed up for lunch with John the next day with a hop in my step and a smile on my face. I didn't feel as confident on the inside, but I wasn't going to let anyone else see that. When I arrived there were already two salads and iced teas on the table, but John did not look happy. I quickly sat down and, in a hushed tone, asked what was wrong.

"We finished the due diligence and everything was just as you promised," he assured me, "I like the deal, and SafeSkin would be a great fit for Kimberly-Clark. But my boss wouldn't give me the authority to enter negotiations with you," he said apologetically. "I know you were counting on me, but I'm sorry to say you'll have to find another suitor. I am sure you will."

It was like an uppercut to my midsection. Completely speechless and suddenly unable to breathe, I was glad I'd already been sitting or I would have fallen. Those were the last words I expected to hear. I had practiced a response for a host of various questions and objections, but never contemplated John would have to pull the plug. We had not even gotten into the price negotiation. "What were their objections?" I inquired, trying to hide my obvious devastation. "Is there anything we could do to convince your boss to reconsider?"

"No," he said simply. "He didn't give me any more information other than he wanted to wait for more time to pass." This was the end. I thanked John for his time and friendship, and went back to my office not knowing what to do. I had no fall-back plan. After calling my father to explain what went wrong, I called my executive team into the conference room. They walked in with chipper faces, anticipating good news coming their way. I walked them through the entire conversation with John, and none of them could believe it. The last meeting had ended so positively, every question was answered to their satisfaction. Silence hung in the air until our CFO, Dave, eventually turned to me. "So Richard, what are we going to do next?"

"I don't know!" I confessed. "I need some alone time to figure out our next move. Let's reconvene tomorrow." I refused to believe this was the end, but had no idea where to turn next. I pretty much knew we would miss our reduced forecast the following quarter and I had to close a deal before then. Otherwise our stock price would take another plunge and even our loyal customers might start believing our competitors that the end was coming, and jump ship before we sank. I was petrified.

All the work we did building SafeSkin into an industry leader was quickly being washed away. My credibility was in question, and it cut me to my core. I knew that many people I respected would start doubting my abilities. Competitors were telling hospitals that SafeSkin was going out of business in attempts to get them to switch providers, and customers were calling to ask what on earth was going on. CM called pleading to increase production, as he was already losing many of his best people. How did I ever get myself into another mess like this?

I felt sick and started feeling sorry for myself, but thinking like a victim didn't do anything to help. Dejected, I picked up the phone and called my father to explain the change in the Kimberly-Clark discussions. "Since when do you ever take no for a final answer?" he snapped back without missing a beat. "You are the one who is always telling me that no is the first step to any sale. If they said no, then they have objections you haven't overcome." He was right, I just wasn't sure how I could find out their objection. "If John can only say no, then get in front of the executive who can say yes and find out what his objections are," my father instructed me.

It was so simple, I didn't know why I hadn't thought of it before. Right then I made the decision to take responsibility for my thoughts, feelings and actions and do something. I picked up the phone and called John, insisting that if he could not say yes to the deal then I wanted to meet with his boss, who was the number two or three executive at Kimberly-Clark. I didn't know exactly how I was going to convince his boss to do a deal with us, but I did know that I had a better chance to change his mind face to face. I felt so strongly that it was the right thing to do for Kimberly-Clark and SafeSkin – now I just needed to figure out a way to make it happen. John didn't understand what I could possibly accomplish by meeting with his boss, but he agreed to set up the appointment for me as a personal favor.

A few days later, I traveled to Atlanta to meet with Senior Vice President Robert Abernathy at the Kimberly-Clark headquarters. When I arrived, his secretary greeted me graciously so I knew the appointment had been made. First win of the day! Fifteen minutes later, Robert shook my hand as I walked into his office. "What are you doing here?" he asked, without even the hint of a smile.

I explained that John had made the appointment for me. "I know you have an appointment, but I have thrown your SafeSkin file into the garbage half a dozen times. How does it keep getting back on my desk?" he protested. "Divine intervention?" I joked, hoping a little laughter would change the energy in the room. He didn't laugh, but he didn't kick me out either.

I used the short amount of time I had with him to explain how our customers wanted to buy gowns, masks and gloves together, making us a perfect fit. "We are Huggies diapers and plenty of other products our customers can trust. Tell me why on earth I'd acquire a company with a product with over 300 lawsuits?" he challenged, defending his customers' trust with a vengeance. "To begin with, we have the absolute highest-quality latex gloves, just like your gowns and masks. Every major glove manufacturer is included in these lawsuits. We, however, are certified hypoallergenic and powder-free. With a highly defensible position and an additional $40 million of insurance to back us up, we are the best, most-trusted latex glove company you could acquire," I confidently asserted.

"But the most important reason Kimberly-Clark will buy SafeSkin," I continued, "Is that our customers want to buy gloves, masks and gowns from one manufacturer, and Kimberly-Clark is their preferred choice." Though I had no idea where these words came from, I spoke with force and enthusiasm, and every claim I made was true. Though he did not acknowledge my comment about buying SafeSkin, I could see Robert's eyes soften and head nod as I described what was best for both our customers.

After a thoughtful pause, his gaze returned to meet mine. "There is no way we can agree on a price," he began matter-of-factly, "And I'd rather wait a few quarters to make sure your business has stabilized. We've seen this scenario way too often, where the stock price continues to freefall for a few quarters before recovering and the business starts to grow again." John had warned me of this objection. I just had to find a way to resume the due diligence and postpone the price discussion until they had invested more time, money and emotions into the deal.

"Robert, may I call you that?" I asked with a respectful smile, gesturing across the desk. "Yes, of course," he assured me, with a notably friendlier tone of voice. "If we don't move on the purchase discussions now, I am certain that another glove company will buy us by the time you are ready," I said, maintaining focus on our shared goals. "Kimberly-Clark is the perfect partner for us; SafeSkin is the perfect partner for you and for both of our customers. I suggest we leave the price negotiation to the end when you finish the due diligence. Once all that's done and you see how much you like our company, I'm sure we can find a price and structure that works for both of us. We can even consider an earn-out for any difference in valuation we may have." The longer I spoke, the more I convinced even myself that he would be crazy not to say yes.

"One thing is for sure," he said with a much firmer voice. "We will never do an earn-out with a small company. It only sets us up for a lawsuit, so get that out of your mind." He hesitated for a moment, and I remained quiet, allowing his silence to envelop the room. Just as I thought I couldn't hold my breath any longer, he looked me straight in the eyes and continued: "You do make a good point: it doesn't cost much more time or money to finish the due diligence. I will instruct John and his team to complete their work and give me a recommendation. If it comes back positive, you and I can talk about how to structure and price a deal that is good for both companies."

Was I hearing him correctly?! I paused in shock for a moment, unsure of how to respond. I pulled my mind together and buried my excitement as I looked him straight in the eyes. "Thank you for your consideration. I am sure we can find a mutually agreeable path forward, and look forward to continuing our conversation." I reached out to shake his hand, and quickly turned around and headed for the door. This is a key point in sales – when someone says yes to what we want, stop selling immediately. Having accomplished what I came for, I didn't want to give him a chance to change his mind. I thanked his secretary on my way out and beelined straight for the elevator.

As I got back into the car to head for the airport, my body just collapsed with relief. Somehow, I had actually pulled it off. Though we weren't out of the woods yet, we were back on track and still had a fighting chance to stay alive. As we took off for San Diego, I settled back into my seat and reflected on my conversation with Robert. I had listened closely to his needs and assessed that he only had three major remaining objections: timing, lawsuits and price. Once he accepted it was now or never and I gave him enough confidence that there was a way around the lawsuits, all I had to do was get him to agree to punt on the price negotiations until everything else was completed.

In the end, being a customer expert and connecting heart to heart with Robert allowed me to get the negotiations back on track instead of being tossed back into the garbage bin again. If I had not understood and acknowledged his remaining objections, he never would have agreed to continue with the process. But I had also learned almost as much about his business as he did, and I was able to paint the vision of the merger between our two companies as a major win for both Kimberly-Clark and their customers.

The remainder of the process went fairly smoothly as we addressed each of Kimberly-Clark's concerns one by one. Though our insurance coverage was more than sufficient, the risk management team was not convinced. They gave us continuous pushback, but it didn't seem to be enough to hold up the deal. Plus, they found our reputation among hospitals and distributors to be impeccable. A senior manufacturing executive was even sent to inspect our manufacturing and quality-assurance processes at our Thailand factories, and reported back that the SafeSkin Thailand facility would be the highest-rated factory in the entire Kimberly-Clark company. Analysis of our sales team came back with an A+ rating. The proof was in the pudding: we had built an incredible company.

A week later, John let me know that his team had given the official recommendation to proceed with the acquisition, and Robert's assistant would schedule a time for us to discuss the next steps by phone. I had hoped to fly back to Atlanta to negotiate the pricing face to face. Not being able to read his facial or body language over the phone made me nervous, but maybe that was why he refused to see me in person. I don't think he planned for our first meeting to turn out the way it did.

Either way, I was ecstatic to get closer to the finish line, and immediately called Neil and Dad to discuss our strategy. Our stock price, which had been as high as almost $50 a year ago and as low as $6 per share in the third quarter, was currently trading between $8 to $10. As soon as I shared the good news that Kimberly-Clark was ready to start price negotiations next Monday, Neil and my father congratulated me on doing such a great job so far. "Relax," I warned. "We're a long way from agreeing on a deal. I need a price range that is acceptable to all three of us and our shareholders."

Neil jumped in without missing a beat. "Take six dollars per share, or even lower if we have to, but just sell the company at any cost! If we miss our financial forecasts one more time we will be a penny stock and no one will want to buy us." Exhausted by our constant crises, and in complete survival mode, he was not about to let this opportunity to sell the company and finally breathe easy slip through our fingers.

"Let them make the first offer," my father calmly interjected. "Then you have a point to begin from. No matter what price he gives you, he expects you to counter at a high price. He might say this is his first and final offer, but tell him you will think about it and get back to him. Be respectful, but appear that you are negotiating from strength." He briefly paused before adding, "And don't let him hear that you are scared shitless!" My father knew just how I felt, which gave me some small comfort. "OK, I will do my best and let you know how it goes."

That entire weekend I kept going over and over the conversation I expected to have with Robert. Would he lowball me with a $6 price? I knew he understood that as a public company it would be difficult to sell to our shareholders a price below the market price of the day. Was he a take-it-or-leave-it negotiator, unconcerned on whether we closed a deal or not? I didn't think so. Kimberly-Clark was a Fortune 100 company in the consumer business with ambitions to expand in the healthcare sector. Our revenues were approaching $250 million a year, which meant a successful acquisition would bring Kimberly-Clark's healthcare business to over a billion dollars – no small feat. I felt they really did want to buy us so I decided to negotiate from a position of strength like my father suggested. No matter what I thought or said, I knew it would be best responding to Robert's offer; he requested the phone call, so I was going to let him begin the conversation.

Monday morning 10 a.m. finally arrived and as I sat down at my desk, I said a short prayer and dialed Robert's assistant. She let me know that Robert was expecting my call. After a very short hold, he came on the phone. "Good morning, Richard. How are you today?" he asked with a smile in his voice.

"Great, thanks, and how are you doing?" I attempted to maintain a casual enthusiasm. "Oh, very busy but all is good," he assured me before cutting straight to business. "John and his team came back with an outstanding recommendation about SafeSkin. I must admit I expected some rundown, patched-together factories like so many I have seen in Asia, but our manufacturing and engineering executives were absolutely blown away by the cleanliness and efficiency of your operations."

My heart lifted as he continued, "I knew about your reputation in the medical industry, so once we got past that nothing else surprised me. You were correct in that our customers and distributors would like to see Kimberly-Clark and SafeSkin join forces, and we would make a formidable force together. The only items left are to agree upon a valuation for SafeSkin, and get board and shareholder approvals from both companies."

Crap. I had forgotten about board approvals. I knew it would be no problem on our side, but their approvals were just another hurdle standing in our way. "I am cognizant that your shareholders need to feel like they are receiving fair value for their shares," he went on, "I have looked at the recent SafeSkin trading ranges, which go from $6 to $8 per share. I think the highest price of $8 a share is fair." My father was correct – I now had a beginning point.

"Robert, thank you for your confidence in SafeSkin, but I don't think our shareholders will see that as a fair offer." I swallowed my fear and continued confidently, "Kimberly-Clark has a great reputation in the market and I'm sure our shareholders are expecting a premium to the price the stock is currently trading at. I know we can work something out, but please allow me to bounce your offer off a few of my more experienced board members and get back to you by the end of the week."

He seemed completely unsurprised at my response. "I understand your position, but I believe our offer is fair. I am traveling until Friday morning this week. Can we talk then?" he politely suggested. "Of course. I will call you the same time Friday if that works for you," I responded as nonchalantly as possible. "Great, have a good week and talk to you then," he said and hung up.

Phew! Somehow my fear and insecurity disappeared when I got on the phone with Robert. It felt more like a negotiating game than a wrestling match for our survival. I picked up the phone and called Neil and my father. "It went just as you predicted, Dad. He offered $8 a share, the same price as the stock this morning, and I said I didn't think our shareholders would approve of it. They expected a premium from Kimberly-Clark and..."

"What, are you crazy!?" Neil interrupted. "Take the $8 and run! If he changes his mind we could end up with nothing. Call him back and accept his offer!" he insisted. I had somewhat expected this response from him, and took a deep breath. "These negotiations are never comfortable, Neil. But I've done this before and need you to trust me on this. Plus, I can't talk to him until Friday anyway, as he is traveling all week. Let me have one more shot at him and then I'll agree to whatever price I need to." I balanced between empathy and conviction. "If I have to backtrack to his offered price, I can always do that!"

"I think Richard is doing fine," my father interjected. "He needs to proceed his way, as these negotiations always take on a life of their own. The good news is that they want to buy the company. Be patient and I know Richard will get the best price we can." Without much other option, Neil begrudgingly agreed. We hung up the phone and I went back to running the company for the week. The continual challenges with customers, shipments and investors were a welcome distraction, but my mind kept jumping back to my

Judgement Day phone call with Robert. I knew that if I pushed too far, we could lose the whole thing.

Every time my mind wandered to Robert's possible response, knots of dread tore through my chest and nervous beads of sweat gathered across my brow. The moment I felt the energy start to leak out of me, I would take a deep breath, consciously bringing my mind back to the present, and focus on something I could affect immediately. I forced myself up and out to the beach for jogs each morning, finding some calm and solace in watching the waves crash. No matter what Robert says, I reminded myself, the waves will continue crashing on the beach and life will go on.

Friday morning finally arrived, and when I went to see what the stock price had done that morning, I just about jumped out of my chair. It had shot up to around $10 per share! I don't know how news had leaked out that Kimberly-Clark was looking to acquire SafeSkin, but with Kimberly-Clark's due diligence and customer calls, it was hard to keep a secret in the medical industry. Robert obviously would be less thrilled. I dialed his number and after a few pleasantries with his secretary, she let me know he was just finishing up another call and put me on hold.

The longer I waited, the more nervous I became. My father and I had developed the strategy that I would ask for a 20% premium on the $8 price he offered, but now that the price was $10 per share, did I dare to ask for the premium on that price? I decided to wait for Robert's opening, then go with my gut instinct. When he finally came on the line, he apologized for keeping me waiting and explained he was talking to one of their lead board members about SafeSkin. I didn't know if that was a good or bad sign. "I agree that shareholders usually expect a premium on the stock price when a company is sold," he cut straight to the point, "But the problem we have here, is that the stock has already climbed to over $10 per share. Has your side been leaking news of our conversations?" he pointedly accused.

"Certainly not, Robert," I assured him. "It's hard to keep a secret in our industry, especially when your team is questioning hospitals and distributors about SafeSkin. Let's see if we can agree to a price so we can make an announcement right away and put the rumors to rest." Again I sat back and waited for him to proceed. He knew how to use a nerve-wracking pause, waiting patiently before responding, "I agree. Let's get this deal done. I can go as high as the current share price of $10 per share, but no higher. I think we are being very fair and your shareholders will be more than satisfied."

My heart just about leapt out of my chest, and I almost jumped at the offer. But something inside me said there was more room to negotiate. Neil and my father would be thrilled with this, but my competitive nature wouldn't allow me to accept it. Before I could even think, I heard myself saying, "Thank you for the offer, and though it is generous, I believe the right thing to do is to give our shareholders a 20% premium on today's price. I know it is more than you expected to pay, but it's the right thing to do." Oh dear lord. I held my breath and couldn't believe I actually said that.

It was too late to take it back, and I was hoping that I could still go back to the $10 price if he flinched at my response. My words hung in the air as he was searching for how to respond. Clearly surprised by my move, he finally responded in a soft, judgmental tone. "Richard, I think that price is way too high and I need the weekend to think it over. I will call you Monday morning to let you know whether we want to go forward with the deal or not. Enjoy your weekend." And just like that he abruptly hung up.

What?! That wasn't how it was supposed to go. I felt horrible. I pushed it too far. Why did I have to do that? What inside me drove me to risk the whole enchilada just to chase an extra few bucks?

What was I going to tell Neil and dad? What would I do if the deal fell apart? My mind was racing a mile a minute, each thought a new dagger to my confidence. I took a few deep breaths to try and slow my mental roll. Focusing on the things I could control, I decided to tell Neil and my father that Robert wanted the weekend to think over the deal and would call me back Monday. I didn't give them all the details of the call, though they requested it, and said I would call them Monday after I spoke with Robert.

That was the longest weekend of my life.

All day long I couldn't stop playing the conversation over in my head. When I finally left the office, I decided not to take any work home with me and to try to avoid as many work calls as possible throughout the weekend. I was so grateful in that moment to have such a supportive partner, one I could both confide in and lean on. After dinner and putting the kids to sleep, Ann and I sat around the kitchen table as I explained the entire call with Robert in great detail. "In all honesty," I admitted, "I shouldn't have pushed him so far. I think I might've blown our last chance to save the company."

She took a moment to take it all in before taking my hand in hers and gazing deep into my eyes. "You have always been extremely successful by following your gut instincts, and that is exactly what you did today. There is nothing you can do to change what happened on the call so just be yourself. You know how to get through these hard moments," she assured me. "Control your thoughts, be positive and visualize Robert agreeing to your terms. It will make for a much better weekend, and if you don't get the response you want, you'll manage the objections and figure out next steps on the phone together." It was as if I were talking to myself. Ann, my father and my mother had a way of believing in me even when I couldn't find a way to believe in myself.

That weekend we took long walks along the beach and I reflected back on those harrowing times nine years earlier, with foreclosure notices and personal guarantees being called. I cultivated gratitude, concentrating in on how far we had come. I meditated and prayed. Every time I started thinking what might happen if Robert decided to pull out of the deal, I caught myself and redirected my thoughts to the present. It was a continual mental battle all weekend, constantly bringing my mind back into the present in order to quell the overwhelming fear for the future. It left me drained and exhausted, but somehow I made it through to Monday. I woke up early, kissed Ann and the kids goodbye and headed into the office to face my fate.

Overall I felt good given the circumstances, as more often than not I was able to visualize Robert agreeing to my terms. Both Neil and my father called me early to wish me luck, reminding me to call as soon as I got off the phone. They knew what was riding on this phone call, they just didn't know how far I had pushed Robert. As 10 a.m. approached, I sat by the phone nervously running my fingers along the ridges of my desk as the clock ticked away, slowly and incessantly. Finally, my assistant poked her head in the door to let me know that Robert Abernathy was on the line. I thanked her, asked her to close the door and took a deep breath. This was it.

"Good morning, Robert!" I greeted him enthusiastically, "I hope you and your family had a great weekend. Were you able to come to a decision about acquiring SafeSkin?" I had decided that I would take a confident and direct approach to get started. "Yes we have," he responded slowly. I held my breath as I waited for his verdict.

"The price you have asked is much higher than we ever anticipated," he began. "However, we also found your company to be much more efficient and the potential for your surgical gloves even bigger than we ever expected. We will agree to pay you a 20%

premium on the opening stock price today (which came to over $12.30 per share). I think your shareholders should be thrilled." Holy shit. Was this a dream? $12.30?! It took every ounce of effort to remain calm and collected as he continued.

"We will need to quickly craft a public statement and make an announcement today indicating the price that Kimberly-Clark has agreed to purchase SafeSkin for, and caution that it requires approval from both boards of directors. Please talk to John and let him know who will be handling the announcement for you. I look forward to combining our two great companies, and strengthening Kimberly-Clark's leadership in the medical industry." I somehow pulled the words together to thank Robert for his confidence and support, and committed to doing everything in my power to push the deal through to completion. The joy, relief and pure adrenaline that pulsed through my body was indescribable. I hung up the phone, collapsed into my chair and released months of stress and anguish with the deepest, most intense shriek I have ever emitted. When my assistant came running in to see what was wrong, I leapt out of my chair, picked her up and gave her a massive bear hug. "We did it!" I shouted, my eyes tearing up in surreal relief. "We're selling to Kimberly-Clark!" As one of the few people who knew just how much stress I was under, Maripat was just as excited as I was, gasping and giggling in joyful disbelief. After sharing the great news with my executive team, we exchanged hugs and high fives like we'd just won the Super Bowl, and even danced a collective little jig.

Before getting too carried away, I reminded everyone that we were not done yet. There would still be obstacles ahead, including a couple of people on the Kimberly-Clark team who were not happy with the deal. "Every 'i' needs to be dotted, and every 't' crossed to make sure we close this thing!" I reiterated, with all the tenacity and enthusiasm of a coach's fourth-quarter pep talk. We needed approval from both boards of directors, and Kimberly-Clark was a huge company with vastly different priorities.

After brief celebrations with the executive team, I called my father screaming, "They accepted our offer! We have a deal, we have a deal!" I was almost hoarse already from all the screaming. "You won't believe the price," I added, giggling as reality continued setting in. "They took the $10 price?" he guessed. "No, they did not," I retorted, trying to hide my glee. "$9?" he guessed again.

"Nope, 12 dollars and 30 cents!" I proudly announced. "How in the hell did you do that?" he exclaimed in amazement. I walked him through the entire negotiation, apologizing for withholding the details. He understood completely and commended me for a job well done.

As I told him I needed to go craft a public announcement and secure both boards' approval, his tone got more serious as he asked for details. "Let me explain the situation to Neil and get back to you with a closing plan." Boy did it feel amazing to be calling with good news. "Remember, Richard, this isn't a done deal yet. Do not let up until the money is in the bank." I told him I was acutely aware of the task at hand, and promised to stay focused until it was complete.

I went through the same conversation with Neil, though he had many more questions. While impressed with my results, he admonished me for risking everything just to get a few more dollars. "Good work, but holy shit, Richard – you could have blown the whole deal!" he scolded me. "Possibly throwing it all under the bus just for a few extra bucks. Just make sure we can close at this price and that their board doesn't try to back out because it's too expensive!" We all shared a cautious sense of relief, conscious that we were still a long way from completing the transaction.

Kimberly-Clark's next board meeting was already scheduled less than a month away. Our executive team made up a detailed list of tasks that needed to be completed before then, and doled out assignments amongst ourselves. But just two days later, before we had the chance to do anything, I received a disturbing call from John Metz stating they were having trouble getting us on the agenda for Kimberly-Clark's next board meeting, meaning we may need to wait another quarter. "We just agreed to a deal. What could possibly hold up adding us to your board agenda?" I snapped, quickly losing my patience.

"Kimberly-Clark has a hard and fast rule that nothing can go on the board agenda unless all the paperwork is distributed to the board two weeks prior to the meeting. It appears that we couldn't complete the necessary paperwork for the board, since a few insurance issues had not been documented before our head of insurance left for vacation yesterday," John calmly explained. I quietly fumed on my end of the line while immediately shifting my focus to finding a solution rather than placing blame for the problem. The head of insurance was one of the biggest voices against our deal. I'm sure he did this on purpose, as he never got over all our pending lawsuits. "I will have the insurance issue resolved this week. You just make sure we get on the agenda!" I insisted.

We had not come this far to fail at the last minute. I called an emergency meeting of our executive team and instructed Bill, our treasurer and lead insurance executive, to get all the insurance issues in order, track down Kimberly-Clark's head of insurance and fly out the next morning to wherever he was vacationing. "Do not come home until you have his signature on all the insurance documents we need," I threatened in an uncharacteristically jarring tone. "And do it quickly!"

Though utterly surprised when Bill showed up at his Puerto Rico hotel room, the Kimberly-Clark executive was cooperative and signed everything we needed. Bill then overnighted the signed paperwork to John at Kimberly-Clark, who walked the documents into Robert's office just two days after he'd called me. With all the documents we needed to present to the board, Robert reached out to a few of their board members who helped to squeeze us onto the end of their board agenda just a few weeks away. It was a dangerous position to be in, as they could often run out of time, but at least we had made it on. All we could do now was cross our fingers and pray.

The following three weeks waiting for approval from the Kimberly-Clark board was excruciatingly draining. I was in touch with John every few days confirming things were still on track. He kept reassuring me that it was a done deal, but I knew better. The deal is only done when the money is in the bank, and if things got derailed there would be no other way of saving the company; we would be too far gone. I had no idea if anyone inside the company would try to convince the board members to squash the deal, or if more pressing matters on their agenda would take more time, bumping the bottom items to the next board meeting the following quarter. Only time would tell.

We had scheduled the SafeSkin board meeting the same day as Kimberly-Clark's, and approved the sale first thing in the morning. For the next few hours I waited by the phone, willing it to ring. Finally, in the early afternoon, Maripat popped in to say that John Metz from Kimberly-Clark was on the phone. There had been so many devastating phone calls over the past 25 years. I held my breath and prayed that this one would make up for all of them.

As Dad and Neil sat on the edge of their seats, anxiously awaiting the verdict, I took a deep breath and answered the phone, "Hi, John, how are we doing?" I inquired with a completely false sense of calm. Thank God he didn't beat around the bush. "After a very full board meeting, they were able to squeeze in our agenda item. Though they had many questions for Robert, he handled it beautifully and as promised, the board unanimously approved the purchase of SafeSkin at the terms we agreed to. The only thing remaining is a ruling from the SEC (U.S. Securities and Exchange Commission) as to whether they will be reviewing the deal for antitrust consideration. Without a review, we could close 30 days after their approval. With an SEC review, it would take an additional 30 to 60 days."

I gave Dad and Neil the thumbs up sign, as I giddily responded, "That is great news, John, thank you so much for your hard work!" At this point I didn't need to hide my excitement. "No, Richard, it was your dogged persistence and determination that finally got this deal done, and we want to thank you for allowing us the opportunity to continue to grow your great company! Let's talk tomorrow and make a list of all the remaining tasks that need to be accomplished before closing."

I hung up the phone and found myself jumping up and down and fist-pumping across the room, "YES! YES! YES!" I shouted as I danced. Neil was smiling broadly as he slouched back in his chair. I could see the months and years of stress draining off his face. Dad was just shaking his head while beaming ear to ear. The rest of the SafeSkin board congratulated the three of us on a job well done while reminding us that the deal was not done yet. They counseled us to track every last detail and not leave any stone unturned until the SEC approved the deal and the transaction was closed.

Dad, Neil and I remained extremely nervous throughout December. Though we had all of the other necessary approvals and didn't feel like we were in danger of any SEC obstacles, shit happens and we kept telling each other that a deal is never done until the money (or stock) is in the bank. I tried to maintain a cautious optimism throughout the month, but couldn't shake the constant, nervous pit writhing in my stomach day and night. With the SEC out for the Christmas holidays, we rang in the New Year with no word back.

Then on one exceptionally fine day in January, we received word that since Kimberly-Clark had recently bought Ballard, a soap company, and since the SEC had reviewed that transaction, they would allow us to proceed to close our deal without further review. What a relief! Thirty days later, on February 8, 2000, the deal was closed and we could finally breathe easy. Thank God we closed the deal when we did and didn't require an SEC review; two weeks after closing the deal and receiving our stock, the stock market crashed. Kimberly-Clark's stock plummeted.

Since we had accepted an all-stock deal for a fixed amount of shares based on the pre-crash price, if we had not closed the deal when we did, we would have lost 30% of the value when the stock fell. Honestly, in the wake of the crash we may not have closed the deal at all. And since our plan was to hold on to the Kimberly-Clark stock long term, the stock market crash didn't have an immediate impact on us. Once again, for one last time, we survived an extremely close call by the skin of our teeth. Boy, did I sleep well that night.

I feel very fortunate that we were able to create a company with a legacy of enthusiasm and respect among clients and team members. Customers raved about our products and employees enjoyed coming to work. They genuinely cared about each other and believed in our mission to protect and serve healthcare workers with the highest-quality latex gloves. To build a company where people truly love each other and that makes a substantial, positive impact in the world is the dream that drew me into the crisis-ridden, unpredictable world of entrepreneurship. And it was worth it a hundred times over.

The rollercoaster of entrepreneurship pushed me, molded me and challenged me to my core. I'd do it all over again in a heartbeat.

Tapestry of Life
November 13, 1998

*Life is a multi-colored tapestry we weave
through heartaches and rejoices
It vibrates from the fabric of our morals
while reflecting the wisdom of our choices.
Though most of us spend our lifetimes chasing love,
our ultimate goal
The path to inner peace and happiness is revealed
by learning to grow our soul.*

*For each love in life is a precious
thread with new lessons we must share
Colored with lasting memories that teach love's
greatest gift, learning how to care.
But another's love is not the path we must
explore to find life's purpose;
When looking to others for our answers we only
find their questions on the surface.*

*We must search within our own hearts to love the only soul we see.
Acceptance of who we are today is the first step to
being who we want to be.
Because life is all about our attitudes and
the point of view we choose to take,
Accepting things we cannot change while taking responsibility for
choices that we make.*

*For once we love our own soul as much as
the one we desperately hope to find,*

*We build the inner strength and confidence
that leaves empty loneliness behind.*

ACKNOWLEDGEMENTS

Nothing great is ever achieved without a trusted team, and the successes depicted in this book are by no means mine alone. It was the hard work, sacrifice and support from the people closest to me that made this all possible. While words cannot describe the depths of gratitude I feel for my incredible network of family, friends and mentors, some thank you's are in order.

First, to my amazing parents. The sacrifices and loving relationship that my mother and father displayed throughout my life are what allowed me to grow into the person I am today. In business and life, they have been my best friends and role models for how to treat others and strive to be the best at everything I do. Though this book is written through my eyes, it is their wisdom and guidance that allowed our businesses to succeed. They gave me the ability to learn from my own mistakes, and everything I have ever accomplished is a testament to the support they have given me.

My best friend, soulmate and incredible wife, Ann, has stood at my side and shaped me into the man I am today. She gave me strength through the darkest times, shared the incredible joy and elation of the highs and has continued to help me grow into a better version of myself. My inspiration, my cheerleader and mother to our incredible three children, she spent years building a loving home while I spent most of my time in the office or on the road.

I could have never imagined the unconditional, life-changing love my three children, Brett, Charly and Maxi, would bring into my life. They gave me hope and reason to persevere even when it seemed like there was no chance of pulling through, and showed me that there is so much more to life than professional success.

There were huge sacrifices made by relatives whose stories are not included in these pages, contributions that were crucial to the success of Guido's. My sister Susie traveled tirelessly and gave up her own career to help the business right when we needed it most. My brother, Jack, worked side by side with me through long days and nights, and his indelible spirit kept us all going through the most challenging times. My big sister Joyce's sage counsel was always there when I needed it. My cousin Idonna brought an infectious sense of humor and tireless work ethic, and her ability to adapt and thrive with the various responsibilities thrown her way was a crucial piece to our success.

Throughout these pages, you've met my Uncle Bob, who is the one who convinced me to dive into this crazy world of entrepreneurship in the first place. His tireless work ethic and unparalleled salesmanship were critical in growing both businesses, and I'm forever grateful for his love and guidance.

My good friend Jim Belasco mentored me through the most difficult SafeSkin years, asking difficult questions that helped me live by my values and vision in challenging times. His mentorship has played a huge role in the creation of this book, as he brought those same tough questions and sage guidance to our writing process.

And finally a special shout-out to my daughter and co-author Charly for pulling this story out of me. She has spent countless hours detailing the emotional journey depicted in these pages, and gave a voice to the stories and lessons through her enrapturing writing style. I understand myself better because of her questioning and guidance, and am overjoyed that together, we were able to share the fruits of that labor with you.

ABOUT THE AUTHORS

Charly Jaffe is a writer and captivating advocate for mental and emotional health, with a sense of purpose that has taken her across industries and continents. Beginning with the hardest problems she could find, Charly dove into international politics and conflict resolution at Georgetown University, studying in China, Europe and the Middle East. Intrigued by the power of story, she shifted into journalism, producing content for *The Washington Post* and *BBC News*.

Realizing that her passion was not to inform, but to transform, Charly joined Google as a strategist. Honing her business acumen and helping companies deliver their message digitally, she led numerous initiatives to enable diverse and marginalized communities to gain more from Google. In 2015, she was awarded the Google's Diversity Impact Award for her efforts.

Her most powerful learnings, however, have come from personal experiences – near death illness, sexual assault, depression, eating disorder and Post-Traumatic Stress Disorder (PTSD). These long avoided obstacles eventually drove Charly off the Silicon Valley career path and into deep study of the human mind and spirit.

After adventuring through Southeast Asia and co-running a yoga school in Australia, Charly returned to the United States and is currently a crisis counselor and graduate student in Columbia University's Department of Counseling and Clinical Psychology. Keeping with her roots in conflict transformation, Charly now focuses where most conflict begins – within.

To learn more about Charly and book her for coaching, speaking or consulting, visit: **www.CharlyJaffe.com.**

Richard Jaffe started Nutri-Foods Int'l in 1975 after graduating from Cornell University with a Bachelor of Science degree in Industrial and Labor Relations. Nutri-Foods manufactured and distributed Guido's Italian Ices and frozen juice bars. After struggling for many years, he enlisted his parents and brother to help, and together they turned the business around, took it public in 1984 and eventually sold it to The Coca Cola Company in 1985. After the acquisition, Richard remained President of Nutri-Foods and served on the executive operating committee of The Coca Cola Foods Division for the next two years.

In 1988, Richard was introduced to a businessman who was starting a latex glove company. With the exploding AIDS epidemic and the government declaration of universal precautions, every healthcare worker needed to wear gloves and change them between each patient. Those two events created an enormous glove shortage. When Richard explored the opportunity, he found a huge problem: the latex used in making gloves had always been treated with chemicals that, if not removed, could cause skin rashes if in contact with skin for long periods. Since nurses and doctors started wearing latex gloves ten hours per day instead of ten minutes per day, he saw a significant customer behavior change he thought a company could take advantage of. His second company, SafeSkin Corp., was born.

In 1989, SafeSkin was granted FDA approval to market a hypoallergenic latex exam glove. Always customer-focused, Richard took the approved product and asked his customers what they liked and what could be improved. The response was consistent: "Give us less powder." Listening to customers' needs, SafeSkin developed the first hypoallergenic, powder-free latex exam gloves — an extraordinary success! Under Richard's leadership, SafeSkin went public in 1993, was voted Forbes Magazine's "Best Small Company in America" in 1996, and was purchased by Kimberly-Clark Corporation in 2000.

Moving from success to significance, Richard turned his attention to philanthropy. In 2000, Richard, his wife, Ann, and Richard's parents, Irving and Eleanor Jaffe, gave the lead gift and led a campaign to raise an initial $36 million to build a new 42-acre campus for the San Diego Jewish Academy. Today, they have helped raise over $75 million dollars for SDJA, and the school now serves over 600 students from pre-K through 12th grade. In 2018, it was recognized as one of the top 50 private schools in the United States, being awarded the coveted Blue Ribbon designation.

In 2004, Richard became a part owner of the NBA's Phoenix Suns and in 2007 he published a book of poetry entitled *Inner Peace and Happiness – Reflections to Grow Your Soul*. Richard currently mentors young entrepreneurs on starting and scaling new ventures. He and his wife have three grown children and currently reside in La Jolla, California.

To learn more about Richard Jaffe and get your own copy of his poetry book, visit: **www.RichardJaffe.net.**